The Isle of Wight, Portsmouth and the Solent

Landscapes of the Imagination

Landscapes

THE ISLE OF WIGHT, PORTSMOUTH AND THE SOLENT

A *Cultural History*

MARK BARDELL

Signal Books
Oxford

First published in 2012 by
Signal Books Limited
36 Minster Road
Oxford OX4 1LY
www.signalbooks.co.uk

A catalogue record for this book is available from the British Library

ISBN 978-1-908493-07-1 Paper

Cover design: Devdan Sen
Design & production: Devdan Sen
Cover images: Jake Foster/istockphoto; Wikipedia Commons
Illustrations: All images Wikipedia Commons except Isle of Wight Tourism/islandbreaks.co.uk 2; Martin Bardell i, x, 13, 134; nen.gov.uk 147; Portsmouth Museums and Records Service 184, *The News* 157, 211
Printed by Short Run Press Ltd., Exeter, UK

Contents

Part Two
EPISODES FROM HISTORY

Preface

When in 1960 my father was posted from Fremington in North Devon to Portsmouth, I moved, aged eleven, from a bucolic backwater to a bustling seaport city. At first I travelled to school in Old Portsmouth from our house in Lee-on-Solent. This meant taking the ferry across the harbour from Gosport to the Hard close by Portsmouth Dockyard and the city's Harbour Station. This was, I grant you, a small voyage but it could be an inspiring one. The harbour entrance was just to the south with the Solent beyond and further up the harbour there were warships tied up alongside with the Semaphore Tower signalling the start of the dockyard's town-scape; a redundant Isle of Wight paddle steamer was berthed near the ferry's pontoon on the Portsmouth side.

The cross harbour ferries were basic craft back then compared with the Cunard-style luxury of today's boats. The main deck—mostly for stand-ing passengers and stacked with bicycles—was open to the elements. There was a warm, fuggy cabin below where passengers could retreat from the rain. The walk to school from the ferry took me past a tattoo parlour—its premises built into the railway embankment. It is still in business but in those days tattoos were for tough nautical types and were in no way main-stream. Further on was the main gate of HMS *Vernon*, home then to the Navy's torpedo school and clearance diving unit and now the Gunwharf Quays shopping and housing development. Further on along St. George's Road the vast bulk of the power station dominated the surrounding area; with its two giant chimneys it was a local landmark and had been a Second World War Luftwaffe target.

Across the road was the Landport Gate (1760), the only surviving gate of Portsmouth's old town. The school was sited at the top of Old Portsmouth's High Street, its main building part of the former Cambridge Barracks. Two doors down the street was the house in which Charles I's favourite and ineffectual commander, George Villiers Duke of Bucking-ham, was assassinated in 1628. You did not need to go looking for history, it came to you.

This book is an attempt to evoke some of that history and some of the personalities who have made Portsmouth, the Solent and the Isle of

Wight so crucial to Britain's past and so important in its collective imagination.

ℰℑ

I want to thank James Ferguson for giving me the opportunity and motivation to write this book and waiting stoically for its completion. I also want to thank Carolyn and Maggie for their encouragement and my son Martin for his continued interest in the project and especially for his involvement in a productive photo shoot on the Isle of Wight.

Introduction

THE VIEW FROM THE TOWER

First let's consider the tower. The top of its spire is 170 metres (just over 550 feet) from its base. That base is supported by 84 reinforced concrete piles driven into the seabed, the longest of which is almost equivalent to the height of Nelson's Column. The building site had a small footprint, and as it was so close to operating shops and restaurants all the materials and equipment initially had to be brought in by sea. Four years in the making, the tower was finally opened in October 2005. Despite being approved as a Millennium Project ten years earlier, political wrangling, controversy over contractual and financial issues and construction difficulties had created a saga of delay. Perhaps because of this protracted uncertainty there was much local scepticism about the tower; but once finished and in use its aptness as a focal image for Portsmouth's city and harbour and its fitness for purpose were apparent. It literally provided a new angle and viewpoint on a familiar historic scene and gave coherence to the sea and landscapes of the Solent, Portsmouth, Gosport and the north coast of the Isle of Wight.

Looking out from the tower's first viewing deck three hundred feet above the harbour, it is possible to review some of the sites and seascapes that are the subjects for this book: seascapes that provided topics and inspiration for the painters J. M. W. Turner and William Lionel Wyllie; the part of Old Portsmouth below that was the setting for the rumbustious, even licentious public goings-on depicted in Thomas Rowlandson's painting *Portsmouth Point* (1800); Portsmouth Dockyard, still its own township within a city; the ghost town archipelago of naval shore stations, ordnance and supply yards; the collar of Victorian forts that encircled the city from the west in Gosport, along the ridge of Portsdown Hill and out to the man-made island forts of Spithead; the resort of Southsea, location of the first garden suburb; the long pier across the Solent at Ryde and the funfair fragment at Clarence Pier, symbols of the heyday of the English seaside holiday; the royal residence over the water at Osborne eight miles distant—the house that Victoria and Albert made for themselves as a family home which was a key site of the queen's long reign. The yachting and marine engineering centre of Cowes is another half a mile westward along the north Wight coast.

Immediately below the first viewing deck the railway snakes round to the Harbour Station. Immediately north, the black-hulled HMS *Warrior*, Britain's first ironclad, is moored to a jetty attended by small fishing boats, with the Semaphore Tower behind and the dockyard stretching out north and west. Beyond, the full capacity of Portsmouth Harbour is apparent with its western side studded by marinas and former naval shore facilities: Priddy's Hard magazine and the victualling depot of Royal Clarence Yard and the Royal Navy Submarine Museum signalling the frontage of the former Royal Navy Hospital at Haslar.

The Wight Link car ferry manoeuvres out of its docking berth close to the harbour entrance. Pilot boats and tug boats go about their necessary business. On a clear day the landmark spire of Ryde's High Victorian Church of All Saints is visible on the heights above the town. Similar conditions allow a sight of Seaview to the east with the looming presence of Brading/Bembridge Down further south. The hovercraft from Ryde heads at speed for its beach landing point near Clarence Pier—a maritime hornet wreathed in spray.

I believe in William Faulkner's dictum: "History is not was, it is." Where town planners have not obliterated built history, cities include sites where the past can be read and where surviving buildings can have an unexpected resonance for individuals in the present. A photograph taken during the First World War in Portsmouth shows wounded German soldiers being led into the hospital in Fawcett Road, a school given a new use for the duration. The author's son attended that school towards the end of the same century, its main block exterior largely unchanged. His mother is of German origin.

The Isle of Wight and Portsmouth may present themselves or be perceived as places that are insular or provincial in a negative sense but they have been placed on the world stage by threats of invasion and as launching points for invasion, as the location for displays of sea power and as the depot for supplying expeditions and military adventures and as a reception centre for the causalities. Local life here has always been placed in the context of events and places over the horizon—places known as the scenes of battle or of events heard about but not known or experienced directly by most of the populace—La Rochelle, Sebastopol, Valletta, Nashua, Trincomalee, Tahiti, Cape Trafalgar, the Falkland Islands, Botany Bay, Scapa Flow, Majuba Hill, Jutland, New Caledonia, Van Diemen's Land, Mombasa…

Yet English provincial landscapes repay the time spent exploring them. As the writer J. B. Priestley—of whom more later—counselled: "Any man from America or Australia might take one glance at the Island as something on a map and then decide to give it a couple of hours. But you can spend days and days exploring the Isle of Wight which if you are really interested, begins magically enlarging itself for you."

Portsmouth was an Admiralty town, a key naval location for what was arguably the first international corporation. Jan Morris' elegiac summary encompasses this corporation's global reach and the varied architectural, maritime, medical, artistic and cultural legacy it has left for the nation:

> The Admiralty possessed vast tracts of land, it administered dockyards, barracks and Admiralty House; around the world, it employed scientists, surgeons, clergymen, architects, accountants, archivists. It governed the island colony of Ascension in the South Atlantic, which rated as a ship, was commanded by a captain of the Royal Navy and was borne on the books of the Admiral Superintendent, and Gibraltar. Samuel Pepys had once been the Admiralty's Secretary. Christopher Wren had designed its naval college, Robert Adam the screen of its headquarters in Whitehall. It had its pantheon of demi-gods: Anson, Howe, St Vincent, Rodney, Nelson himself, whose effigy on top of his column in Trafalgar Square, within sight of the Admiralty offices, might be considered the central icon of the kingdom.

Many of the people who also appear in this book are drawn from history's B list of military and artistic celebrities. They were celebrated and significant people in their time but not so much written about now. Yet in terms of contemporary historical and biographical recognition and appreciation, many of the names that go around come around.

To use Karl Marx's famous dictum, "The philosophers have only interpreted the world in various ways: the point is to change it." The artists and writers have interpreted and portrayed the world, the engineers and the architects have materially changed it. So the imaginations also considered here, alongside the interpretive and suggestive power of artists, are the innovatory and creative imaginations of marine, military and civil engineers, of landscape designers and of architects.

This introduction looks out from one contemporary architectural sculpture—the Spinnaker Tower—and it can exemplify this approach. It was built on the site of a former shore station HMS *Vernon* and designed to be the centrepiece of Portsmouth's turn-of-the-twentieth-century waterfront regeneration, Gunwharf Quays. It is another material example of Portsmouth's long post-Second World War change of use from a naval and army company town to a provincial commercial hub, yachting centre and a Channel ferry port. This particular shore station has been re-made into a small civilian town with apartment blocks, a casino, clubs, restaurants, shops, an art gallery and a small marina, and includes a customs house ironically turned into a public house and all clustered beneath an iconic observation tower. The Tower signals this transformation and serves as a dramatic seamark.

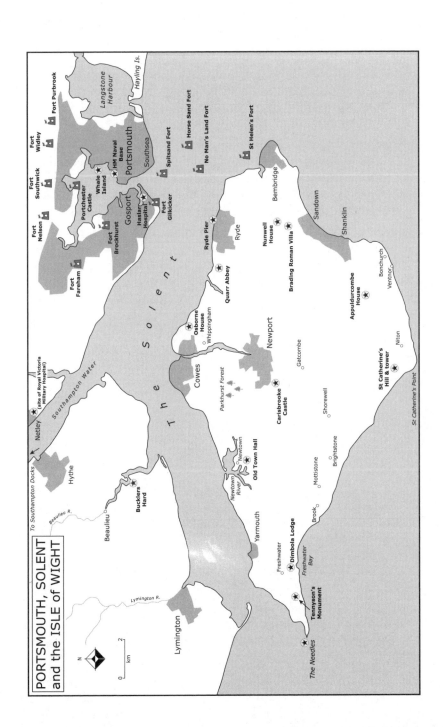

PORTSMOUTH, SOLENT and the ISLE of WIGHT

N

0 km 2

Lymington

Lymington R.

Beaulieu R.

Beaulieu

Bucklers Hard

Hythe

To Southampton Docks

Southampton Water

Netley (site of Royal Victoria Military Hospital)

Fort Fareham

Fort Nelson

Fort Brockhurst

Portchester Castle

Whale Island

HM Naval Base

Gosport

Haslar Hospital

Fort Gilkicker

Fort Southwick

Fort Widley

Fort Purbrook

Langstone Harbour

Hayling Is.

Portsmouth

Southsea

Spitsand Fort

Horse Sand Fort

No Man's Land Fort

St Helen's Fort

The Solent

Ryde Pier

Ryde

Bembridge

Sandown

Quarr Abbey

Nunwell House

Brading Roman Villa

Shanklin

Osborne House

Whippingham

Cowes

Parkhurst Forest

Newport

Gatcombe

Bonchurch

Ventnor

Appuldurcombe House

Carisbrooke Castle

Shorewell

Niton

St Catherine's Hill & tower

St Catherine's Point

Old Town Hall

Newtown

Newtown River

Yarmouth

Brook

Mottistone

Brighstone

Freshwater

Dimbola Lodge

Freshwater Bay

Tennyson's Monument

The Needles

Part One

LANDSCAPES AND SEASCAPES

England's only surviving medieval lighthouse, St. Catherine's Hill, Isle of Wight

Chapter One
THIS SCEPTRED ISLE
THE ISLE OF WIGHT

Jack Priestley was sitting on a coach that had just left Southampton bound for Bristol when he saw a roadside poster map which said: "You are only 12 miles from the lovely Isle of Wight." This set him thinking about the island that he had visited for the first time that summer. It was an autumn day in 1933 and the writer was on the second leg of a personal quest to observe and report on the state of the nation. His one man's "rambling but truthful account" would be published the following year as *English Journey*. The result of his thoughts is a paean of praise to the Island (leaving out the Cowes, Osborne, Ryde area, which has "little charm"):

> The rest of it (Lovely Island) is the English South-country at its best in miniature—Lilliputian downs and all—with an island quality adding a lightening of the horizon in whichever direction you look. Tennyson is its poet, Victoria its queen... The island population—excluding the summer yachtsmen and all the deck hands and stewards and other men who have to play with yachtsmen—consists chiefly of an amiable and slow peasantry not to be hustled but said to be good in a crisis, and elderly gentlefolk tucked away in charming old manor houses or converted farms... If you wish to study the English countryside of the more genteel novelists, you can have it neatly arranged and spread out for you on the Isle of Wight. There is not much bad poverty there, even now, and a good deal of homely enchantment: the Downs high above the Channel; the sub-tropical Undercliff, well away from Farringford but very close to the landscape of Tennyson's poetry; sunsets and the Needles; rooks in the old elms; and the spring, bright with daffodils, that has always haunted English poetry... The island would make a superb national park of the American kind, but then I suppose if you compare it with the real England of our time, it already is.

J. B. Priestley (1894-1984) was the son of a Bradford school master, who left school at sixteen and worked as a clerk in a wool firm. He enlisted in September 1914 and survived four years in the trenches despite being wounded twice. He recalls in *English Journey* that Southampton was one of his embarkation ports for France. The writer John Braine said after his death: "I think the real Jack Priestley died in 1914 somewhere on the Western Front... and what all those millions of words were really written for was so that he wouldn't remember the 1914-18 war." After completing a degree at Cambridge Priestley embarked on a career as a writer, initially as a short story writer, then as a playwright and novelist, with his breakthrough coming in 1929 with the publication of *The Good Companions*—one of the bestsellers of the century. In addition to novels he wrote biography, social commentary and fourteen plays, and was a broadcaster and a performer on the American lecture circuit. He was also a political activist and a founder member of the Campaign for Nuclear Disarmament. He became a celebrity writer and intellectual despite the contemporary handicaps of a middle-class provincial background

Priestley does a familiar thing, seeing the Isle of Wight as part of a former England, a better England, not part of some bland suburban uniformity. Other parts of the country such as Cornwall, Devon and the Lake District also provoke this response, nostalgia for the lost arcadia that was England. It is true and not true at the same time. But what has made the Isle of Wight something of a time capsule is simply its physical detachment from the mainland. Living on an island has in the past reinforced a sense of separateness. Islanders would refer to themselves as "caulkheads" (a "caulk" being a tot of rum) distinguishable from "overners" or mainlanders. The Island (it is usually capitalised) is itself a fascinating geological object.

The Isle of Wight is England's largest island, over three times the size of Jersey and one hundred and forty times the size of Lundy. In area it comprises about a tenth of the county of Hampshire. Shaped like a diamond, its maximum extent east to west is 22 miles, that from north to south thirteen miles. The Island's coast is indented by small harbours, bays, creeks and "chines"—deep, ravine-like clefts from the Anglo-Saxon *cine*, a chink or fissure—cut into cliffs by the action of fast streams. A central chalk ridge (its highest point over 403 feet) from the fragmented stacks of the Needles in the east to Culver Cliff in the west bisects the Island. To the north is an area of Tertiary Lowland, well wooded with many copses and

Low tide at Hanover Point

woods and the Parkhurst Forest, and still mostly rural despite the presence of the Island's three main towns: Ryde, Newport and Cowes. The northern lowlands have extensive areas of mud flats and salt marshes—the tidal marshes of the Newtown river and its nature reserve provide three hundred acres of natural estuarine habitat.

The area to the south of the chalk ridge is Greensand Lowland, a mix of wooded ridges and expanses of lowland including the flat area of Sandstone Belt with more undulating Wealden and Greensand lowland to the south, and to the south-east the chalk downs of the Southern Coastal Hills between Dunnose Point and St. Catherine's Point. The coastal area of the south-east below the southern hills is the Undercliff, essentially a six-mile area of landslip. Chines score the southern coast created by streams with steep gradients. It has been estimated that the central ridge was connected to the mainland and Dorset's Isle of Purbeck until that link was breached seven or eight thousand years ago. Previously at the end of the last Ice Age, around 10,000 years ago, sea levels rose due to glacial melting and formed most of the contemporary outline of the Island. The part of the contemporary Isle of Wight that most resembles the prevalent landscape 7,000 years ago is the marshland area of the Newtown Estuary.

If it is a draw for geologists the Island is an equal magnet for botanists and ornithologists. R. J. Berry in his book *Islands*, in the *New Naturalist* series, states that the Hampshire biota (the flora and fauna of a region) was most likely established before the Island broke away from the mainland; and as "Hampshire is botanically the richest county in Britain", so the Isle of Wight would be similarly endowed as a "preserved microcosm of Southern England". While the Island is a rare habitat for the red squirrel, it is also a primary breeding ground for many types of bird: kestrels, waders, herons, diving birds, gulls, ducks and many others. Its insular status means that the maritime influence on the Island's weather is prevalent and a variety of microclimates coexist in a relatively small area.

Middle Stone Age man led an itinerant life hunting, snaring and fishing: and Mesolithic remains have been found in the Newtown and Bembridge harbour areas. Bronze Age barrows have been discovered on Brook Down, signs of an Iron Age fort on Chillerton Down and recovered vessels suggest the incursions of the Belgae from Gaul. The Romans are in evidence from AD 43 or early 44 on an island they named Vectis; the fine Roman villa remains at Brading, located on a site occupied continuously since the Iron Age, certainly date from c. AD 44. Here twelve rooms were arranged on three sides of a courtyard—a campus that included a hall with "tessellated pavement" and frescoes, a central heating system and a bath block. The surviving mosaics are striking depictions of the Roman cultural landscape: Medusa's head, Orpheus playing his lyre surrounded by animals, Bacchus, a water nymph, two sparring gladiators, Perseus and Andromeda both making sure not to look at the eyes in the head of the slain gorgon-Medusa, Ceres the goddess of corn, Lycurgus King of Thrace being strangled by Ambrosia who has been turned into a vine by Mother Earth to evade the king's advances... The Romans' occupation of other lands meant their gods and mythology came with their armies. The Island had fallen easily to Vespasian in AD 43 and Vectis, as the Romans called it, seems to have become a peaceful posting on the edge of an empire which would stretch from Mauretania on the North African coast to Assyria and Mesopotamia in the east and Britain in the north.

After the Romans left in the early fifth century it was in AD 530, according to the *Anglo-Saxon Chronicle*, when the Anglo-Saxon kings Cerdic and Cynric took possession of the Isle of Wight by force and "slew many men at Wihtgarasburh", perhaps Carisbrooke. It is from one of Cerdic's nephews, Wihtgar, that the name Wight emerged—possibly. Historians and archaeologists are not sure and chroniclers of earlier centuries gave differing versions. The *Anglo-Saxon Chronicle* says that Christianity was brought to the Island by the son of King Wulfhere of Mercia through a devastating invasion in 661. Bede, writing in his *Ecclesiastical History of the English People*, claims that it was still pagan in 686 when Caedwalla King of the West Saxons "laid waste the Island" in the Christian cause of eradicating idolatry. Possibly. It also seems that historians' own disputations are part of a saga that began a long time ago.

Nineteenth-century excavation at Chessell Down north of Brook found an Anglo-Saxon cemetery containing late fifth- and sixth-century pagan graves. Similar Anglo-Saxon graves have also been found, according to Lloyd and Pevsner, "inserted into Bronze Age round barrows along the central chalk ridge". "It also appears safe to assume that in late Saxon times the Island's central place was most probably at Carisbrooke."

CARISBROOKE CASTLE

Viewed from a low-flying air balloon today, Carisbrooke Castle could be seen as a parchment with much of the Island's history etched onto it. From the medieval stone keep to today's English Heritage flag it represents in built form fear of invasion, defence, status, governance, conservation and tourism. This fortress, situated on a flat-topped hill on the outskirts of Newport within a defensive landscape that has been altered and improved over centuries, provides landmarks in earth and stone of successive periods of English history from Anglo-Saxon times to the Civil War and beyond. Our circling balloon would afford clear views of the massive earthen ramparts faced by stone, with a flanker battery on the south-west corner. Entrance to the castle is via a bridge across a perimeter ditch to a large medieval gatehouse. The castle walls which date from the twelfth century provide walkways along the northern and southern sides. The stone keep is visible on its earthen mound or motte; in Norman times this would have been enclosed in a bailey defended by a ditch and a palisade. The construction of such a motte using layers of flint and rammed chalk is illustrated in the Bayeux Tapestry (c.1067-77).

Within the castle walls the key buildings—the Great Hall, the Constable's Lodging and the chapel—are all grouped round a spacious courtyard, as are the privy garden next to the chapel and the bowling green set

Carisbroooke Castle: Hall and chamber block with the top of the keep on the motte behind

amid massive terraced banks at the eastern end of the castle. Less obviously identifiable are the stone shell of Carey's Mansion and the well house. In his time as governor of the Island Sir George Carey had built (1584-86) a mansion of thirteen chambers befitting his status. Display of status was an optional add-on; but the viability of the castle was something else because in the age of siege warfare access to water was crucial for any garrison's survival. The castle's surviving well and treadwheel is located in its own building in the courtyard of the Great Hall. Constructed by Carey in 1587, it was a replacement for a similar well building that dates back to the end of the thirteenth century. The treadwheel was probably worked originally by prisoners; the first recorded alternative power source was a "horse" or "ass" seen by the traveller Celia Fiennes in 1696. Fiennes (1662-1741) was a pioneering woman traveller, journeying to most parts of England on horseback and recording what she saw in her journal, exhorting others to "Spend their tyme in Journeys to visit their native land, and be curious to inform themselves and make observations of the pleasant prospects, good buildings, different produces and manufactures of each place." Since then the well has been continually operated by donkey power and donkeys still perform this task today.

The T-shaped Great Hall and the adjacent chamber block provided accommodation for over 700 years until the end of Second World War; since 1951 the Great Hall "complex" has been a museum. Dating the origin of the Great Hall has proved difficult but it was built most probably in the time of Countess Isabella de Fortibus, from 1262 when she took over stewardship of the castle through inheriting all her brother's estates in Devon, Hampshire and the Isle of Wight after he had been poisoned. The castle was under Isabella's control until her death in 1293 when it was sold to Edward I. During the Hundred Years War (1337-1453) French raids ensured that the castle was in the front line. Yarmouth Castle to the northwest, a single "arrow-head" stone bastion completed in the mid-sixteenth century, was the last of Henry VIII's coastal forts designed to keep the French at bay.

Isabella had made the castle her main residence as well as an administrative hub, a garrison, a law court and prison. She added a chapel to the Great Hall, a great chamber for herself, a further chamber for the Constable and a herb garden. The Great Hall and these adjacent buildings were subject to restoration schemes from 1856, initially under the supervision of Philip Hardwick (1792-1870), who, among other improvements, inserted medieval-style windows in the Constable's Lodgings. Hardwick was one of the doyens of classical mid-Victorian architects, surveyor to numerous mercantile and charitable enterprises, designer of much of the Lincoln Inn Fields legal campus and architect of London docklands warehouses and the Albert Dock traffic office in Liverpool; he was also a founder member of the Institute of British Architects (1834) and designer of the propylaeum or "Doric Arch" that signalled the entrance to Euston Station (demolished 1961-62).

The bowling green at Carisbrooke is linked to the castle's role in a significant chain of events in England's political and constitutional story. This lush green field flanked by formidable banks dates from the time of King Charles I's detention here in 1648, when a bowling green was fashioned for his recreational use. The Civil War battle at Naseby on 14 June 1645 had been a decisive victory for the parliamentarians and the king surrendered to the Scots at Newark in May of the following year; he was handed over to the English in February 1647. What followed was a royal progress in reverse. From February to June the king was a prisoner of the English parliament at Holdenby House in Northamptonshire. He was under house arrest but Charles could go hunting and he developed an enthusiasm for bowls. From June until November the king was the prisoner of the New Model Army in a variety of great houses in East Anglia and Hertfordshire before being transferred to Hampton Court. It was from here that he made his escape on 11 November and took a boat across the Thames to join a group of conspirators waiting with horses. At this point the flight took a comical turn as the party argued about what to do next: make a daring ride to London to rouse the populace, take a boat to France or to Jersey or…? As it was they rode to the Solent coast, appeared to get lost and spent two nights at Titchfield House before crossing to the Isle of Wight and spending a night in the Plume of Feathers hostelry.

The new plan was this: that the king would surrender to the Island's governor Colonel Robert Hammond, a parliamentarian but someone dismayed with the radical politics within the New Model Army who had asked for a posting away from the capital. Surely he would be sympathetic to the king's plight, and the likely "open prison" conditions at Carisbrooke Castle would enable Charles to negotiate his way back into military contention. On 22 November Charles put himself under the protection of Constable Hammond, and at first everything seemed to be going according to his plan. On Boxing Day he managed to sign a settlement of military alliance, called the Engagement, with the Scots parliamentary commissioners, despite his prisoner status. He was also allowed to ride round the Island. The king's coach was shipped over in December together with his library. When not scheming or playing bowls, Charles read voraciously—devotional theology, Shakespeare and the poetry of Edmund Spenser.

The Second Civil War saw a Scottish army cross into England in July 1648 to be decisively routed at the Battle of Preston in August. In the interim there had been some popular agitation in Newport to get the king released. In March Charles had tried to escape from his castle apartments only to get stuck in his bedchamber window. Colonel Hammond was now compelled to become a proper jailor. The army then demanded that exemplary justice be meted out on the deposed monarch. Abdication was offered but Charles continued to count on the probability of foreign military intervention—a final calculation in a history of miscalculations. On 1 December the king was moved to Hurst Castle, just on the mainland, and thence to Windsor Castle and finally to St. James' Palace. Significant numbers among the parliamentarians were angry at the king's willingness to squander English and Scottish lives for his lost cause. His "show trial" began on 20 January 1649 at Westminster Hall where the king stood accused of the charge that "he levied war against the present parliament and the people there represented". Found guilty, he was beheaded ten days later on a platform in front of the Banqueting Hall in Whitehall. For the next nine years the English political scene was "a world turned upside down", with a new republican ideology first as a Commonwealth then as a Protectorate in a hostile wider world.

Across the courtyard from the shell of Carey's Mansion stands the Chapel of St. Nicholas with its own Privy Garden. A church has occupied this site since 1086 and it predates the motte-and-bailey castle, as the Domesday Book testifies. The present building was designed in 1904 by Percy Stone as a memorial chapel to commemorate the 250th anniversary of Charles I's execution. This royalist commission was perhaps no surprise as the Island's governor at the time was Princess Beatrice, the youngest daughter of Queen Victoria.

Percy Stone (1856-1934), endowed with an almost Dickensian job-specific name, trained as an architect, moved to the Isle of Wight in the 1880s and stayed. He built new churches, restored older ones and designed war memorials and the memorial to Queen Victoria in Newport. Stone worked on excavations at Quarr Abbey and Carisbrooke, wrote poetry and published the seminal work *The Architectural Antiquities of the Isle of Wight* in 1891. His reconstruction drawings in this tome could well have been instrumental in his getting the job rebuilding St. Nicholas.

The interior has the feel of a small Oxford college chapel, a bright, well-lit, optimistic space with continuous stalls on either side of the tile-floored nave under a polygonal wagon roof with painted panels, accompanied by sculptured figures on the cornices. The porch at the west end includes a small antechapel that houses a bust of Charles I created by Bernini with its inscription "Remember". The reader may feel some ambiguity as to what exactly it was about the king that the onlooker is exhorted to remember. At the Restoration, parliament declared Charles a martyr and his name was added to the Anglican calendar of saints; in 1894 the Church of England discreetly removed his name from the feast day calendar.

It was decided after the First World War that the chapel would be the

Island's war memorial so now there are 2,000 inscriptions of the names of the dead from two world wars on stone panels between the windows of the nave. This and other war memorials throughout the country are still able to elicit feelings of poignancy and regret almost a hundred years after the start of the Great War. The chapel's altar painting was created and installed on Princess Beatrice's instruction to commemorate her son Maurice who was killed at Ypres in 1914.

LIGHTHOUSES AND SMUGGLERS

The poet John Keats stayed in Canterbury House in Carisbrooke during April 1817 and when he was not walking the "Primrose Island", he sat in his room with its view of the castle, struggling with the composition of the start of *Endymion*. His poem "On the Sea" begins:

> It keeps eternal whisperings around
> Desolate shores, and with its mighty swell
> Gluts twice ten thousand caverns, till the spell
> Of Hecate leaves them their old shadowy sound.

Keats was alert to the sea's destructive and mercurial nature; and the nineteenth century witnessed both the increasing portrayal of shipwrecks and sea rescue in art and the launching of a national rescue service. The life of a seaman was no soft billet. As the biographer of the "Lighthouse Stevensons", Bella Bathurst describes it: "two hundred years ago, almost half of all British seamen died pursuing their trade, either killed by the punishing life on board ship or sacrificed to storms and drownings." In the time between two pictures—Turner's 1805 painting *The Shipwreck* and Winslow Homer's watercolour and gouache *The Wreck of the Iron Crown* painted in 1881—seafaring off Britain's shores became safer. Turner's depiction of three rescue boats struggling to stay afloat in a cauldron of waves was partly inspired by the wreck of the *Earl of Abergavenny* off the Dorset coast in 1805, a tragedy in which the poet Wordsworth lost his brother John, the captain. When the large three-masted schooner the *Iron Crown* was aground off Tynemouth Winslow Homer ran to the beach to make sketches. The resulting picture shows a self-righting lifeboat being rowed up a mountainous wave toward the stricken ship.

Professional seaman William Falconer (1732-70) wrote the first sea-

St. Catherine's Point Lighthouse (1838-40) on the Niton Undercliffe with coastguard cottages

dictionary, *An Universal Dictionary of the Marine*, in 1769, and an epic marine poem, *The Shipwreck*, published to popular acclaim in 1762. It is a combination of gothic horror and technical detail:

> In vain the cords and axes were prepar'd
> For now the'audacious seas insult the yard;
> High o'er the ship they throw a horrid shade,
> And o'er her burst, in terrible cascade.

On 27 December in the year his *Dictionary* was published Falconer was a passenger on the warship *Aurora* which set sail from Cape Town harbour. It disappeared without trace.

The novelist John Fowles in his introduction to *Shipwreck* (1974), a compilation of nineteenth-century photographs of Cornish maritime disasters, has a singular take on the sea and its moods:

> I happen to live over the sea myself, I watch it every day, I hear it every
> night. I do not like it angry, but I've noticed that most urban and inland
> people adore it so. Storms and gales seem to awaken something joyous

and excited in them; the thunder on the shingle, the spray and spume, the rut and rage. No doubt this is partly a product of a life where the elements have largely receded out of daily notice; but I think it goes deeper, into a kind of Freudian double identification, in which the wrath of the sea is interpreted both as super-ego and as id. It is on the one hand a thing without restraint, a giant bull in a salt ring: on the other it is the great punisher of presumption…

Many people living in coastal areas believed they had a right to salvage goods and materials from a wreck. Yet some—"wreckers"—were active in causing ships to run aground and cold-hearted in their priorities: loot over lives. Three developments in the nineteenth century helped combat this coastal maritime anarchy: the building of lighthouses, the establishment of a coastguard and lifeboat service and the development of lifeboats and life-saving apparatus.

The Isle of Wight has three lighthouses—the oldest from 1314 is the only surviving medieval lighthouse in England, a 35-foot stone octagonal tower sitting atop St. Catherine's Hill on the Island's south coast. Legend has it that Walter de Godeton built St. Catherine's Oratory to atone for plundering a French ship that had run aground in Chale Bay. The medieval light tower's "replacement", built between 1838 and 1840, is sited at the edge of the land at St. Catherine's Point on Niton's Undercliff. Its necessity was demonstrated by the figure of over a hundred ships wrecked in Chale Bay between 1750 and 1850.

The Needles Light is perched at the seaward end of the iconic chain of fin-like chalk stacks—a 102-foot-high red and white granite tower built between 1857 and 1859. Prior to this shipping avoided the western approaches to the Solent; but rounding the island by an easterly route had its own dangers. Trinity House, the lighthouse authority, had been petitioned for decades since 1780 to grant a patent for the construction of a lighthouse on Needles Point. Finally it decided to build the lighthouse itself and in 1853 its consultant engineer prepared plans.

The construction work started in July 1857 with the local workforce of quarrymen standing constantly in sea water for the first eight weeks on the Needles Point Rock to construct the granite base. The ground floor would be the main entrance and oil store. The floor above would be the provisions store, with the floor above that comprising the dining and

The Needles Light

cooking area and the living quarters with the sleeping accommodation on the next floor. The floors were built of chequered steel plate and covered with slate. The lantern was housed in a 23 foot high glazed unit. After improvements in the 1950s the light from the Needles lighthouse was visible from a range of fourteen nautical miles. Both the Needles and St. Catherine's Lighthouses had been in the front line in the Second World War, regularly strafed by the Luftwaffe with the loss of three keepers at St. Catherine's in a bombing raid. A helipad was fitted on top of the Needles light in 1987 and the lighthouse keepers left the lighthouse for the last time when automation was introduced at the end of 1995. The Needles lighthouse remains a familiar icon of England's built southern coast.

There was a groundswell of opinion in the early years of the nineteenth century that more should be done to advance and co-ordinate life-saving measures for those at sea, for both humanitarian and economic reasons. Henry Greathead, a South Shields boat builder, had invented the lifeboat in 1789, an invention celebrated in paintings and engravings. Lightships were introduced and in the first decade of the century Captain George Manby of Yarmouth pioneered new methods of launching and securing lines to stricken ships to allow crew and passengers to be taken off.

Again Turner illustrates and publicises this in a painting: *Lifeboat and Manby Apparatus Going off to a Stranded Vessel Making Signal of Distress*. A more effective rocket for firing off Manby's line from a mortar was pioneered in 1827 by a resident of Carisbrooke, Mr. J. Dennett. In 1824 an organisational first was launched with the founding of the National Institution for the Preservation of Life from Shipwreck (later the RNLI).

Two years earlier another service, the Coast Guard, had been set up. This was formed ostensibly to prevent smuggling and to supervise coastal shipping; but it would also contribute to sea rescue. Smuggling has a history as old as sea trade itself; Daniel Defoe had written of Lymington in 1724: "I do not find they have any foreign commerce, except it be what we call smuggling and rougueing, which I may say is the reigning commerce of all this part of the English coast." Certainly during the Revolutionary and Napoleonic Wars (1793-1801 and 1803-15), when England was virtually cut off from trade with mainland Europe, smuggling became part of a significant shadow economy. Distribution often took place through pubs. The chines of the Isle of Wight's south coast such as Blackgang Chine were good entry points with handy beaches, brushwood camouflage and obscure paths inland.

Smugglers were seen by some as folk heroes—men from the lower orders taking their share. Yet whatever the romantic gloss and folk tale mythologising, they were bandits nonetheless, especially those in mounted and armed gangs who escorted the packhorses carrying the contraband to urban traders. The goods incurring high taxes were especially valuable— silk, tobacco and brandy—and these smugglers could be ruthless. One outfit from Kent, the Hawkhurst Gang, travelled to Poole to mount a raid on the Revenue Store to take back a large consignment of tea that had been intercepted by a Revenue Cutter. Some of the gang were later convicted and executed for the murder of informants. By the late 1780s the punishment for smuggling was transportation, a sentence that meant months in the prison hulks moored in Portsmouth Harbour before the seventeen week sea voyage to Van Diemen's Land.

In 1831 the Coast Guard absorbed an experimental shore-based service, the Coast Blockade, set up by the Admiralty to intercept smugglers as they landed. The Coast Guard and the Excise men equipped themselves with more fast cutters to match the boats the smugglers used. This amalgamated force needed permanent residences and the result was a necklace of Coast Guard stations and houses around the Isle of Wight's coast. These stations had their own armoury—ammunition, rifles, pistols, cutlasses and swordsticks—and were also equipped with a galley and a gig. There was a flagstaff for hoisting semaphore signals; in the 1890s the Post Office telegraphy system connected the stations, just as wireless would in the new century. The Island was a key location in the genesis of wireless telegraphy when Guglielmo Marconi set up "the world's first permanent wireless station" at the Royal Beedles Hotel at Alum Bay from where successful transmissions were made to Poole and ships forty miles out to sea. With the Coast Guards it was understood, officially or unofficially, that they would also assist when vessels were in distress.

This archipelago of protective stations survives discreetly. Twenty-four stations were operational in 1850 with two additions—the Needles and Culver Down—in the first decade of the twentieth century. All were closed by 1960. Those buildings that remain, and which are mostly converted to new use, include: in East Cowes a smart terrace of buff and red brick houses formerly for coastguards and the chief officer's house built in the early 1880s on "recovered land", now the Esplanade; a special boat house built on Ryde pier at the seaward end from where the galley and the gig could be launched and housed; another terrace of former coastguard houses still standing at Seaview with a seafront that looks out to Horse Sands and No Man's Land forts; houses on the ridge of Culver Down overseeing Sandown Bay; at Blackgang on Chale Bay and off Military Road at Brightstone and at Brook a former coastguard station and houses survey the English Channel; coastguard houses at Freshwater stand proud in Coastguard Lane (built 1859); and the Needles coastguard houses on West High Down, currently owned by the National Trust, are let as holiday homes; others survive at Totland scanning Totland Bay and at Yarmouth, at Newtown and at Gurnard west of Egypt Point.

THE RAMBLING ISLE

Two early and unlikely activists for rambling were the Lakeland poet William Wordsworth (1770-1850), who used the outdoors as his study, with walking as his means of composition, and his fellow poet Samuel Coleridge Taylor (1772-1834), who was arguably the first modern fell walker. By the early decades of the twentieth century rambling in England and Wales had become a popular recreation and a popular cause. After the

1932 mass trespass on Kinder Scout, located on the Duke of Devonshire's Peak District land, and the subsequent arrests of the organisers, the Ramblers Association was set up in 1935 as a campaign group for walkers. After the Second World War all local authorities were required to trace all rights of way and Ordnance Survey included these on their maps.

Rambler activism and promotion has continued with the 1997 mass trespass protests "Forbidden Britain" organised by the Ramblers Association, by the campaigning for more National Parks and the increased provision by local governments and tourist authorities of walking trails. Here the Isle of Wight has been in the forefront. An island, half of which has also been designated an Area of Outstanding Natural Beauty by the Countryside Commission, is crisscrossed by short- and long-distance routes and trails for walkers. There are over 500 miles of maintained public rights of way that include thirty miles of Heritage Coast walking paths (the highest quality designation).

Since 1967 the Isle of Wight Ramblers have been key players in developing the Island's rambling routes network. In 1999 the organisation received a national award for the best kept footpaths and in 2011 it won the Queen's Award for Voluntary Service. The citation highlighted its work "campaigning for greater access to the countryside and encouraging community participation in walking activities." Inspired by the Ramblers' example, the Council launched the Isle of Wight Walking Festival, a regular May fixture over the last ten years, featuring over sixty events including town trails, a 24-hour round the island walk, a speed dating walk, a Jimi Hendrix garden tour, a night walk through Parkhurst Forest and rambles exploring the Western Yar, the Undercliff and manor houses. Another walking festival is now a regular feature in the autumn. Of the long-distance walks the existence of the Tennyson Trail was to be expected, less so the Robert Hooke Trail.

Robert Hooke was a driven, specialism-defying polymath scientist and inventor. Born on 18 July 1635 in Freshwater, he was the son of the curate of All Saints' Church, John Hooke. Robert was a sickly boy and was kept at home for most of his childhood. Here he made scientific toys such as sundials and clocks. His father died in October 1648 a month before Charles I was to be moved from detention at Carisbrooke to his trial in London. Robert was sent to be a pupil in the harsh regime at Westminster School. Despite his poor attendance he mastered sufficient mathematics, Greek and Latin to enable him to secure a place at Christ Church, Oxford, albeit as a poor scholar. He paid his passage combining the duties of a chorister and a servitor to richer fellow students. He studied mathematics and mechanics under Dr. John Wilkins (Oliver Cromwell's brother-in-law) and learnt dissection from Dr. Thomas Willis. Willis recommended him to a wealthy amateur Robert Boyle. He was initially Boyle's research assistant and through his patron—one of the founders of the Royal Society—secured the post of Curator of Experiments. This is how progress is made.

Hooke was sociable but could be self-centred and difficult, even antagonistic. He managed to cross Sir Isaac Newton, who was arguably the greatest scientist of his day but also someone who could nurse a grudge. Newton outlived Hooke by twenty years and, it seems, managed to get Hooke's contributions deleted from the annals of science. Just for the record, Robert Hooke "contrived and perfected the air pump"; through his book *Micrographia* he introduced the public to the microscopic sights of nature; he made innovative studies of light and of capillaries; his inventions included the hygrometer (an instrument that measures the humidity of the atmosphere), an anemometer that could measure wind strength and a universal joint that silenced the movement of a pendulum. He was a pioneer in the science of meteorology and he articulated Hooke's Law of Springs. (The Island Planetarium at Fort Victoria on the trail includes a Robert Hooke exhibition.) After the 1666 Great Fire of London Hooke was made City Surveyor and played a significant role in restoring the City. He was not an extravagant man; after his death in 1703 an iron chest in his rooms was found to contain notes and coins that amounted to almost a million pounds in today's money.

The Robert Hooke Trail starts in Yarmouth and directs you south along the east bank of the River Yar. This and the causeway after two miles remind the walker that West Wight was a separate island in the seventeenth century. Crossing the causeway brings you to All Saints' Church, where Robert's father was a curate, and down Hooke Hill to a memorial stone passing the site of his childhood home. The walk continues south to Freshwater Bay where it is likely that the young Robert dug for fossils. His sickly childhood precluded much schooling but he taught himself to be an excellent illustrator with pen and pencil. The walk can then be traced north passing St. Agnes Church and Golden Hill Fort (1868)—one of the string

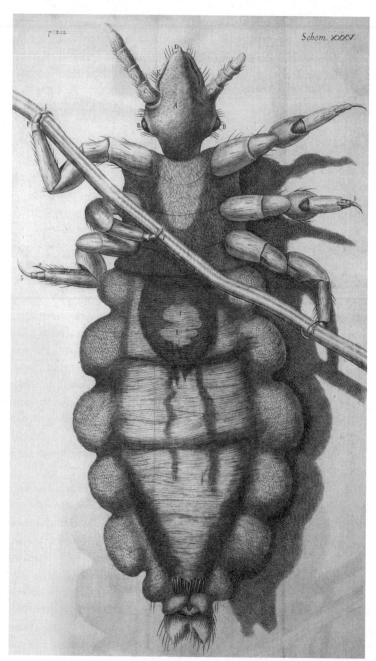

A louse from Hooke's *Micrographia*

of Solent area defensive forts known as Palmerston's follies—to reach Fort Victoria, on the north-western tip of the Island, with its planetarium and Robert Hooke exhibition.

COUNTRY HOUSES

No imagined landscape of England would be complete without country houses and gardens; and naturally the Isle of Wight is furnished with these. Deer parks such as the King's Park at Watchingwell on the south-east side of Parkhurst Forest were Saxon legacies in the Norman record of manorial tenure, value and resources, the Domesday Book. By medieval times small enclosed areas of wood pasture were created to supply venison and as status symbols. There were parks at Swainston, at Wootton, at Nunwell (from the sixteenth century, which the owner Sir John Oglander described thus: "of a rude chase I have now made it a fit place for any gentleman") and at Appuldurcombe (from the early eighteenth century). Manor houses at Barton, Stenbury, Wolverton near Shorewell and Mottistone were built on medieval, moated sites.

The lives and histories of buildings shadow wider community developments. So, for instance, Barton Manor was a seventeenth-century house located on the site of a thirteenth-century Augustinian oratory and acquired by Queen Victoria and Prince Albert when they occupied Osborne House; it was then redesigned by the designers of that same house, Albert and Thomas Cubitt. Barton Manor is not far from St. Mildred's Church at Whippingham, essentially the Royal Family's parish church. Stenbury Manor in the parish of Godshill is also seventeenth-century and is set against a downland background. Wolverton is one of three manor houses at Shorewell. Built at the end of the sixteenth century with an E-plan frontage, a walled forecourt and garden, it also includes an unusual mid to late-eighteenth century Chinese Chippendale staircase in the south wing. The long barn and the former stables are probably seventeenth-century. One of its neighbours, North Court (built c. 1615), with its fine brown sandstone façade, was once set in enterprising landscaped gardens (from 1795 on) that had included a temple, a mausoleum, summerhouse, conservatory and Alpine bridge, but not now. The gardens were, however, recreated in the latter decades of the twentieth century and the rescued house, stables, coach house, bath house and knot garden remain. As with North Court, the sixteenth/seventeenth-century Mottistone Manor at

Brighstone had to be rescued from some dereliction in the 1920s. The Manor Garden is now a National Trust property with a twentieth-century design that includes a modern Mediterranean planting scheme, an olive grove and a cabin retreat that was the drawing office of the architects working on the restoration.

The house at Nunwell, just to the west of Brading, was the home of the Oglander family from the sixteenth century until 1980, and the family had held land at Brading since the beginning of the thirteenth. The best-known family member was gardener and diarist Sir John Oglander, who was a keen royalist and friend of Charles I. Sensibly he mostly occupied himself with estate matters. He writes in his *Commonplace Book* about the origins of his local realm: "I built the house at East Nunwell, together with brewhouse, barn, stable, Warren, gardens, orchards, Hoppegardens, bowling green and all other things thereunto adjacent in 1609." He goes on to enthuse about his work planting two orchards with "pippins, pear-mains, putles, hornies... Cherries, damsons, plums... and in the upper garden, apricocks, mellecatoons [melons] and figs". The book also contains sensible advice for his descendants:

> Have a small warren for some rabbits when thy friends come. Build a pigeon-house and fit up a fishpond or two that at all times thou mayest have provisions at hand. Pale in place to breed or keep pheasants and partridges in. I paled all my warren round about my houses in compass 12 acres.

The present house is set in beautiful parkland but lacks some architectural coherence due to expansion and improvement from the 1750s to the 1920s. It does include a fine library and main staircase with an impressive former stable block to the south-west.

The grandest of these houses is Appuldurcombe House, now a shell but a wonderfully restored and preserved shell managed by English Heritage. It is set in a beautiful landscape/dreamscape in a valley near the village of Wroxhall, two miles north-west of Ventnor and surrounded by downs. The site of the house affords panoramic views of Stenbury Down and Appuldurcombe Down to the west and St. Martin's Down to the east. The Tudor mansion was demolished and rebuilt in the early eighteenth century by Sir Robert Worsley and the park later remodelled for his heir

Engraving of Appuldurcombe Park

Sir Richard Worsley in the 1770s. There are portraits of Sir Richard Worsley and Lady Worsley, formerly Seymour Dorothy Fleming, painted by Sir Joshua Reynolds, around the time of their marriage in 1775. They both look the part: he booted and spurred with a large sword and she, determined and elegantly dressed with a fine feather hat and carrying a long riding crop. Both figures are beautifully rendered and stand out against a vague rural landscape that looks like an unconvincing theatre backdrop; but what it certainly does do is declare landed aristocracy. Their marriage lasted seven years before a divorce followed Lady Worsley's admission of having taken 27 lovers.

There remains some uncertainty about the identity of the principal architect for the current house but it seems probable that it was John James (c. 1673-1746), who served apprenticeships as a carpenter and as clerk of works to Nicholas Hawksmoor at Greenwich Hospital and later rose from Master Carpenter to Surveyor of the Fabric of St. Paul's Cathedral. The elaborate decorative treatment at Appuldurcombe with Portland stone for the features and dressings includes, for example, a circular window crowned by a figure and foliage with hanging stone drapery either side above the main door all flanked by considerable Corinthian columns and the roof adorned with pairs of linked chimneystacks; these would seem to be something of a departure from James' normally "plain and unadventurous" designs. The house was in the English baroque architectural style with the ends of the building given emphasis by projecting pavilions.

The new landscape was designed by Capability Brown, with sweeping slopes and tree clusters surrounded by a stone wall and ha-has to prevent the deer from straying. Features such as an obelisk on Appuldurcombe Down and a folly of a gothic "castle" on St. Martin's Down (probably not part of Brown's scheme) did not survive the twentieth century but the Freemantle Gate does. This triumphal arch was the main entrance to the estate's serpentine carriage drive which was also devised by Capability Brown.

The eighteenth century was the heyday of Appuldurcombe House. After Sir Richard's death the estates were inherited by his niece Henrietta. She married Baron Yarborough, the founder and first commodore of the Royal Yacht Squadron. His seat was at Brocklesby Park in Lincolnshire but Appuldurcombe became a useful base when he was sailing at Cowes. The estate was sold in 1855 after the significant works of art were shipped to Lincolnshire. The new absentee owner leased the house to a joint stock company with the idea of converting it into a hotel, but this did not happen. From 1867 until the 1890s a Rev. Pound ran a school here for young gentlemen. It was then occupied between 1901 and 1908 by refugee French Benedictine monks while they awaited the completion of their new home at Quarr Abbey. From 1909 until 1952 the house was unoccupied except for use by troops in both world wars. The decision was made in 1952 to preserve the building from dereliction and decay, and first the Historic Buildings Commission for England and then English Heritage have pursued a programme of repair and preservation at Appuldurcombe.

MERCHANDISING THE PAST

It is important also to recall that while these landscapes can provide inspirational places for contemporary visitors, the expansion and improvement of many rural parklands involved trampling on the rights of estate tenants through clearance, eviction and the demolition of their dwellings. This sanitising and packaging of the past in the interests of present-day tourism is the one of the main themes of Julian Barnes' 1998 satirical novel

England, England. It tells the story of Sir Jack Pitman, arts patron and leading entrepreneur—"less captain of industry than a very admiral"—working to realise his last grand scheme to assemble in one giant theme park the essential component parts of Englishness or at least versions of them: the Royal Family, pubs, real ale, cricket, Robin Hood, Anne Hathaway's cottage, Wembley Stadium, *The Times*, Queen Victoria, smuggling, the class system, Cotswold cottages and London fog, and to represent these attractions and experiences in one condensed site. He decides the perfect location to be that "pure diamond, little jewel", the turbot-shaped Isle of Wight, described by one of Pitman's researchers as a "mixture of rolling chalk downland of considerable beauty and bungaloid dystopia".

This version of England required the Isle of Wight to be independent of mainland England so Sir Jack manages to persuade the necessary English and international courts that Edward I's acquisition of the Island from Isabella de Fortibus in 1293 was unlawful and to get this annulled. He duly becomes the Island's governor. *The Times* is then published in Ryde, Jane Austen's house and Ann Hathaway's cottage are relocated, Battle of Britain planes fly over Tennyson Down and its three golf courses, retro weekends are introduced at Osborne House, a replica of Buckingham Palace is built with stand-in royals appearing on the balcony and a recreated street of typical former Island dwellings called Bungalow Valley is built as a reminder. Immigration officers check arrivals' creditworthiness and those with an insufficient credit rating are sent back to Dieppe. Visitors are required to take out health insurance for the duration of their stay—there is no system of socialised medicine in this other England. The tourist experience is designed to be a reassuring one, a sanitised version of Olde England produced by a pure market state. Writing at the end of the 1990s, Julian Barnes seems to have been rather prescient about today's political and economic developments.

⁂

Jack Priestley acted on his sense of enchantment for the Island and moved first to Billingham Manor, Shorwell, in 1933. He added a pavilion to an infill between the two wings of this stone and brick house; and in this study "like the bridge of a ship" from where he could survey the rolling countryside he wrote much of his autobiographical book *Rain upon God-*

shill. After the war he moved back to the Island in 1948 and acquired Brook Hill House further west along its south coast—an early twentieth-century coursed rubble-and-stone house with fine views south over the English Channel and west towards Tennyson Down. In 1953 he married the archaeologist and writer Jacquetta Hawkes. They moved back to the mainland in 1959.

During the dark days of 1940 the BBC had invited Priestley to give a series of talks after the evening news. These radio broadcasts were given the name *Postscript* and made him into one of the earliest media celebrities. The first talk was about the heroic role played by pleasure steamers and ferries in the rescue of the British Expeditionary Force from the beaches of Dunkirk; one of the ships he talked about was a vessel the author had used pre-war, the ferry paddle steamer *Gracie Fields* which operated between Cowes and the mainland. It did not return from Dunkirk. In a later talk he underlined again the crucial civilian contribution to the war effort through the recruitment of a third of the population into the Home Guard.

Some argued that his talks had made Priestley the voice of the nation. His non-toff background, his still vivid recall of service in the Great War and its aftermath, his research into social conditions in the 1930s Depression and from that his sympathy for the needs of the ordinary citizen came across strongly to listeners. However, it was Priestley's explicit emphasis that the country was fighting for a different post-war social and economic future with equality of opportunity and democratic fairness as objectives that did not please many in government and in parliament. *Postscript* was taken off the air after eighteen talks. J. B. Priestley's vision of a different social landscape was not shared by many in the war cabinet and certainly not by Winston Churchill—but it was shared by a majority of the post-war electorate.

Chapter Two

COASTING

THE PRESENCE OF THE SEA

In the summer of 1982 just as Britain was going to war with Argentina in a deadly dispute over imperial real estate in the Falkland Islands, Paul Theroux, an American novelist, travel writer and author of *The Family Arsenal* and *The Great Railway Bazaar*, set out on a journey of personal cultural discovery. This was planned as a sequence of walks and train journeys clockwise round the coasts of Britain from Gravesend (last resting place of the American Indian princess Pocahontas) to the end of the pier at Southend-on-Sea.

The resulting book, *The Kingdom by the Sea*, was part travelogue and part commentary on the British and Britishness. The author acknowledges the contribution to the genre of Daniel Defoe, William Cobbett, Henry James, Charles Dickens and Robert Louis Stevenson, who had all turned their pen to a form where the writer is journeying as a cultural reporter. Theroux prefaces his own account with an adaptation of Charles Dickens' dedication in *American Notes*, his journalistic documentary on the young republic published in 1842. "I dedicate this Book to those friends of mine in Britain who, giving me a welcome I must ever gratefully and proudly remember, left my judgement free: and who, loving their country, can bear the truth, when it is told good-humouredly and in a kind spirit." Given that Dickens' account was a critical even disparaging description of contemporary America, readers of Theroux's book could consider themselves forewarned.

It does seem as if Theroux's personal journey travelogue is something of a riposte to Dickens. It is undeniably the case that English people can be insular, misanthropic, small-minded, chauvinistic, foreigner-averse, negative, even curmudgeonly... Need I go on? Our author manages to find ubiquitous evidence of this Little England negativity and insularity, sourced from grumbling conversations in trains and on park benches, even from graffiti.

The author is more judicious on landscapes or at least some landscapes. It is hard not to agree with his take on the Isle of Wight's Ventnor, "an English town in an Italian setting, the town tucked under bluffs and struggling along terraces and dropping from ledges". Ryde invites a similar description. He experiences travel on the Ryde to Sandown railway on a "hand-me-down pensioned off" London underground train and notes that Henry James had described this as "an objectionable conveyance". The earlier American writer/transplanted English resident had deemed Portsmouth to be "dirty, sordid and dull" after a two-hour visit in 1879. Theroux, writing a hundred years later, agreed. He concluded: "Portsmouth was its harbour" and beyond that, "it was pointless to look behind the harbour for anything better." So our intrepid traveller ignored Dickens' birthplace (deliberately?), two Frank Matcham theatres, the first garden suburb, the surviving dockyard architecture of the world's first industrial site and a collection of Victorian forts and barracks that rivals any similar military historical site. The author's verdict would have done nothing to undermine some popular negative clichés about the city.

Theroux is at least aware of his subjectivity when he writes, "it is every travel writer's conceit that no one will see what he has seen: his trip displaces the landscape and his version of events is all that matters." But, of course, there is what he has not seen. Henry James says in his introduction to *English Hours* (1905), "it takes passionate pilgrims, vague aliens and other disinherited persons to appreciate the 'points' of this admirable country." In truth the English writers Daniel Defoe, J. B. Priestley and George Orwell did this better.

In the same year as Theroux's jaundiced journey Jonathan Raban, English novelist and travel writer and author of *Soft City* and *Old Glory: an American Voyage*, set out to sail single-handed round the coasts of England. The resulting book, *Coasting*, was part sailing travelogue, part autobiography, part state-of-the-nation documentary. The author is now a resident of Seattle in America's Pacific north-west. In 1996 he set off to sail the thousand-mile sea route of the Inside Passage from Puget Sound to Alaska. The resulting book, *Passage to Juneau: a Sea and its Meanings*, is a history of that region told through the story and mythology of the region's Native Americans and through accounts of 1790s voyages of the British ship *Discovery* under the captaincy of George Vancouver. It is also an exploration of the sea and of the author himself.

The two coastal waters and coastal walking authors from 1982 did meet when Paul Theroux came aboard Jonathan Raban's boat in Brighton marina, an episode described in Theroux's book. Raban commented later that the American writer's description was not what he remembered, and added, "the memory… is a great maker of fictions."

Both books are episodic accounts of the lone traveller seeking enlightenment offshore or just charting an escape. In *Coasting* Jonathan Raban places himself in the tradition of writing about single-handed sea voyages and he explores some of its history. He locates its origin in the high-minded endeavour of John MacGregor (1825-92), whose book *The Voyage Alone in the Yawl 'Rob Roy'* is an account of designing, building and sailing the boat to France. Published in 1867 it became a bestseller. Mac-Gregor was an evangelist and a philanthropist, a rescuer of London street urchins, vice-president of the Ragged School Union and co-founder of *Boy's Own Paper*. He had certainly experienced enough to be a role model for a *Boy's Own Paper* hero. As a man from a family with ample means he was able to give up a career in the law to devote his life to philanthropy and travel. Other bestselling books recounted his solitary journeys by canoe through the rivers of the continent and even kayaking down the Suez Canal and up the River Jordan. He helped to popularise canoeing in England; as Raban suggests, MacGregor "turned sailing a small boat into a species of high moral endeavour". Not content with just making converts to cruising he also used his cruises for other missionary purposes—handing out bibles on landfall.

Two near contemporaries inspired by MacGregor's maritime missionary zeal were Empson Edward Middleton and London stockbroker and yachtsman R. T. McMullen. Middleton taught himself to sail during a week on the Solent after reading *The Voyage Alone* and he had built a larger version of the yawl *Rob Roy*. His pioneering single-handed voyage round the British Isles, recorded in his book *The Cruise of the Kate*, was also motivated by his "aggrieved loneliness". Raban believes the sea provided "a kind of correlative to this yachtsman convert's inner state and…he found himself more at home at sea than he had ever been on land."

The other disciple of lone yachting, Robert McMullen, well known for his account of coastal sailing *Down Channel*, certainly had clear ideas about ranking competence. "Yachting proper" was the pursuit of professional mariners. Yacht sailing by amateurs he dismissed as "idle recreation". Mc-

Mullen's finale as a yachtsman took epic involvement with the sea to a new level. On 14 June 1891, alone on his yawl *Perseus* somewhere in the English Channel, he suffered a fatal heart attack. *Perseus* was subsequently spotted off Cherbourg by a French fishing boat, still keeping its steady course to the west. "The dead man," writes Jonathan Raban, "his limbs locked in rigor mortis, was keeping a firm grip on the tiller. If a member of the French lower orders (a category which had given McMullen no end of trouble during his life) had not unsportingly intervened, he might well be still sailing today."

Another opinionated maritime refugee, Hilaire Belloc (1870-1953), poet, author, short-term Liberal MP, Catholic and self-declared anti-Semite, published *The Cruise of the Nona* in 1925, an account of a pessimistic prophet recently bereaved who escapes to the sea to get a better handle on the country. He declares mystically that from a boat "the majesty of the land itself takes its true place and properly lessens the mere interest in one's fellows. Nowhere does England take on a personality so strongly as from the sea." Certainly single-handed sailing is an exercise in back to basics and taking stock. As Raban himself observes, concentrating on the essentials can include both survival and statehood: "Setting up house in a boat four things matter—food, water, fire and weather." Like a latter-day Robinson Crusoe, "Inside your timber stockade, you begin to construct your civilisation from scratch. You start by keeping warm and end up with do-it-yourself Theology."

YACHTS AND SAILORS

The Victorian/Edwardian-era writers referred to were all living through a time of expansion in modern yachting. Yachting has been associated with royalty from the time of the pharaohs and their sumptuous barges, but the "commoner yachtsmen", the first to handle their own vessels, were the Dutch in the seventeenth century. Their small practical vessels, developed initially for government service, were called *jaght schip* (or "speeding ship"). Charles II was given one by the Dutch on his restoration as king in 1660; and as an enthusiastic and capable sailor he had two dozen yachts built for Royal Family use. In English the single word yacht described the vessel spelt as pronounced in Dutch. The oldest yacht club was probably the Water Club of Cork launched in 1720. Clubs promoted sailing and the Navy; indeed, some clubs were called squadrons with a commodore as a club official. As participation in yachting grew the clubs were able to provide maritime instruction, technical advice and safe anchorages. The oldest surviving yacht club, founded in 1815 at Cowes on the Isle of Wight, became by royal warrant the Royal Yacht Squadron just before the Battle of Waterloo.

Modern yachting developed from the 1850s. In that decade the horizons widened from yachting expeditions—whole oceans and the Arctic were the new challenges. The Marquis of Dufferin set sail for Spitsbergen in 1857. Almost two decades later, in 1874, Lord Thomas Brassey (publisher of Brassey's *Naval Annual*) and his wife Annie began a half a million-mile voyage in their 170-foot schooner—an odyssey recalled in seven books. Amateur yachtsmen cruising in small boats grew in number and prompted the setting up of the Cruising Club in the 1880s to provide "a library of charts, pilot books and other technical information".

Significant too was the growth of yacht racing from 1850 to the early decades of the twentieth century, which prompted developments in yacht design and technology. It was the visit of the yacht schooner *America* to the Isle of Wight in 1851 that initiated a long-standing international fixture and fired the starting gun in the competition over the vessels' design. A race around the Isle of Wight was proposed by the Americans to the Royal Yacht Squadron, and it was *America* that prevailed in the first significant international yacht race. The resulting trophy was given to the New York Yacht Club and it was "deeded" as "a perpetual international challenge cup" so that the club that won the trophy should next accept a challenge from another country's yacht club. The civil war in America meant the next race was not held until 1870 and subsequently the New York club successfully defended the cup in twenty-eight races between that year and 1980; Australia carried off the trophy in 1983. The America's Cup played its part in stimulating yacht design generally and in particular the career of a local Solent yacht designer Charles Nicholson.

Nicholson was born in Gosport in May 1868, joined the family firm of Camper and Nicholson in 1886 and rose to become one of the most versatile and innovative yacht architects of his day. He helped make the yard at Gosport and then later at Southampton the best in the country, designing everything from twelve-foot dinghies to yawls and cutters for offshore cruising, J-class America's Cup challengers, a 699-ton schooner and clipper-stem steam yachts. He was equally able to turn his design flair to building flying boat hulls in wood and wooden cargo vessels during the First World War. Most of the blueprints of his designs were lost when the Gosport Yard was virtually destroyed by bombing in 1941; but many of his designs live on in the sublime images taken by the celebrated marine photographer, Beken of Cowes. Frank Beken of Beken & Son, chemists by appointment "to his late majesty", became interested in marine photography in the 1890s, inspired by the majestic yachts he could see from his shop window. His photographs were celebrations of the golden age of sail and his name became an identifiable brand. His son Keith was equally inspired and continued to practise his father's camera craft.

The racing of yachts large and small boomed in the years between 1890 and 1930 and so did their design. The Americans and Canadians were pioneers in the "one design" concept for small boats but a significant dinghy designer was English and based in the Isle of Wight. Uffa Fox (1898-1972) was born in East Cowes, the son of a carpenter who worked on the building of Osborne House and Lucy Cobbold, who was a housekeeper to Queen Victoria. Apprenticed at fourteen to the Cowes boat-builders S. E. Saunders, builders of fast motor boats, hydroplanes and flying boats, Uffa Fox learnt too from his time in the Royal Naval Air Service during the First World War. After the war he set up on his own as a boat designer and builder, designing a small dinghy, the International 14 in 1928, which was especially fast for its class. He advertised his new designs through his success as a contestant in the annual Cowes Week races. During the Second World War Uffa Fox designed and built the first parachuted airborne lifeboat; and after the conflict he became something of an ebullient, sometimes temperamental, celebrity, more widely known as a boat designer for royalty and as a writer. He wrote manuals about yachting and yacht design and latterly his autobiography.

Until the 1950s yacht racing was an elite sport; subsequently it became more democratic. By the 1960s most boats under eighty feet were built with fibreglass hulls, a less expensive material. Also some countries, exemplified by New Zealand, developed youth-training programmes and new events for women and youth sailors, and the Olympic Games widened the participation in competitive sailing. The 1960s witnessed the rise of extreme sailing and speed sailing. Business became increasingly interested in the sponsorship potential of single-handed races across oceans; and more sailors wanted to emulate the feat of Nova-Scotia born sea captain Joshua

Slocum, who in 1898 had completed the first solo circumnavigation of the globe. Two of the aspirants were British.

Francis Chichester's (1901-72) unhappy childhood propelled him into migrating to New Zealand, where he combined being a land agent and property developer with learning to fly. The navigational skills he acquired through flying would be translated into similar capabilities at sea. After returning to England Chichester made a solo flight to Australia from England completed in nineteen days and subsequently embarked on another solo flight from New Zealand across the Tasman Sea. During the Second World War he was a navigation officer at the Empire Flying School and afterwards ran a firm publishing maps and guides. In 1960 at the age of 59, a year after recovering from lung cancer and still searching for another "life intensifying experience", he won the single-handed transatlantic race. When he reached 65, and between August 1966 and May 1967 he sailed solo 29,600 miles around the world in 226 days in the yacht *Gipsy Moth IV* purpose-built for a circumnavigation attempt. He made one stop—in Australia. After his return to Plymouth and a hero's welcome he was knighted at Greenwich by Queen Elizabeth II.

Alec Rose (1908-91) was a less flamboyant figure but equally determined. He had served during the Second World War in the Royal Naval Reserve escorting Atlantic convoys and on landing craft during the Normandy landings. Together with his wife Dorothy he ran a greengrocers shop in Southsea from the early 1960s and became increasingly involved in learning the ropes of ocean yacht racing. In 1963 Rose bought the 36-foot ketch *The Lively Lady* and the following year put himself to the test over 36 days in the *Observer* single-handed transatlantic race. By 1966 he was ready for a solo circumnavigation attempt and set off before Francis Chichester but suffered a collision with a freighter in the Channel during the second night out which resulted in his attempt being postponed until 16 July of the following year. He completed his voyage 354 days later, making landfall at Portsmouth just short of his sixtieth birthday and welcomed home by an estimated 250,000 packing the Seafront and the Common. He too was knighted for this daring exploit.

In subsequent decades the pace and frequency of these extreme sailing attempts accelerated, especially after the developments in the 1980s of satellite navigation and satellite systems. More recently one intrepid pioneering yachtswoman also based in the Solent/Isle of Wight area, Ellen (now Dame Ellen) MacArthur, caused her own storm. Ellen followed her 2002 record-breaking solo transatlantic race time when, in February 2005, she beat the then solo non-stop circumnavigation record time of just under 73 days set by François Joyon in 2004. After 27,354 nautical miles sailed she beat Joyon's time by 1 day, 8 hours and 35 minutes (plus 49 seconds). She was subsequently presented with the award of Dame Commander of the Order of the British Empire.

In her account of that journey, *Race against Time*, Ellen recalls the relentless exhausting roller coaster ride dominated by the elements with sleep coming in small packets of twenty minutes. The lone yachtswoman stares into the shifting unlit unknown:

> Imagine driving a car, fast, off-road at night in lashing rain. You're forced to hang on to the steering wheel just to stay in your seat, and you have no idea what's coming next, as you have no headlights. To make matters worse you have no windscreen wipers clearing your view. In fact, you have no windscreen. No roof. That's how it feels sailing fast in the Southern Ocean at night.

Satellite communication can take the extreme edge off loneliness; but to achieve their goal and to go where few others have gone before, unusual mental and physical stamina is demanded of the lone yachtsman and woman. In one exhausting period, west of the Falkland Islands, Ellen was forced to make twelve sail changes in twelve hours.

Exhaustion and loneliness are conditions the circumnavigating lone sailors have to cope with, and with depression too. Donald Crowhurst had set out from Teignmouth on 2 October 1968 on his own solo Golden Global odyssey. His boat was poorly prepared and the sailor was escaping business failure. He was looking for a proving experience and possible prize money but he could not face failure and was perhaps not self-sufficient enough to cope with his isolation. Communications technology then was limited and ocean sailors could sail beyond its reach. When Crowhurst realised he was falling behind in the race he made up the daily tallies of miles covered and gave fictitious reported positions. Essentially he coasted around in the Atlantic waiting for his competitors, who really were sailing round the globe, to catch up. He plotted his own imagined successful circumnavigation but became trapped by despair in a vast seascape. Sometime in early July 1969, when Crowhurst realised he could not convincingly stage his triumphant return, he stepped off his trimaran *Teignmouth Electron* somewhere in mid-Atlantic.

While these yachts slice through the water emitting sounds only from a billowing sail, another vessel on duty in these coastal waters squats on the sea's surface and can be heard some way off. This is the Portsmouth to Ryde hovercraft bumping its way across the Solent connecting the Isle of Wight to the mainland in ten minutes—the longest-lasting continuous commercial hovercraft service in the world. This craft supports its own weight through a fan which generates an air cushion contained beneath its hull. The vehicle's ability to land on beaches as well as hard surfaces has made it effective in remote wilderness lakes and it has also proved practical for military and civilian uses.

The hovercraft was designed by Sir Christopher Cockerell (1910-99), whose father was director of the Fitzwilliam Museum in Cambridge and mother was an artist and illustrator. Christopher himself was more interested in science and building his own crystal set. Having completed an engineering degree at Cambridge and post-graduate research in radio and electronics he worked for Marconi Wireless and Telegraph and was part of the team that designed the first BBC outside broadcast vehicle. After designing a radio finder for the Cunard liner *Mauretania*, he was one of the "boffins" recruited by Bomber Command at the start of the Second World War. His team built a new radio navigation and communication equipment prototype in eleven weeks which was ready to be installed in bombers in June 1940. Cockerell subsequently did similar work on radar location for the Royal Naval Fleet Air Arm in the run up to D-Day.

After the war Cockerell declined offers of promotion into more bureaucratic work and in 1947 set up his own caravan and motorboat building business near Lowestoft. Research into water drag led him to patent his invention of an amphibious hovercraft in December 1955. After his years spent lobbying government officials, the Ministry of Supply visited the marine engineering firm Saunders-Roe on the Isle of Wight to investigate the feasibility of building Cockerell's craft. Under the aegis of the National Research Development Corporation and its subsidiary Hovercraft Development Ltd., Cockerell, as a director and technical consultant, worked with the Saunders-Roe design team at Osborne.

The first model SRN1 was unveiled for the press in June 1959 and the following month crossed the Channel as part of the fiftieth anniversary celebrations of Blériot's first successful flight. Interservice military trials at Lee-on-Solent to test the hovercraft's potential began in 1961. From the mid-1960s cross-Channel hovercrafts operated for thirty years. Christopher Cockerell received a knighthood and a CBE and was made a Fellow of the Royal Society. He did, however, continue to voice his strong views on the relatively low status of engineers and inventors in British society.

The Hovertravel Portsmouth to Ryde passenger service has been an ever-present since 1965. It is now the only scheduled hovercraft operation in Europe. Its main rival, a catamaran, has to dock at the end of Ryde pier, a third of a mile from the esplanade. In contrast the hovercraft has no problem negotiating Ryde beach at low tide. Its amphibious capability is used by the US Navy in landing operations and by coast guards, rescue services and the police in, for example, Scandinavia and Canada. This noisy hybrid craft scuttling across the waves would never have attracted the attention of a Beken photographer. But it does the job—in ten minutes.

ARTISTS AND GEOLOGISTS

Whether British artists have been held in any higher esteem is open to debate. Certainly the sea and the coast increasingly preoccupied artists in the nineteenth century. The Fine Art Society held "The Sea Exhibition" in 1881; it included the work of James Clarke Hook (1819-1907), who portrayed fishermen as noble artisans, often depicted passing on their skills and virtues to their children, and the painting of HMS *Black Prince* in a storm, an ironclad battling the waves, a watercolour from the official Marine Painter to the Queen. Hook had influenced Edouard Manet to paint *Toilers of the Sea* and the American painter Winslow Homer, who moved to Cullercoats on the north-east coast in the year of the exhibition, to make studies of fisherfolk. The latter's studies of fisherwomen, for example the heroic woman depicted in his watercolour and graphite study *Inside the Bar* (1883), seem to anticipate the proletarian heroes of twentieth-century Soviet art. This dramatic portrayal of the fishing community could be traced back to the start of the nineteenth century when J. M. W. Turner was working on paintings of those who go down to the sea in boats; his *Fishermen on a Lee Shore* from 1802 was typical of his earlier more naturalistic period.

Turner was a restless, energetic travelling artist and the Solent, Portsmouth and Isle of Wight were places that provided subjects for him in his "apprenticeship" years and later. In 1795 at the age of twenty he was commissioned to make drawings of ten views of the Isle of Wight for the engraver John Landseer. A watercolour of the cliffs at Alum Bay was also a product of that expedition. The first oil painting he exhibited, at the Royal Academy in 1796 entitled *Fisherman at Sea*, was confirmed by his sometime travelling companion, the engraver E. Bell, as "a view of flustered and scurrying fishing-boats in a gale of wind off the Needles". In 1828 he went to stay at East Cowes Castle, the country seat of the architect John Nash, filling four sketchbooks with drawings of Solent yacht racing and two oil paintings of the castle and regattas.

If the coast and coastal waters provided fishing folk and yacht racing as fertile subjects for artists, so too did landscapes of coast and seashore and the idea that the coast was a frontier. Equally the sea itself was a fount of poetic inspiration in the nineteenth century. Jane Austen, sometime resident of Southampton and visitor to Portsmouth, has a character in her last, unfinished novel *Sanditon* (1825) lecture the heroine about the sea:

> He began, in a tone of great Taste and Feeling, to talk of the Sea and the Seashore, and ran with energy through all the usual Phrases employed in praise of their Sublimity... The terrific Grandeur of the Ocean in a storm, its glassy surface in a calm, its Gulls and its Samphires, and the deep fathoms of its Abysses, its quick vicissitudes, its direful Deceptions, its Mariners tempting it in Sunshine and overwhelmed by the sudden Tempest...

Austen may have been satirising pretension, cliché and boastful rhetoric but contemporary poets were inspired by the sea as metaphor for life and death, the power of nature, the heroism of sailors and fishermen or just the emotion that can be aroused by contemplating the sea from the land. The Royal Academy would include quotations from poems in its exhibition catalogues; and some painters wrote their own poetry. Turner was one. On an expedition to the West Country to make drawings for engravings in 1811 he composed a poem that could be used to accompany them. In part he refers to the "hollow" of Lulworth Cove:

> To a few fishing boats give anchorage ground
>   ... but no security to those
> Who wish from stormy sea in save repose
> Whoever lucklessly are driven
> From Portland seeks an eastern haven
> Must luff against the south west gale
> And strike for Poole alone the tortured sail.

As part of his fieldwork Turner scribbled poetry alongside the drawings in his sketchbook.

For poets such as William Wordsworth and Alfred Lord Tennyson, the calm coastal sea could be seen as eternity, but a poet who had lost his faith in Christianity, Algernon Charles Swinburne, celebrated instead the joy of swimming in "A Swimmer's Dream" written in 1889, the same year as Tennyson's "Crossing the Bar".

> A dream, and more than a dream, and dimmer
> At once and brighter than dreams that flee,
> The moment's joy of the seaward swimmer
> Abides, remembered as truth may be.

In the 1850s up to the publication of Charles Darwin's *On the Origin of Species* in 1859 and most certainly after that, the literal truth of the biblical story of the Creation came under increasing scrutiny. Amateur geologists, collectors of specimens and beachcombers were growing in numbers during the Victorian era, and coastal formations could provide evidence in the Creation/Evolution debate. A painting such as William Dyce's *Pegwell Bay, Kent: a Recollection of October 5th 1858* depicts a scene of geological sleuthing with Victorian ladies searching the rocky beach at low tide for razor shells, bright algae, zoophytes, agates and fossils.

Geology was a subject of popular discussion in the early nineteenth century, and study and debate were informed by beautiful publications such as the two-volume *A Description of the Principal Picturesque Beauties, Antiquities, and Geological Phenomena, of the Isle of Wight* (1816) with engravings both sublime and instructional by Thomas Webster. One depiction by Webster of Scratchell's Bay and the Needles and an aquatint by William Daniell of the Elegug-Stack on the Pembrokeshire coast (from his book *A Voyage Round Great Britain*, 1813-23) are as atmospheric as Turner's 1832 storm-tossed painting of *Staffa: Fingal's Cave*. As Turner experienced it, the work of a maritime artist involved discomfort and sometimes danger. Even Webster, when making his drawings off the Isle of Wight's south coast, would seek out a rock exposed at low tide and sit sketching there for a couple of hours soaked by spray, to be finally forced back to his boat by the incoming tide.

Charles Lyell's popular *Principles of Geology* (1830-33) gave the subject drama in his accounts of the significant erosion wrought by the sea's action on England's southern and eastern coasts. Paintings such as E. W. Cooke's *Bonchurch Pier and Cliffs* (1856) bear witness to this scientific warning.

THE FORTIFIED COAST

But if some sea cliffs were under threat from nature they also provided a barrier. Shakespeare in *Richard II* has John of Gaunt declaim:

> This fortress, built by Nature for herself,
> Against infection and the hand of war…
> This precious stone set in the silver sea,
> Which serves it in the office of a wall,
> Or as a moat defensive to a house,
> Against the envy of less happier lands.

As in previous centuries the likeliest targeted coastline was the stretch from East Anglia round to Plymouth, with the Thames to the Solent the most vulnerable section. For much of nineteenth the likely suspects remained the French; and the invasion threats posed by Napoleon Bonaparte and his ambition of world domination prompted the building of Martello towers from Suffolk to Sussex between 1805 and 1812. Yet throughout the century there was the greatest public confidence in the Navy and its fighting men, often fishermen, who served willingly/voluntarily or not. This sentiment was celebrated by paintings such as James Clarke Hook's *Hearts of Oak* (1875) where a fisherman sits with his family on the shoreline carving a boat for his son—also fashioning solid, dependable values in a new generation. It was celebrated too in poems such as "Rule Britannia" and a chorus in a David Garrick play from the mid eighteenth century which include:

Heart of Oak are our ships
Heart of Oak are our men;
We always are ready;
Steady, boys, steady;

The perceived threat posed by the new French president Louis Napoleon after December 1848 triggered an arms race and much debate about coastal defence, with the Duke of Wellington pressing for better coastal defences in the new era of steamboats and steam battleships. In an ode to the duke after his death in 1852, Tennyson showed he was as capable of writing poetry about coastal defensive landscapes as about the sea as a metaphor for the afterlife:

Remember him who led your hosts;
He bade you guard the sacred coasts.
Your cannon moulder on the seaward wall;
His voice is silent in your council hall.

The fear of possible French invasion continued over the next two decades, despite an interval of two years (1854-56) when Britain and France were allies in the Crimean War. One local consequence of this sustained panic was a controversial scheme for the fortification of Portsmouth and the eastern Solent. During the government's investigation into the best use of military resources in the county's defence Crimean veterans had recalled witnessing the Russian sea forts that protected the naval base at Kronstadt. When the Royal Commission on coastal defences reported in February 1860 it concluded that a Channel protection fleet was too expensive and that a sufficient field army to counter any invading force was unfeasible because of existing colonial commitments worldwide. So the answer was forts.

The then Prime Minister Lord Palmerston, against cabinet opposition, supported the Commission's plan for the protection of Portsmouth. The Chancellor, William Gladstone, opposed this very expensive scheme and threatened resignation. Palmerston allegedly suggested to Queen Victoria that it was better to lose Gladstone than to lose Portsmouth. The scheme went ahead and in the 1860s the first phase of the plan saw a ring of six forts built along Portsdown Hill. Set low in the landscape these polygonal-shaped forts were state-of-the-art Victorian technology. Their guns faced northwards and their role was to guard Portsmouth from landward attack. Five smaller land forts guarded the westerly approaches to Gosport. Other existing forts, such as Fort Cumberland and Southsea Castle, were incorporated into the scheme.

The Portsdown forts were finished in the early 1870s. They were defined by a unique, often French-derived, technical vocabulary: terre-plein, barbette, bastion, caponiers (structures designed to cover the forts, ditches against infantry attack), counterscarp, redan (a V-shaped outwork), ravelin, glacis (an earthwork parapet that sloped gradually to the natural surface of the surrounding ground), revetment, traversing platform and enceinte (the space enclosed by the fort). The Spithead sea forts in the eastern Solent were to present a more formidable engineering challenge.

The challenge was met by John Towlerton Leather (1804-85), aka "Contractor Leather", a contractor of railways and sea defences, a hydraulic engineer and one of those engineer "heroes" in the mould of Brindley, Brunel and Stephenson. Born in Liverpool he was schooled in his uncle's engineering office at Beeston colliery in Yorkshire and set up his own business as a civil engineer and surveyor in Sheffield, building reservoirs, Leeds railway lines and the Tadcaster viaduct. In 1849 he was appointed sole contractor of the Portland breakwater, a scheme to enclose the largest area of deep water of any British artificial harbour and a project not finished until 1872. He had subsequently involved himself with work on a suspension bridge, Fens drainage, steam engines and the Portsmouth Dockyard extension scheme. Perhaps the reader can pause briefly to consider these practical Victorian entrepreneurial engineering polymaths. They needed to have an up-to-date working knowledge of "geology, mineral resources, hydrology, the strength of materials, metallurgy, maths, levelling, map making" as well as entrepreneurial and marketing skills.

On the strength of his curriculum vitae's diverse engineering feats and his work as the contractor for the Portsmouth Dockyard extension, John Leather was given the Spithead Forts contract in 1861. There was a three-year delay because of the need for more seabed exploration as some of the original chosen sites proved unsuitable due to mud and quicksand. The planned five island forts were reduced to four: No Man's Land, Horse Sand, Spitbank and St. Helens. Each fort was circular with a hollow centre

Spitbank Fort

built on a sandbank with foundations of stone and concrete twenty-one feet below the seabed. The circular stone rampart was fifty feet thick made variously from Cornish granite, Portland stone and pebbly sandstone inside. Iron plates were built into the masonry.

Gun emplacements apart, the forts comprised shell and cartridge stores, a coal store, soldiers' and officers' quarters (congested accommodation for up to one hundred and fifty men on Spit Bank Fort), a laundry and an artesian well for fresh water all grouped round a circular central courtyard. In 2007 one fort, No Man's Land Fort—the third across from the Southsea shore—was on the market for £4 million. The Victorian sea fort had been made into a corporate events residential venue complete with twenty-one bedrooms, heated indoor pool, Jacuzzis and two helipads. Clearly the fort as real estate had character, unique vistas and few prospects of noisy neighbours—shipping aside; but perhaps the name was not a selling point.

The result of two decades of construction was a distinctive fortified land/seascape—a Victorian port city guarded from military incursion by sea forts and by forts in its hinterland. Still these forts came to be dubbed "Palmerston's follies", as this grand scheme was deemed to be obsolete on its completion in 1880. This should not have come as a complete surprise given that the American Civil War joust between the Confederate and Union ironclads the *Merrimack* and the *Monitor* back in 1862 had ushered in a new era of naval warfare. The international configuration of alliances and mistrust had also changed. After France's humiliating defeat at the hands of Prussia in 1870, the north German state had decided to become allied to the southern German states—a move that would bring about full German unification. There was a new power to fear on mainland Europe.

Fishing boat on Southampton Water

Chapter Three

THE SOLENT

DEPARTURES

The Solent is a former river valley which became a strait, shaped like a boomerang with the bend at Cowes on the Isle of Wight's north coast. The western waters stretch to the Needles Channel and are guarded by Fort Albert on the Island's coast and Hurst Castle located on a spit arcing out from the mainland. The eastern arm of the Solent stretches from an imaginary line drawn from Cowes to Hill Head on the mainland coast to another line plotted north from St. Helen's Bay on the Island's north-east coast to the southern shore of Hayling Island. These waters include Spithead—traceable from a line between Gosport and Ryde stretching eastward to include Spit Sand and Spitbank Fort to the north and Horse and Dean Sand to the east. These eastern approaches are kept under silent surveillance by the now redundant Palmerston forts sited from just off Southsea beach across to Bembridge Ledge.

These stanzas of Alfred Lord Tennyson's poem "Crossing the Bar" were composed on a ferry crossing from Lymington to the Isle of Wight. The poem was a reflection on his own death and was published in 1889, three years before that event came to pass:

> Sunset and evening star,
> And one clear call for me!
> And may there be no moaning of the bar,
> When I put out to sea,
>
> But such a tide as moving seems asleep,
> Too full of sound and foam,
> When that which drew from out the boundless deep
> Turns again home.

Twilight and evening bell,
　And after that the dark!

And may there be no sadness of farewell,
　When I embark;

For tho' from out our bourne of Time and Place
　The flood may bear me far,
I hope to see my Pilot face to face
　When I have crost the bar.

Twenty-three years later and a few miles round the coast to the north east, the RMS *Titanic* would leave the port of Southampton on her maiden and last transatlantic voyage bound for New York.

RMS *Titanic*

The name of this ship has entered the language as a myth, a simile, as a satirical comment, and more often as a warning against hubris. On her maiden voyage she was the largest liner afloat—an icon of British marine engineering and the result of the competitive race for passengers during the early twentieth-century vogue for North Atlantic luxury travel. The main British contenders were Cunard and the Oceanic Steamship Navigation Company, more commonly known as the White Star Company. Certainly that company's liner *Teutonic* had made an impression on the German Kaiser Wilhelm II at the Solent Naval Review in 1889 and arguably gave impetus to the naval armaments race between Germany and Britain up to the outbreak of the Great War—that and the new British fast-build *Dreadnought* class battleship launched from Portsmouth Dockyard.

　The White Star Line had been taken over in 1902 by the International Mercantile Marine, an American conglomerate created by the financier millionaire J. Pierpont Morgan. This exercised the British government which was concerned at the potential loss of part of the maritime fleet for military use in any future conflict, and it offered Cunard the Royal Mail concession and favourable loans to build new ships. So Cunard laid plans to build two fast liners, the *Lusitania* and the *Mauretania*. The luxury and speed of these two vessels captured the public imagination; and the *Mauretania* retained the speed record for crossing the Atlantic (the Blue

Riband) for 22 years from 1907 to 1929.

In response White Star initiated its own plan to build three grand liners, first the *Olympic* and the *Titanic*, and then the *Gigantic*. The company also moved its operations in 1907 from Liverpool to Southampton. The south coast port had a double high tide due to its midway location on the English Channel and to the Atlantic pulse, so giving it longer access periods for shipping—over 17 hours of deep water out of the 24. From the mid-nineteenth century Southampton had also become the British government's main packet station and then the emigrant station for Canada, South Africa and Australia. The company would be able to attract some of the emigrant traffic from mainland Europe and to use both the new tidal dock opened in 1905 and the other dock expansion projects initiated by the London and South-Western Railway Company. Being nearer to London and to the continent would be crucial for future maritime expansion. If Cunard's *Lusitania* and *Mauretania* would dominate the Liverpool docks, White Star calculated that their new titans would do the same at Southampton. Within five years of White Star's south coast relocation Southampton became the busiest port in the country.

The *Olympic* and the *Titanic* were built at Harland and Wolff's Belfast shipyard. The author of *Dracula*, Bram Stoker enthused over "the large gantry... wide enough to cover two great ships." In fact, the structure was 840 feet long and 250 feet wide with its own lifts, overhead and side cranes and sloping walkways.

The increasing size of passenger ships was also captured in fiction and had become a contemporary topic in campaigning journalism. In 1907 the American author Morgan Robertson wrote a novel about a huge 40,000-ton liner—*Titan*—which sank after colliding with an iceberg. There were insufficient lifeboats on board and the loss of life was heavy. This safety issue had previously been articulated by W. T. Stead, journalist and editor of the *Pall Mall Gazette*. Stead was a defender of civil rights and an active participant in the world peace movement who used his reformist periodical to run exposés of the inadequate state of the British Navy and, most controversially, the reality of child prostitution. In 1886 he published an article that drew attention to the inadequacy of lifeboat provision on liners.

Yet the prevailing mood at the time of the *Titanic*'s maiden voyage seemed to be one of excitement at the prospects opened up by innovation in maritime engineering and ship design. Beryl Bainbridge, in her 1996 novel about the ship's last four days, *Every Man for Himself,* has the narrator Morgan recall a fellow passenger "enthusing over the magnificence of the ship, comparing it in concept and visionary grandeur to the great cathedrals of Chartres and Notre Dame. 'A cathedral,' he reiterated, waving his cheroot in the direction of the stained glass above the bar, 'constructed of steel and capable of carrying a congregation of three thousand souls across the Atlantic.'"

The keel plates of the *Olympic* were laid down at the start of January 1909 and those of the second vessel—yard number 401, the *Titanic* to be—at the end of March that year. The *Olympic* was launched on 20 October 1910 and made a triumphant maiden voyage from Southampton to New York in June of the following year. Three months later the liner was steaming clear of Southampton Water and had turned eastwards into the Solent when she was in a collision with a Royal Cruiser HMS *Hawke.* The Navy ship's ram bow gouged a hole in the liner's starboard side; so *Olympic* was forced to anchor overnight in Osborne Bay and was towed back to Southampton by tugs the next day. Her commander was Captain Edward John Smith who could trace a seagoing career back over four decades, but not one that had been free of accidents. He would in the following year undertake a final pre-retirement voyage as the master of the *Titanic.*

The *Titanic* had thundered down the slipway in less than a minute on 31 May 1911. Completion of her fitting out was delayed as repairs were carried out on the *Olympic,* but after fairly perfunctory sea trials, the *Titanic* set sail from Belfast to her "home" port of Southampton where she docked on Wednesday 3 April. There began the processes of provisioning, interior decoration, coaling the ship—made more difficult by a recent coal strike—and recruiting the seagoing crew. Thus many of the ship's company would be local men; seven hundred of the nine hundred crew gave Southampton addresses, with perhaps forty per cent being Hampshire-born.

Wednesday 10 April 1912 was the departure date for the *Titanic's* maiden voyage to New York. Embarkation times and boat train arrival times were staggered for different classes of passenger. Of the 329 First Class passengers forty-eight were millionaires. Of the 710 Third Class passengers, most were emigrants. One was Charles Warren, a brick-layer from

Portsmouth who was going to America ahead of his family to reconnoitre employment opportunities.

At midday the ship cast off, and then narrowly avoided collision with the *New York* after the smaller ship's stern cable had broken in the resulting surge of water activated by the *Titanic*. This could be considered an omen for those who would later look for one. The giant liner steamed ahead down Southampton Water, past Netley Hospital and Calshot Spit, past the Light vessel, past Lutterel's Tower, and the rented home of Guglielmo Marconi (the wireless inventor who had almost been a passenger on that maiden voyage), then out into the Solent to steer a course parallel to the northern shore of the Isle of Wight, past Osborne House on the starboard side and then the developing skyline of Quarr Abbey, stopping to allow the pilot to disembark at the approaches to Spithead before steaming through the string of Spithead forts and out into the English Channel. The ship headed toward the northern coast of France, anchoring in the Cherbourg roads overnight and on the following day in the roads off Queenstown in southern Ireland to land mail and embark passengers before heading out into the North Atlantic.

The voyage and its end are both the stuff of record and of legend. Just after 11 p.m. on 14 April the liner was south of the Grand Bank in a zone where during the spring ice from the Arctic Ocean is typically carried south by the Labrador Current. The fatal iceberg was spotted when only 500 yards ahead and evasive action was too late and insufficient to avoid the contact which opened up a 300-foot gash on the starboard side of the vessel. From then the "unsinkable" *Titanic* was doomed. The two Marconi wireless operators signalled the ship's distress for two hours. The subsequent government enquiry into the loss of the *Titanic* revealed that another White Star Line ship was only a few miles away as she was sinking but did not alter course to rescue passengers. No explanation for this was forthcoming.

There were not enough lifeboats for everyone on board and when the stern of the ship accelerated vertically into the deep at 2.20 a.m. 824 passengers and 673 crew members were left to die in the icy waters. The sea temperature was 0°C (32°F); the survival time in the water was some fifteen minutes. The ship which responded to the SOS signals, RMS *Carpathia*, arrived on the scene around 3.30 a.m. and picked up the survivors over the next four hours.

Memorial to the musicians on the *Titanic*

Only 210 of the ship's crew of 898 survived. Particularly hard hit by these losses were the Southampton districts of Northam and Chapel. The names of the crew who had survived were posted outside the White Star Line offices, the ironically-named Canute Chambers. One contemporary resident wrote, "Nearly every house in Northam had lost a son or husband... every blind was drawn." Captain Smith went down with his last command. Of the 1,324 passengers 500 survived. The journalist W. T. Stead had been en route to New York to speak at a peace conference. He was not one of the survivors; and neither was the ship's designer Thomas Andrews.

What happened to the other two ships in White Star's trio of titans? The *Olympic* continued in service until she was taken to the breaker's yard in 1933. The projected *Gigantic* was launched as the *Britannic* in 1914. Quickly requisitioned by the Navy she was sunk by a mine in the Aegean Sea two years later.

The city of Southampton has been reluctant to exploit the *Titanic* for cultural heritage purposes; the Maritime Museum's display is low key.

There are discreet memorials around the city to the ship's crew, its postal workers and musicians. A bronze and granite memorial to the engineers was sited on the edge of East Park and unveiled in April 1914—four months before the start of the First World War, a conflict that would leave its own legacy of thousands of memorials.

In 2012 the city of Southampton opened the SeaCity Museum in the former magistrate's court wing of the Civic Centre. A large hall is devoted to recounting the city's maritime past, the rest of the building plus the new extension devoted to the story of RMS *Titanic*. The superbly designed museum uses spaces to evoke a response as well as to show and tell. The old courtroom is an appropriately atmospheric space for recreating the Board of Trade Inquiry into the disaster. In another room the floor is covered by a street map of Southampton highlighted to show every street that suffered human loss in the sinking. One loses count of the numbers. A beautiful model of the liner *Queen Mary* dominates one end of the maritime museum wing.

The city's docks had developed eastwards from the Town Quay in the nineteenth and early twentieth centuries to meet the increasing volume of passengers and cargo and demands for more maintenance infrastructure. By the 1920s and 1930s Cunard and the White Star Line had built four large transit sheds that enabled passengers to leave their ships and board departing boat trains on the quayside. A floating dry dock large enough to accommodate any contemporary liners was opened in 1924. The docks expanded westwards on reclaimed land in the 1930s, and included in the Western Docks development were eight new berths, one specifically for the Union Castle Line's Southampton to Cape Town service, later used by Imperial Airways for their flying boat service to the Middle East, India and the Far East, the Solent Flour Mills, a symbol of the city's trading significance, and rail carriage sheds where train carriages could be cleaned, heated and made ready for disembarking passengers. In the late 1960s a container terminal was built further west at Millbrook. Containers would be the shape of the future.

The Ocean Terminal which replaced the Cunard/White Star sheds was opened by then Prime Minister Clement Attlee on 1 July 1950. This complex afforded embarking and disembarking passengers some luxury with escalators and luxury leather upholstered seating. It also announced that Southampton had now become Britain's premier port.

THE *QUEEN MARY*

A part of Southampton's Western Docks development plan included the George V dry dock built specially for the liner *Queen Mary* when she was scheduled to come into service in 1936. Work started on the construction of the *Queen Mary* for Cunard at the John Brown yard on Clydebank in December 1930. The consequences of the Depression brought the work to a halt at the end of December the following year. Eventually the government was persuaded to approve the necessary money for the ship's completion as long as Cunard was amalgamated with the White Star Line; and work started again in April 1934. On 27 May 1936 the *Queen Mary* left her home port of Southampton bound for New York on her maiden voyage. It would be the beginning of three decades of trans-Atlantic service.

The *Queen Mary* was the largest vessel yet built at 1,019 feet long and with a gross tonnage of 81,237 tons. At her launch the Poet Laureate John Masefield had penned a poem, "Number 534" (her unnamed shipyard designation), which evoked "a rampart of a ship,/Long as a street."

The ship's name was in honour of Mary of Teck, King George V's consort, but this was kept completely secret until the launch ceremony on 26 September 1934. One version of events relates that Cunard had planned to call the ship *Queen Victoria* as the company had a convention of baptising its vessels with names that ended in "ia". When, however, Cunard officials requested permission from George V to name the ship after "Britain's greatest queen" the king loyally—and unexpectedly—remarked that his wife would be very pleased and flattered. Alarmed at the prospect of royal disapproval, the company representatives had no option but to pretend that they had always intended the liner to be named the *Queen Mary*. Whether or not the anecdote is true—and Cunard officially denied it was—if the ship had been named *Queen Victoria* it would have broken the tradition of royal names being used exclusively by the Navy.

Much rested on the commercial success of this ship and so in the marketing drive much was made of her dimensions. She was longer than the Eiffel Tower and just 230 feet shorter than the Empire State Building. To help the lay mind to further comprehend her scale a postcard image displayed the ship inserted into the central London cityscape around Trafalgar Square with the stern of the *Queen Mary* wedged against the Garrick Theatre in Charing Cross Road and her bows inserted into Whitehall. Size was also combined with speed, and the *Queen Mary* set a new record time for a trans-Atlantic crossing between Southampton and New York of four days and 27 minutes in August 1936. She would hold the Blue Riband for the next fourteen years.

Allied to her power and presence the *Queen Mary*'s artistic designers had been recruited to create original and elegant interior spaces that would provide a unique shipboard world. Thirty-three artists contributed to the ship's decorations, which featured Doris Zinkeisen's 1,000-foot square painted mural for the Art Deco semi-circular Verandah Grill, her mural panels for the cabin-class ballroom, and ivory and plaster friezes and wood reliefs. Bertram Nicholls' large painting *A Sussex Landscape* dominated one wall of the 118-foot-long English club-like long gallery and faced Algernon Newton's equally idyllic landscape painting *Evening on the Avon* hung on the wall at the after end. There were sculptured bronze doors, carved gesso panels, Kenneth Shoesmith's large painting of *The Madonna of the Atlantic* for a drawing room that was sometimes used as a chapel, Dame Laura Knight's mildly surreal painting of backstage, *The Mills Circus*, mural and wooden screen carvings and two paintings by William Wadsworth: two dockscapes with the decidedly surreal *The Sea* and the more conventional but still idiosyncratic *Dressed Overall at the Quay*. The *Queen Mary* is in both paintings heading over the horizon in the direction of the harbour. Mac-Donald Gill's large—15 by 24 foot—korkoid and warm brown mural map dominated the cabin class restaurant and showed the ship's winter and summer routes between Bishop's Rock and Nantucket with a portion of the Manhattan skyline and a manhattanised London cityscape. The ship was all about England and Englishness as Cunard had intended it should be.

Passengers could shop at a modern version of the Burlington Arcade with its W. H. Smith and Austin Reed men's clothiers outlets, and the beautiful public spaces were a modernist Art Deco re-working of the gentleman's club. It might be a truism to say that the liner's cabin-class ratings mirrored the class system of contemporary society; but it was true nonetheless. If you were cabin-class you were awarded staterooms at the top end that included a bedroom, a sitting room and a bathroom. Specially-commissioned artworks were specific to this class, and the rooms were panelled in light wood with statuettes included. Tourist class was designed with more people per cabin in mind, and with less use of wood and narrower beds. The third-class cabin included folding upper berths and lacked en-suite bathrooms or toilets. The designers must have been doing some-

Queen Mary as a troop ship in New York harbour

thing right to provoke this response of snobbish satire from the novelist Evelyn Waugh in his novel *Brideshead Revisited* in which the book's hero Charles Ryder describe the ship thus:

> I turned into some of the halls of the ship, which were huge without any splendour... I passed through vast bronze gates on which paper-thin Assyrian animals cavorted; I trod carpets the colour of blotting paper; the painted panels were like blotting paper too—kindergarten work in flat drab colours... all over the blotting paper carpet were strewn tables designed perhaps by a sanitary engineer... the whole place hummed from its hundred ventilators and vibrated with the turn of the great engines below.

Bookings suggested that the passengers of less refined sensibilities were nevertheless prepared to book their passage. But the outbreak of the Second World War changed the ship's glittering course. The Germans declared on 3 September 1939 that the *Queen Mary* was a "belligerent ship" and therefore a target for planes, warships and U-boats, and this when she was in mid-Atlantic and bound for New York. She made it to New York and stayed docked there over that winter. The *Queen Mary* was then painted battleship grey and pressed into war service. In March 1940 she set sail for Sydney via Cape Town where the furnishings and fittings were removed and she was then converted into a troopship. Her war service would include bringing Australian troops back to Scotland, delivering British troops to Suez and increasingly acting as a transport for American troops between New York and the Scottish port of Gourock. In 1943 she took Churchill and a delegation to New York.

The ship was fitted with sonar detection devices, anti-aircraft guns and she usually had a cruiser escort. Yet it was her speed—in excess of thirty knots (34.5 mph) that was her best protection. The *Queen Mary* sailed hundreds of thousands of miles in her five years of war service but she managed to avoid enemy engagement. She survived the Battle of the Atlantic—a theatre of conflict where over 2,800 ships were sunk. Over-crowding did become a problem, however. In the lead up to D-Day the ship was transporting an entire division across the Atlantic in five days; the record number for one crossing was 15,740 GIs, with 943 staff somehow finding room aboard. The liner also acted as a hospital ship taking wounded servicemen and women back to the United States and later carried GI brides and children to their new stateside home. The ship was demobilized on 29 September 1946. One thousand and five hundred men from the John Brown yard were then sent down to the Thorneycroft works at Southampton and in ten months the ship's refit was completed.

The *Queen Mary* returned to service in July 1947 with her red Cunard colours restored and 10,000 pieces of furniture and interior fittings re-installed. In those immediate post-war years the *Queen Mary* and the *Queen Elizabeth* alternated weekly on the Atlantic run and would usually pass each other in mid-ocean—deliberately close up for dramatic effect. The current advertising slogan "Getting there is half the fun" had a strong appeal in the era before the dominance of air travel. Travel on this floating piece of England was glamorous and the celebrated signed up for the crossings. The roll call of celebrity was long and the stars would expect to be photographed on board: Clark Gable, Marlene Dietrich, Charlie Chaplin, architect Frank Lloyd Wright, Noel Coward, Rex Harrison,

Douglas Fairbanks Jnr., Marion Davies… But this was a sea-going party that would end. The Americans built a liner of their own, the *United States*, which won the Blue Riband on her maiden voyage in July 1952; and her newness and speed enticed passengers such as the controversial Duke and Duchess of Windsor away from the *Queen Mary*. From the later 1950s to mid-1960s North Atlantic passenger air traffic numbers quadrupled. There was also labour unrest. Crew stewards faced back-breaking work loading stores and 18-hour days when at sea. Dock workers' unions in New York and Southampton organised strikes. By the mid-1960s the two Cunard ships were losing money, and one had to go. The Californian city of Long Beach made an offer for the *Queen Mary* that could not be refused by Cunard. She would become a static object used as a hotel, conference centre and tourist attraction. The *Queen Mary* was beached indeed.

On 16 September 1967 the *Queen Mary* left Southampton on her 1000th Atlantic crossing and her last to New York. Just over a month later she left Southampton for the last time to the sound of a Royal Marine band and a huge crowd ashore and on the accompanying flotilla; fourteen navy helicopters were flying in an anchor salute formation above. Forty days out from Southampton and after a 14,559-mile voyage via Cape Horn the *Queen Mary* arrived at Long Beach for her new incarnation. For many people who had lived through the war the ship was a symbol of the country's defiance and survival. Most people would not have been on board and most of the ship's working life had been over the horizon; but it was perhaps that people felt the ship had done her bit too—the *Queen Mary* had been through what they had been through.

When the Southampton's Ocean Terminal was demolished in the 1980s it was confirmation of the demise of the trans-Atlantic liner trade and recognition that the future lay with cruise ships and containers.

SOUTHAMPTON: IMPERIAL TROOP PORT

The Solent has been a prime conduit for military expeditions since the Hundred Years War with Portsmouth and Southampton key ports of embarkation. From Agincourt through to D-Day via the Napoleonic Wars, the Crimean War, the Boer and First World Wars, this part of southern England became the crucible for changes in the military logistics of sea transport. Outposts of empire needed replenishing, relieving and sometimes reinforcing.

For most of the nineteenth century Portsmouth was the main port for trooping—rotating military personnel in the East. Until 1894 the Royal Navy ran its own Indian Troop Service, two ships operating between Portsmouth and Suez and three more between Suez and Bombay. The opening of the Suez Canal in 1869, under British control, proved a huge benefit, shortening the journey to India via the Cape by weeks and thousands of miles. The estimates for the trooping season between September 1868 and March 1869 show the scale of just routine movements of troops to and from one part of the British Empire: 10,800 officers and men out, 11,980 back. Morale and the prospects of home are crucial in any army. As Rudyard Kipling put it:

> They'll turn us out at Portsmouth wharf in cold an' wet an' rain
> All wearin' Injian cotton kit, but we will not complain.
> They'll kill us of pneumonia—for that's their little way—
> But damn the chills and fever, men, we're goin' 'ome to-day!

Commercial shipping lines such as Peninsular and Orient (P&O) and the Union Line were involved in this transportation; and when the Navy's own vessels became obsolete in the 1890s it was decided to hire from shipping companies and move the Indian Troop Service operations to Southampton. This port had already become a significant point of troop despatch in war and emergency situations. By November 1854 during the Crimean War 20,000 men had been sent from both Portsmouth and Southampton to the Black Sea peninsula.

The conflict was to be remembered as much for participants at the side of the stage as for those on the field of battle. W. H. Russell of *The Times* was the first journalist ever to write as a war correspondent and Roger Fenton operated as the first accredited war photographer. It was Poet Laureate Alfred Lord Tennyson who immortalised the heroic folly of the cavalrymen sent into the "Valley of Death" ("Theirs not to reason why/Theirs but to do and die") during the Charge of the Light Brigade at the Battle of Balaclava. Images and descriptions of war did have some influence on perceptions of war, but it was Florence Nightingale who had the most impact through her nursing endeavours in the war zone and her political campaigning about the inadequate state of the medical support services at home.

Yet it was the two wars at the turn of the twentieth century and during its second decade that demonstrated Southampton's new position at the heart of modern military mobilisation and despatch overseas. In the first four months of the South African War, from the beginning of October 1899 to the end of January 1900, 112,000 army regulars were sent to Cape Town from the Hampshire port. This testament to industrial efficiency was just a preface to what was to come. For Rudyard Kipling, a strong admirer of local empire entrepreneur Cecil Rhodes and military adventurer Leander Starr Jameson, South Africa was another theatre where Britain's imperial destiny was played out. Yet this theatre of operations introduced a new repertoire that included guerrilla warfare and concentration camps and made household names in Britain of places on the South African veldt: Kimberley, Pretoria and Mafeking.

RICHARD EURICH

Just inland from Hythe on Southampton Water and just up the road now from the giant refinery at Fawley and on the edge of the New Forest is the village of Dibden Purlieu. It was here at Appletreewick that the artist Richard Eurich (1903-92) lived and worked until his death. Born in Bradford, both his parents were "of a socialist and Quaker persuasion". He went to Bradford School of Arts and Crafts and then to the Slade School of Fine Art (1924-27). At the latter his talent as a draftsman was recognised and encouraged by Henry Tonks, the legendary Professor of Fine Art. Eurich was not a disciple of any particular artistic orthodoxy or stylistic tendency but rather he followed the advice of fellow painter Christopher Wood "to paint the things you love, and damn all the fashions which come and go", and among those subjects, then and throughout Eurich's career, were harbours and the sea.

Eurich's influences were Turner, Dürer, Cézanne, Christopher Wood and the Dutch marine artist Willem van der Velde. The influence of Wood was apparent in paintings such as *Lyme Regis* for his Paintings of Dorset Seaports exhibition in 1933. This exhibition was a success. He attracted an agent, sold work and made enough money to get married and move from rented property in London to the newly-built cottage situated on land set beside the New Forest and affording a view of shipping movements around Southampton Docks. It suited him but being out of the metropolis meant being out of the loop, particularly in the post-Second World War years.

Richard Eurich continued to produce paintings with nautical themes that attracted increasing public interest and higher prices. His 1936 oil painting *Solent Fort*, showing No Man's Land Fort with the skyline of Ryde in the background and an aircraft carrier, a paddle steamer and various sailing craft negotiating a choppy Solent, was priced at 100 guineas. Eurich continued to paint harbour scenes after the outbreak of the war; in 1940, the year he was recruited as a war artist, he made oil paintings of real harbours: *Robin Hood's Bay in Wartime* and *Fishing Boats at Whitby* and of an imagined snow-covered dock, *December, Work Suspended*. Official war paintings included *A Destroyer Escort in Attack* (1941) and *Bombardment of the Coast near Trapani, Sicily by HMS* Howe *and* King George V. The first portrayed destroyers at speed in a wholly convincing seascape; the second put on display the awesome firepower of contemporary battleships. As part of his war work Eurich could still display some eccentricity smuggled into the final composition. In *The Midget Submarine Attack on the* Tirpitz, *22 September 1943* he paints a convincing, even beautiful panorama of the fjord where the German battleship was at anchor and into this scene he introduces a sea monster. Closer to home, his *Night Raid on Portsmouth Docks 1941* shows a scene imaginatively witnessed from the vantage point of the Semaphore Tower looking to the north-east with buildings glowing red like logs in a fire illuminated above by searchlight beams. The artist used his own experience of raids on Southampton Docks to compose this disturbing dream image.

After the war Eurich continued to paint harbours, including *Coast Scene with Rainbow* (1952-53), a dramatic scene of an unspecific harbour that draws on his pre-war research of south coast harbours and shows the influence on his work of Turner; and *The Queen of the Sea, 1911* (1954), which was an imaginative recollection of the painter's boyhood after a visit to Whitby in that year (the artist's boyhood self is visible through a hotel window). Eurich did work for Shell and BP including illustrating guides to Cornwall, Caithness and Anglesey. He also increasingly painted the Solent, including *Gathering Storm* (1969), a silhouette of a tanker beneath a threatening sky, *Dark Solent with Tankers* (1980), *White Solent* (1981) the near abstract *Yachts in a Squall* (1980) and the strange *Moment of Sadness* (1981), set on a harbour side with a dark-suited clown carrying a banjo and the figure of fellow performer/daughter standing hesitantly beneath an uncertain sky in part illuminated by a lighthouse.

Richard Eurich continued to defy classification. He had never been in the swim of the metropolitan art scene and instead worked at his art—every day of the week if possible, for seven decades. His skilled draughtsmanship, visual memory and spatial awareness, together with a unique visual imagination, made him an original artist. After a major 1979 retrospective touring exhibition elicited a favourable review from *The Times*, Eurich commented: "the critics are always rediscovering me." Still, the artist had experienced a brush with fame. In his role as official War Artist to the Admiralty, Eurich had painted *Withdrawal from Dunkirk* in May 1940 which showed beleaguered British troops being rescued from the beaches of Dunkirk by destroyers, drifters, naval tugs and pleasure steamers set against the backdrop of a funnel of dark cloud created by Luftwaffe bombing. This painting was shown to great acclaim as part of a contemporary exhibition at the National Gallery in London and subsequently at the Museum of Modern Art in New York. There is also another war painting portraying an event of crucial national consequence which had local resonance and which confirmed Eurich's importance as an artist.

Eurich was able to visualise how a landscape or seascape would look from an inaccessible or imagined viewpoint; and this is apparent in his painting *Preparations for D-Day 1944* where his panoramic view of the largest armada ever assembled in history was his own realistic but imagined composition and not an attempt to record faithfully the original huge and complex scene from any recognisable place. A column of military vehicles trundles through a screen of trees toward the open red doors of a landing craft. Beyond the embarkation point ships are anchored in the grey dawn light on a grey/green sea all the way across to the brighter horizon. These are more a collage of remembered features than any real identifiable places, in which the brooding island on the horizon should be familiar but is not. Nearer the embarkation shore a line of barrage balloons start to cavort like porpoises. Eurich would have known all about the sixteenth-century Flemish painter Pieter Breughel's busy, peopled landscapes and had learnt from him.

In a letter to a friend during early July 1944 Eurich commented on the censor's decision not to pass the painting for public display: "The funny part about it is the whole thing is a creation of my own and has no relation to the facts at all—I saw so much of everything that was going on here I realised it was impossible to render things as seen so I set to recreate the thing in my mind from odds and ends remembered." Clearly censors were not necessarily recruited then on the basis of their empathetic understanding of artistic creativity.

THE D-DAY MUSEUM

On Portsmouth's southernmost point stands Southsea Castle and two hundred yards inland is the D-Day Museum, which houses an equally important collage of the Normandy Landings. Designed by Sandra Lawrence, the Overlord Embroidery is 83 metres (272 feet) long and was made by 25 embroiderers at the Royal School of Needlework. It was five years in the making, and is a masterpiece of visual storytelling. At its simplest it is a wonderful comic book collage that requires no further explanation. This means it can be appreciated by almost any age group and by visitors with little prior historical knowledge or speaking any language. Closer attention reveals how carefully-wrought is its conception and design with a familiar cast of characters from history, and how it draws on contemporary images using a palette of colours that are both vibrant and subtle.

A selection of images includes: the pre-invasion contribution of air raid wardens, fire fighters in the cities and the women of the Land Army; echoes of Stanley Spencer's Clydeside shipbuilders; the local underground operations room where aircraft movements are plotted on a room-sized map; Field Marshal Rommel, the Channel coast commander inspecting the Normandy coastal defences; checking kit and rations in a military encampment north of Portsmouth; British agents landed at night by Lysander aircraft bringing guns for the French Resistance fighters; a British tug boat captain as an emblem of the merchant navy's role; some 5,400 ships and craft steam in formation towards the beaches headed by flotillas of minesweepers and protected by squadrons of Allied fighters and preceded by Lancaster bombers and Horsa gliders carrying airborne units; the surrendering young German soldier wearing the Iron Cross, copied from a contemporary photograph; the deadly hide and seek combat of the *bocage* countryside; a front line Advanced Dressing Station and a Field Hospital behind the lines; a field of dead German soldiers with inertly neutral cows and blazing military equipment; the wreckage of the city of Caen pulverised by artillery and Bomber Command.

The *Mary Rose*, shortly before her sinking

THREE SHIPWRECKS

The eastern end of the Solent has in the past been the scene of naval conflict and loss. The Tudor warship the *Mary Rose* was the "great ship" of Henry VIII's navy; weighing 600 tons and with eighty guns she was the flagship of the Lord High Admiral and had been named after the king's sister Mary Rose. On the morning of 19 July 1545 Henry stood on the battlements of Southsea Castle (commissioned by the king and the last word in contemporary defensive architecture) watching his fleet engage with the French invasion fleet as if witnessing a nautical joust. Soon into the battle and a few hundred yards away the pride of the king's navy turned to fire a second broadside at the French when water flooded in through her open gun ports and she capsized and sank like a sounding lead. Only thirty of the crew survived from a complement of around 400 with the distinct probability that there had been many more on board. One of those drowned was the vice-admiral and ship's captain Sir George Carew. The reasons for the disaster are unclear and often debated: over-manning of the vessel causing it to sit too low in the water, a sudden squall, the undisciplined "knavery" of the crew or a drunken brawl onboard.

In 1968 the wreck's location was discovered by MIT's Professor Harold Edgerton using side-scan sonar. In 1979 the Mary Rose Trust was formed to dive on the site and devise a way of recovering the ship; and in 1982 sections of the ship were lifted to the surface and returned to Portsmouth. This was a seminal event in the modern history of nautical archaeology. Among the trove of objects recovered were a tabor drum and a shawm (a woodwind instrument), navigation instruments including compasses, divider callipers and sounding leads, and a barber-surgeon's chest with instruments such as a copper syringe. The *Mary Rose* is one of three significant warships on view to the public in Portsmouth Dockyard and she remains the only sixteenth-century warship on display anywhere.

Over 200 years later the eastern Solent was the scene of another maritime disaster. The first-rate 100-gun HMS *Royal George*, returned from service during the American War of Independence and was anchored at Spithead. It was the morning of 29 August 1782. Almost the complete crew were on board together with women and children visitors and dockyard craftsmen. At 7 a.m. the stores tenders arrived with the dockyard workers who were to install a cistern pipe for cleaning the decks. The ship had to be heeled over for a hole to be bored in the side. Guns were run out or pulled back to facilitate this procedure. The carpenter noticed that the ship seemed to be settling in the water. Just as orders were given to reposition the guns so the ship could be righted she capsized and sank. Nine hundred lives were lost including Admiral Richard Kempenfelt; three hundred survived.

Several artists wanted to tackle the subject of the sinking of the *Royal George*. Rowlandson visited the disaster site and made a sketch. The last drawing master of Portsmouth's Royal Naval College, John Christian Schetky, interviewed some of the survivors and exhibited his painting at the Royal Academy in 1840. S. Horsey's engraving shows the stricken vessel keeled over with ships arriving and boats being rowed to the scene.

On 3 June 1859 the transport ship *Eastern Monarch* arrived from Bombay and caught fire in the Solent; only a handful of the 547 passengers and crew survived. Richard Beavis' (1824-96) oil painting of the *Burning of the Eastern Monarch off Fort Monckton, 1859* captures the desolation of this maritime tragedy.

There is perhaps something especially poignant that these tragedies with such high death tolls were the result of ships sinking so close to land. The contemporary poet William Cowper wrote of the *Royal George* disaster in "Toll for the Brave":

> His sword was in his sheath
> His fingers held the pen
> When Kempenfelt went down
> With twice four hundred men.

Chapter Four

THE NAVAL HERITAGE

PORTSMOUTH HARBOUR AND THE

GOSPORT SHORE

The shaping of the coast around Portsea Island created an ideal anchorage. To the south Portsmouth Harbour is sheltered by the Isle of Wight and, according to Patricia Haskell, "the Solent's twin entrances create a convenient tidal pattern at Portsmouth, with a seven-hour flood and a five-hour ebb." A 1716 map of Portsea Island, separated from the mainland to the north by Port Creek, shows the fortified town at the harbour entrance—roughly the extent of Old Portsmouth in modern times and separated from the Dock, a modest dockyard development to the north, by an extensive Mill Pond. The rest of the island is farmland with significant salterns on the eastern side and the Great Morass to the south where part of Southsea Common and part of the suburb of Southsea would be located over a century later.

A six-inch (revised 1873-74) Ordnance Survey map of the western half of Portsea Island shows significant urban development in Portsea, neighbouring the dockyard, and served by its own Harbour Station. All the new building is on the western harbour side of Portsea or tracing a line along the northern edge of Southsea Common eastwards. For much of its route across the island the London and South Western Railway still passes through a semi-rural landscape.

HARSH RECRUITMENT

The popular picture of the eighteenth-century British Navy is often dominated by images of drunkenness, flogging and the press gangs. Run ashore riotousness was certainly part of the everyday scene in ports. Thomas Rowlandson's engraving *Portsmouth Point* (c.1800) depicts lewdness, sexual assignations, rolling out the barrel and general debauchery—all played out at the harbour end of Old Portsmouth's High Street.

Portsmouth Point by Thomas Rowlandson

Discipline was a crucial factor at sea. The captain was charged with enforcing it so that the ship could be properly manned to deal with the everyday perils of the sea and the crew would be an effective unit going into battle. The command structure had to stay intact, and mutiny was an unspoken background fear. Punishment options were few. Locking sailors up was not viable in already cramped shipboard conditions. Deprivation of pay was pointless as that was the normal state of affairs. The form of punishment required was deemed to be a swift deterrent act which would be harsh and visible—flogging. The man found guilty would be tied spread-eagled to an upright wooden grating, stripped to the waist and subjected to the prescribed number of lashes from a cat-o'nine-tails, carried out before the whole assembled Ship's Company.

It is not hard to imagine why naval recruitment did not attract the manpower required, especially in times of war. More forceful measures were needed and the principal one was the operation of the press gang—enlistment by kidnap. Gangs of seamen under the direction of an officer were given quotas of men to be seized. They would trawl the streets, alleys and taverns of ports and seaside towns looking for likely recruits to seize, ideally sailors and fishermen but also landsmen. Some groups were supposed to have immunity from impressment. One such were the Sea Fencibles, men recruited into the maritime militia raised in coastal areas during the invasion scares of the Revolutionary (1793-1801) and Napoleonic (1803-15) Wars. Manpower requirements in the Navy during these conflicts meant that desperate recruitment measures were resorted to including the offer of a small reward for the recovery of deserters, the taking of men from the courts and prisons and even the collaring of Sea Fencibles. Certainly Gosport was not immune from these incursions, but one building beyond Haslar Lake bears testimony to a more enlightened Royal Navy.

HOSPITAL AND DEPOT

Looking after sick and wounded naval personnel had been an already inadequate affair before 1650, relying on the desultory administration of parish relief when the Dutch Wars between 1652 and 1674 provided too many casualties for the scandalously insufficient provision to be ignored any longer. A commission for sick and wounded seamen was set up in 1653 and subsequent commissions were set the task of finding accommodation and care for convalescent seamen in different areas of the country. In 1665 the author, essayist and Commissioner for Kent and Sussex John Evelyn spelt out the obvious—that thousands were dying for lack of accommodation. The necessary solution entailed the building of naval hospitals. The Secretary to the Navy Samuel Pepys agreed. Evelyn devised a set of plans for a hospital at Chatham but the scheme was abandoned. As Evelyn wrote in his diary, everyone involved was "earnest it should be set about speedily; but I saw no money!" Lack of money and outbreaks of peace meant that the Navy persisted with a system that involved contracting to lodging houses and the requisitioning of civilian hospital beds. This was inconsistent, unfair and open to abuse. Finally, in 1740, their Lordships of the Admiralty began to consider the possibility that it might be for the public good to "erect hospitals at the Publick expense". In September 1744 an order in council from George II directed that hospitals be built in Portsmouth, Plymouth and Chatham. It would be the one designated for Portsmouth, built on the Haslar farm site at Gosport, that would be the first finished and occupied purpose-built navy-run hospital.

The Royal Naval Hospital at Haslar was begun in 1746 and finally completed in 1762. Then it was the largest brick building in Europe. The main group of buildings formed a U-shape of three- and four-storey blocks "in fairly austere Georgian style in dun brick" (Pevsner and Lloyd). Intricate sculpture in Portland stone adorned the pediment above the central block's entrance comprising the Royal Arms, figures depicting Navigation pouring oil on a wounded sailor and Commerce distributing money, fruit and flowers with various emblems of shells, zephyrs and Asclepius the Greek god of Medicine. A rail track ran up and into this entrance passage allowing horse-drawn carts to bring supplies and patients from a jetty that served the hospital. To the south-west of this main block is St. Luke's Chapel located on an axis with the hospital's main entrance and built on a small mound at the end of a tree-lined walk. On the roof above the blue and gold clock in the chapel's pediment is an octagonal bell turret itself surmounted by a weather vane. The chapel and other eighteenth-century residences for senior medical officers to the south of the main hospital completed an integrated and human-scale hospital campus. The water tower of 1885, built as some Italianate fortress, still remains a powerful building and a clear landmark.

Part of the wing facing the sea included a section referred to in early documents as the "lunatic asylum". There was also an adjacent piece of land between the hospital and the sea wall described as the "lunatics' airing grounds". This area of grassy banks sloping down to the sea and topped by a summer house gave the patients fine views of the Solent and the Isle of Wight beyond. A purpose-built "mental department" was built on the sea wall in 1910 and fulfilled its function until patients were moved to the hospital at Netley in the early 1960s.

The Haslar Hospital was in an isolated position as the centre of Gosport could only be easily reached by ferry. When a bridge was built at the end of the eighteenth century the subsequent increase in drunkenness among patients and staff led the hospital's governor to request it be dismantled. A toll bridge was operational from the nineteenth until the mid-twentieth century. The current low-level, single carriageway bridge, controlled by traffic lights, still gives the feeling of journeying to Haslar Hospital from Gosport a sense of restricted access.

A walk from the ferry gardens into the town of Gosport will bring you to an abandoned barracks and the overgrown ruin of a railway station. Both are architectural mementoes of early and mid-Victorian otherness. St. George's Barracks in Clarence Road (1857-59) consists of two-storey

The Haslar Hospital

blocks with a dominant veranda running the whole 57-bay length of each block. Legend has it that somehow architectural drawings got mixed up and those intended for a barracks designed for the Far East, possibly Hong Kong, were sent to this site in the less tropical climes of Gosport. One block still remains now incorporated into a housing development.

Across the park from the barracks in Spring Garden Lane it is possible to see the shell of Sir William Tite's Gosport Railway Station (1842) through the site's perimeter railings. Its history encapsulates the wider story of the nation's railways from the Victorian high noon to the closures of the 1950s and Dr. Beeching's major surgery on the network in the 1960s. This was the Gosport terminus of the London and Southampton Railway and Yard, and the remnants of a fourteen-bay Tuscan colonnade in Portland stone suggest its former glory. To complete a landscape of architectural memory is a Victorian pillar box near the station entrance, octagonal in shape with an ogee top. From the main station a branch line ran down to the station designated for Queen Victoria's use in the former Royal Clarence Victualling Yard.

Walking back towards the harbour along Mumby Road and heading north up Weevil Lane takes you past the Royal Clarence Yard, a vital supply depot in the Navy's heyday now converted into a housing and business development. The impressive stuccoed entrance gateway topped with the Royal Arms dates from 1828 when all the Navy's victualling operations were brought together on this seventeen-acre site. It had been a naval supply yard in the eighteenth century—a grey clapboard cooperage the unique survivor from that era. In the following century the yard grew into a sort of township with residential houses for superintendents, artificers' quarters, offices, a police station, an apple orchard, a kiln, a steam mill, a slaughterhouse, storehouses for rum, tea, tobacco and cocoa and enough open space to accommodate herds of cows brought here on cattle drives by drovers who then camped out in the yard. Livestock was killed on site in the slaughter house just across from Burrow Island and this became the dumping ground for the bovine body parts left on the abattoir floor; its named was changed in popular parlance to Rat Island.

The Royal Clarence Yard combined the distribution of supplies with the making of them too. As with so much else connected to the Navy, its supply and production processes provided the blueprints for later developments in the civilian economy; as John Sadden has argued, the Royal Clarence Yard and equivalent yards at Deptford and Stonehouse (Plymouth) could be considered "the first large-scale food processing factories in the country". Key buildings were the brewery and the granary, the latter the most powerful architectural presence in the yard. Attributed to the architect John Rennie the Younger, this brick and stone dockside building from 1853—four storeys tall, its first floor supported by iron piers—was also used as a mill and bakery of ship's biscuits aided by steam-powered mixers.

The hard tack "Gosport Biscuit" was a staple of sailors' diet and millions of them were produced every year; fresh bread for seagoing crew had to wait until the first decade of the twentieth century and electric ovens. Other staples included cheese, peas, oatmeal, oatmeal beer, watered rum and in particular salted meat—an item that was increasingly supplanted by canned meat from 1847 onwards. As the whole supply chain was vulnerable to fraud and dishonesty, frequently corrupt suppliers meant corrupted meat. Perhaps more edifying, even edible, were the contents of the book stores: bibles, prayer books and biographies of Nelson. The yard was closed in 1995 after the development of deep refrigeration and contracting out of Navy functions had left it with no viable role.

Nearby the Forton Fuel Depot provided another key supply role, particularly for the coal-driven Navy. One of its most dramatic contributions to the seascape was the introduction in 1904 of the giant coaling vessel *C1*. This supply leviathan, longer than a football pitch and moored initially off Rat Island, acted as a coaling wharf; supplied by colliers it transferred the coal to ships and tenders using a boom arm attached to high derricks. Further north on the Gosport shore is Priddy's Hard, the former gunwharf and magazine yard suitably isolated from Gosport by the Forton Lake inlet.

EXPLOSIVE HISTORY

The Square Tower in Old Portsmouth (begun in 1494) was designed for artillery but was used as a gunpowder magazine from the late 1500s. Unease gradually increased among the local population at the reality of living in such close proximity to anywhere up to 12,000 barrels of gunpowder. The Master General of Ordnance was petitioned in 1716 but it was a full fifty years later that a serious and damaging explosion forced the Ordnance Board to act. A remote piece of land on the Gosport shore had been acquired to extend the local fortifications but was now designated as the new site for a powder magazine together with storehouses and a cooperage; Captain Archer, the Commanding Engineer at Portsmouth, was given the task of preparing plans and estimates. Ten years later, in 1777, Priddy's Hard (so named after a former owner of the land, Jane Priddy) was the source of armaments for ships in the harbour. The powder magazine was complemented by a bomb-proof magazine across the harbour at Tipner Point and floating magazines in the form of "powder hulks", retired wooden warships.

Two gunwharves had emerged north of the Camber on the Portsmouth side on reclaimed land by the start of the nineteenth century. The centrepiece of the later Gunwharf (1814-), the Grand Storehouse, was an imposing red brick and stone building with a clock tower and cupola. It was used to store rifles, small arms, boarding hooks, "gun carriages and every description of ordnance store". Typically for the period its forecourt was filled with rows of mortars and cannons, cannonballs and shells. The ordnance and weaponry were taken off ships returning from a commission, stored, cleaned and maintained.

During the late eighteenth and nineteenth centuries Priddy's Hard developed as a magazine depot to include the small enclosed Camber Basin and a laboratory and powder magazines. In the early 1800s small sailing craft, "powder hoys", transported barrels of gunpowder between the powder works at Horsea Island in the north of the harbour, the powder hulks at anchor, Priddy's Hard and any ships moored in the Solent. Priddy's Hard, together with Upnor and Chattenden on the Medway near Chatham and Bull Point and Ernesettle at Devonport, became the country's main ordnance depots. These in turn were part of a countrywide archipelago of ordnance stores and mining depots—Greenock, Falmouth and Pendennis Castle, Ditton Priors, Fort Victoria, Tipner Point and Marchwood—names whose purpose and meaning would be as obscure to a civilian as the names of lower league grounds would be to a football abstainer. As the global reach of the Royal Navy was extended worldwide, Priddy's Hard also became part of an international network in which similar activities were carried out at the magazine at Malta, in the caves and tunnels under the Rock of Gibraltar, in the Keep Yard at Bermuda and the magazine at Simon's Town on the Cape of Good Hope.

At the high point of its operational importance Priddy's Hard extended over a 25-acre site. A narrow gauge railway connected different sectors of the site in the early 1880s and by 1913 the depot was joined to the national rail network. Apart from the original gunpowder magazine, most of the buildings are brick and of a utilitarian appearance that does not betray their function. The Proof House was where a sample ten per cent of the depot's production of detonators, primers and igniters were tested. The muffled thump of explosions that emanated from this building on a regular basis gave some idea of its purpose. There were cordite magazines and guncotton magazines and a laboratory complex which housed all the operations involved in the filling or emptying of shells or cartridges. Most of these buildings had redoubts attached or sited nearby.

During the Second World War the workforce grew threefold to 3,700 of whom 1,700 were women workers. Women had also been recruited during the First World War and the depot's laboratory workers managed to supply all the players for the Gosport ladies' football team of 1917-18. Coming to work in this quarantined township required more than just clocking in. Work in any "clean" rooms or walkways involved changing into magazine-provided clothing in the Shifting House. These work clothes were typically for women cream jackets with bone buttons, baggy cream trousers with trouser braces and leather shoes. A red spot on caps identified a "contact" or TNT worker. As a museum panel spells out, the men and women of Priddy's Hard RN Armament Depot "have hoisted and stored, pored and filled, worked metal and sewed, coopered and calibrated, fused and proofed, checked and maintained, packed, guarded and supervised."

After the depot had been painstakingly searched and declared free from explosives the main gates closed in 1989. Five years later the Ministry of Defence sold Priddy's Hard to Gosport Borough Council; and the current visitor attraction, Explosion: the Museum of Naval Firepower, was opened in 2001. A recent visit to the museum impressed with the conscientious telling of the depot's story and the imaginative displays of the difficult subject of armaments—from the Colt Service Revolver to the Bofors guns, torpedoes and beyond. The author recalls a visit to the almost deserted site in the mid-1990 when people were allowed to wander amid the largely dilapidated and overgrown landscape; and what it brought to mind were pictures of those abandoned frontier towns of the American West. Maybe it is because of the museum site's isolated location away from the beaten tourist paths, but at the time of writing the museum is scheduled to close.

A ROMAN FORT, PRISON HULKS AND NAVAL SHORE STATIONS

At the head of the harbour to the north-east is the strangely anonymous piece of land known as Horsea Island. During the late 1890s a huge torpedo range (by 1904 it was 3,345 feet long) was built here employing convict labour to work on the thousands of tons of rock transported from the chalk pit at Paulsgrove. In recent years it has been the home of the Defence Diving School.

To the west of the torpedo proving waterway is Portchester Castle situated on a low promontory and dominating the north end of the harbour. Originally a Roman walled fort from the late third century AD enclosing a nine-acre site, its original walls and bastions survive as does the medieval castle enclosed within its walls—a keep and inner bailey dating from the twelfth century. An Augustinian priory was sited in the south-east corner of the outer bailey in 1133 but moved within two decades. What does survive is a small Romanesque church set in a churchyard. The castle was then an intermittent royal residence, a place where military expeditions were assembled and increasingly over the centuries a military prison.

In the late eighteenth century the fine view of the harbour from the

View of the Harbour from Portchester Castle keep

top of the keep would have included the hulks of former warships being used as floating prisons for French prisoners in the Napoleonic Wars and, after the sailing of the First Fleet in May 1787, civilian prisoners waiting transportation over 12,000 miles to the fatal shores of New South Wales and Van Diemen's Land. Ambroise-Louis Garneray's oil painting from c. 1810, *Prison Hulks in Portsmouth Harbour*, shows a landscape of various hues of grey with the only brightness coming from the sails of small craft. Grey prison hulks looking like giant coffins are at anchor in a line at the top of the harbour facing toward its entrance. These hulks were part of the solution to a criminal incarceration crisis in the second half of the eighteenth century. With the start of the American War of Independence in 1776 that country was closed as a convict destination and the existing gaols in Britain could not cope. Old naval hulks were pressed into service and prisoners sentenced as far away as Dorchester were made to walk to Portsmouth in chains to board a hulk moored in the harbour. Convicts were brought ashore to work on the construction of Fort Cumberland and other defensive projects. When this floating gulag still did not solve the

The floating bridge on the Gosport shore and a view of the Harbour entrance and Old Portsmouth beyond, c.1895

problem of a shortfall in prison places, an experimental transportation plan was drawn up—to send convicts to the other side of the world.

Travelling south on the M275 as you pass the Trimast sculpture and the Tipner Bridge masts—motorway icons that signal your entry into the modern city—it is possible to glimpse a scrap yard which extends under the road bridge to the harbour shore. This is Tipner Point and the site in the nineteenth century of a naval deposit magazine; it was transferred to the Army in 1890 and sold by the Ministry of Defence to a scrap merchant in the early 1970s. Only a tabloid Voltaire would have noted the ironic symbolism of this change of use at such an important gateway to the Island and to the city of Portsmouth.

As the modern M275 continues south and snakes past Stamshaw, with the greyhound stadium to the east, Whale Island comes into view to the west. This island is a seventy-acre geographical construct that emerged from the thousands of tons of spoil dug out to provide the dockyard with its latest basins and dumped on the mud banks to the north. HMS *Excellent*, the Navy's School of Gunnery, was transferred here in 1890 from a redundant harbour-bound warship that had become its college. This artificial spoil-created island uniting Whaley and Burrow Island then became the latest part of the Navy's infrastructural complex. The emerging island was identified by one gunnery lieutenant as a possible site for a shore based School of Gunnery; Captain Jacky Fisher (later the First Sea Lord) agreed and so eventually did the Admiralty.

Another shore establishment township duly grew, and HMS *Excellent*, with its barracks, canteens, clothing store, drill shed, football pitches, gymnasium, pigeon house, reading room, sick bay, tennis courts and washrooms, soon became the largest gunnery school in the world. A floating bridge and a low-tide causeway together with ferry boats first connected the island school with mainland Portsmouth; a swing bridge introduced in 1900 replaced all these. Training in the use of heavy guns was not conducive to the civilian ambiance of Portsmouth Harbour and the complaints of Queen Victoria at Osborne had to be taken into account, so the gunboat classrooms steamed out into the open sea for those lessons.

Naval shore establishments were adaptable townships where change of use was an expected scenario; they could be assigned new roles and identities, expanded, downsized, closed and abandoned given the vagaries of international relations, defence spending and the development of weaponry. Under a new dispensation during the First World War, Gunwharf became a mining school and it was the establishment that developed wireless telegraphy for the Navy. A submarine escape training tower became part of

Gunwharf Quays

the landscape. The Grand Storehouse became the Vulcan Building, which during the inter-war period housed the departments of mine and torpedo design as part of the new shore establishment of HMS *Vernon*. This building, the Custom House, the main gate, a crane and a few torpedoes are the sole survivors from the site's most recent makeover into the leisure, retail and housing development of Gunwharf Quays clustered beneath the Spinnaker Tower—the replacement name for the Millennium Tower when build overruns had taken away the relevance of the original name.

PAINTERS OF PORTSMOUTH

Portsmouth Harbour always provided good subjects for artists. John Christian Schetky's oil painting *The Arrival of the King of France in Portsmouth Harbour* (1844) shows the French ship besieged by an armada of small craft. John Cleveley the Younger's coloured engraving *View of His Majesty's Dockyard at Portsmouth* uses a different palette of colours of almost comic book intensity. Joshua Cristall's *An Exact Representation of Launching the Prince of Wales Man of War, before their Majesties at Portsmouth*, an engraving of 1794, has a touch of the surreal about it. The ship bedecked with giant flags careers down the launching ramp stern into the water; its decks are packed with a cheering hat-waving throng and even the giant figurehead looks agitated. Their majesties are stowed dockside in what looks like a box at the opera.

More modern and more controversial for some at the time were the paintings of the French artist James Jacques Joseph Tissot. His *Portsmouth Dockyard, c.1877* depicts a boat outing in the harbour with a Highland regiment sergeant sitting in the bows flanked by two attractive ladies with parasols seen from the perspective of the oarsman. The bows of older ships with strange figureheads loom on the darker side of the boat with a lighter vista, more modern ship and brighter water on the other side. In his 1876 oil painting *The Gallery of HMS 'Calcutta' (Portsmouth)* a young officer and two young women in figure-hugging white dresses survey the dockyard scene. The woman nearer the viewer with her fan is leaning against the rail in a very un-Victorian pose that makes the picture seem more like a modern magazine photo shoot. The suggestiveness involved was remarked on by some contemporary critics, which did not notably do Tissot's reputation any harm.

The English artist Thomas Rowlandson (1757-1827) was himself no stranger to gambling and tavern life. He also worked as a portrait painter and a book illustrator and was ever ready to embrace satire and lampooning. A graduate of the Royal Academy, he was dubbed "the ingenious caricaturist" by the London press. A biographer John Hayes said of him that "he revelled in the comedy of everyday life," and his images came to shape the public view of late Georgian Britain. He was always keen to include in his visual storytelling images of the human appetite for food, drink, entertainment and sex; his watercolour *Jack Ratlin's Tavern, Portsmouth* 1784 alludes to all these subjects. Research for this and the 65 other watercolours, subsequently published in book form as *Tour in a Post Chaise*, was carried out during his twelve-day investigatory journey to Portsmouth and the Isle of Wight in the autumn of 1784. Rowlandson's watercolour, pen and wash picture *Lord Howe's Victory, the French Prizes Brought into Portsmouth Harbour* depicts most of the crowd on the sea front welcoming the ships in an orderly fashion. But Rowlandson could not resist including a disorderly gaggle of latecomers—women of ample proportions and coarse-looking men—trying with difficulty to mount the ramparts. The usual careering dog is in attendance.

CROSSING THE HARBOUR

Getting across the harbour, getting around it or even beyond it, has always afforded business opportunities. The wherrymen of the later eighteenth and nineteenth centuries took passengers in their boats. These included sailors from their ships for a run ashore and back, courtesans to and from ships anchored in the Solent, sightseers out to the prison hulks or across to witness Nelson's last departure, tourists to view HMS *Victory* or people who simply wanted to cross the harbour. But in 1840 the watermen's transport monopoly was challenged by another product of the Victorian engineering imagination: a floating bridge. Built in Bristol, it was towed round to Portsmouth and set to work immediately. This clanking iron vessel was powered by two sixteen-horse power engines and ran across the harbour from Old Portsmouth to the Gosport Hard over two chains with attached balanced weights to mitigate the motion of the water in rough weather. It could carry passengers, carriages, horses and cattle and provided a link for rail passengers from the Gosport terminus while Portsmouth waited for its own rail terminus. It was an immediate success and the watermen were left protesting.

J. M. W. Turner, who liked the modern and liked machines, wrote in his diary of the floating bridge: "it is a large, flat-bottomed boat, similar to the busses of the Middle Ages. The deck is covered with road-stuff so that carriages drive on board the same as it were a continuation of the road itself." Another contemporary visitor W. S. Gilbert, the parodist and librettist collaborator of Sir Arthur Sullivan, was less fascinated by this maritime contraption and relied on a boatman to take him round the harbour as he sought background material for the opera *HMS Pinafore*.

By the end of the 1860s some of the watermen had their own steam launches, so the floating bridge company introduced passenger steam launches in 1871. Four years later the Gosport and Portsea Watermen's Steam Launch Company was launched to provide some commercial opposition. The timing was good as in the following year (1876) the new Portsmouth Harbour Station was built and the provision of a free public landing stage and gangway was written into the railway company's contract. Now waterborne passengers from Gosport could be provided with a direct link to London-bound trains.

Another rival watermen's company started up—the Port of Portsmouth Steam Launch and Towing Company—using the same cross-harbour route. This resulted in a fares war together with verbal jousting and argy-bargy on the pontoons. A truce was called in 1888, the departure times of each company's launch were synchronised and the takings equally shared. The floating bridge company survived the loss of two bridges and introduced new launches. The different ferry companies all benefited from special events—Fleet Reviews, Portsmouth FC's home matches and Navy Week—a "see the ships, meet the men" invitation from the Royal Navy floated in 1927 and retained as a more regular fixture.

In 1931 some of Gosport's local politicians proposed the building of a coastal road linking Southampton and Portsmouth with a tunnel taking the traffic under the harbour. A motorway connection was built but the ferries still cross the harbour. The crossing currently takes four minutes and the ferries are substantial enough to be employed on Solent cruises. The author remembers using the Gosport ferry to get to and from school in the early 1960s—with the bicycles stacked forward against the chain railings and many of the passengers placed on a main deck open to the weather. The floating bridge company ceased operating in 1959 because many of its commercial customers had ceased using the service and due to the mounting costs of maintaining the bridges. They were broken up for scrap. W. A. Jefferies' (1907-70) painting *Floating Bridge* recalls this distinctive industrial reminder of an earlier Portsmouth Harbour.

W. L. WYLLIE: MARITIME ARTIST

Hard by the harbour entrance on the Portsmouth side is Tower House the former home of sailor, marine artist and maritime social and historical activist William Lionel Wyllie (1851-1931). The London-born son of an artist, William (or W. L.) had shown an early love of sailing and the sea and a precocious artistic flair—going to art school at fourteen with no prior formal education, and then to the Royal Academy at fifteen and winning a Turner gold medal two years later. In the early 1870s and during the following decades he worked as an illustrator for the *Graphic* while gaining a reputation especially as a watercolour painter of maritime subjects and for his etchings. Wyllie was influenced by James McNeil Whistler and was a disciple of Turner, publishing a book on the master in which he wrote: "The man who strives to rival Turner must go out and study nature face to face as he did. On the mountain side, in crowded cities, or afloat on the ever-changing ocean." Like Turner he was prolific, worked fast and was capable of making "stylish sketches even in a small boat on a choppy sea". His seascapes were atmospheric and his ability to reproduce ships and craft convincingly was appreciated by those who worked with them; a captain of a Thames barge wrote to the artist in 1908: "The pictures were grand. I have not seen many barges drawn except yours that are anything like barges."

Wyllie did work for the White Star Line and after his move to Portsmouth in 1907 increasingly for the Royal Navy. The Wyllies acquired a property in Capstan Square by the harbour mouth and adjacent to the Round Tower. The capstan in question had been the one that operated the "mightie chain of yron", the boom that had stretched across the harbour entrance. The property was a three-storey former Yacht Chambers and as part of the conversion the Wyllies added a tower high enough to allow the artist to look over the Round Tower to the Solent and the Isle of Wight beyond. Directly by the edge of the harbour and by its entrance this house was about as close to being at sea as any house on land could be.

During an interview for an article in the *Pall Mall Magazine* Wyllie explained that he used telescopes to help in his work and on display in the studio were two telescopes—both trained up the harbour, one on the

Victory and the other on one of the new Dreadnought battleships. A painting of that period was the watercolour of the Dreadnought HMS *Bellerophon* in Portsmouth Harbour with *Victory* in the background (1909), a romantic impressionist depiction of the Royal Navy vessels including the iconic Trafalgar flagship, the latest trend-setting battleships, steam tugs and an early submarine all rendered in a limited palette of blues, greys and browns.

In 1907 the painter was instrumental in setting up the 1st Portsmouth Sea Scouts at Lord Baden-Powell's suggestion; Wyllie supplied the scouts with a cutter and relevant tackle and encouraged them to use the store on his property and the beach in front of Tower House.

During the First World War Wyllie was given permission to sail aboard Royal Navy ships. He sailed with and painted the Grand Fleet and was in effect a war artist. He never saw action as fate intervened when he applied for permission to sail with HMS *Invincible* after sketching on board while the ship was in harbour. The necessary paperwork from the censor's office did not arrive before the battleship's departure for the North Sea, where she was sunk at the Battle of Jutland. All five of Wyllie's sons served in the Great War, two did not return. Robert was listed missing in November 1914 at Messines, and William was killed at Montauban in July 1916.

After the war Wyllie immersed himself in the study of British naval history, was the illustrator and author of *Sea Fights of the Great War* and was appointed Marine Painter to the Royal Victoria Yacht Club at Ryde. He had been a founder member of the Society for Nautical Research and these maritime enthusiasts formed the Save the Victory Committee to campaign for the rescue of Nelson's flagship from further deterioration at her harbour mooring by raising money for her transfer to the dockyard and subsequent restoration. *Victory* was towed to a dockyard basin on 12 January 1922. A proud poster made by the artist for the Southern Railway Company in 1928 shows the *Victory* in her new dry dock berth with HMS *Renown* at the quayside in the background.

At the age of 79 and in collaboration with his daughter Aileen, the artist worked long hours for nine months to finish a panorama oil painting of the Battle of Trafalgar that measured 42 by twelve feet; it was the result of thorough research that included a visit to the scene of the battle. William Wyllie died suddenly in London on 6 April 1931. After a service at Portsmouth Cathedral he was buried in St. Mary's churchyard within the walls of Portchester Castle. His coffin was been taken there from Point beach at Old Portsmouth in the stern of a cutter rowed the length of the harbour by sea scouts from the troop he had started. His last voyage was watched by large crowds, buglers on HMS *Victory* sounded a salute and flags on the battleships *Nelson* and *Warspite* flew at half mast.

MORE MODERN TIMES

The city was slow to recover from the damage wrought by 67 bombing raids between 1940 and 1944 (see Chapter Eleven). It was clear after the war that the Navy and the dockyards would be downsized and in the decade from 1981 manpower was cut by almost two thirds. From 1969 Portsmouth Polytechnic became one of the city's major employers. Nautech made electronic autopilots for yachts. Marconi produced electronic warfare equipment. Shipbuilders such as Vosper-Thorneycroft were forced to diversify. IBM located its UK headquarters set in parkland on a polder at the top of North Harbour. In 1968 Albert Johnson Quay was part of the enlargement of commercial container freight docks on reclaimed mudflats on the north-eastern shore of the harbour. To the north of these docks the Continental Ferry Port was built in the late 1970s to accommodate cross-Channel operators such as Brittany Ferries. By the mid-1980s this had become the second largest south coast ferry port after Dover.

Marinas stretch from Haslar up the harbour's western side to Port Solent in the north. Below the Spinnaker Tower's viewing platforms a marina shares Old Portsmouth's Camber dock with the Isle of Wight car-ferry terminus.

Part Two

EPISODES FROM HISTORY

Chapter Five

PORTSMOUTH DOCKYARD

NAVAL POWERHOUSE

Portsmouth has a port gifted by nature, a sheltered harbour edged by malleable/flexible mudflats and tapering to a narrow mouth that could in earlier times be secured by a chain of iron; an island to the south provides a sheltering buffer and allows a further large anchorage and roadstead beyond the harbour entrance. Situated on the south coast across the Channel from France's Normandy coast, the port was well-placed for any contest with the usual enemy. Yet the country's cultivation of a new enemy—the Dutch—and the ensuing mid-seventeenth-century wars with them meant that ports on the Thames and north Kent coast—Deptford, Woolwich and Chatham—were then strategically more important. As such, despite this ideal environment and location the history of the development of Portsmouth does not trace a continuous regular upward trajectory. It was a combination of the consistent growth of the Georgian and Victorian navies, the need for shore facilities and support infrastructure, driven by Britain's increasing ambitions overseas and her emergence in the nineteenth century as the foremost imperial power, that made Portsmouth the premier naval port.

After the Norman Conquest Portsmouth was one departure point for France and ships were serviced here. Medieval expeditions against France, now a hostile country, often left from here; although Henry V designated Southampton as the muster point for ships. Henry VII recognised the harbour's strategic importance and in 1496 the country's first dry dock was completed, close to the present No. 2 Dock which contains HMS *Victory*. A storehouse, forge and smithy were added to what became the first royal dockyard. One ship—the *Sweepstake*, was launched from here.

Shipbuilding continued for a while under Henry VIII—the ill-fated *Mary Rose* was constructed here in 1509—but Portsmouth's role latterly was that of ship repair. Its overland distance from the "store of ordnance" at the Tower of London favoured the development of naval port and other facilities on the Thames and the Medway. Nor was there a substantial mercantile class in the town so victualling had to be organised through London or Southampton. There were also problems with the inadequate local supply of skilled workers; and the area was vulnerable to French incursions. When Spain was the most pressing enemy in the time of Elizabeth I, the new Thames yards at Woolwich and Deptford (both established in 1513) attracted all the investment funding. They were better sited strategically for any attacks on the Spanish Netherlands and better situated to protect the capital.

The dockyard fared little better under the early Stuarts. Two failed expeditions to relieve the siege of La Rochelle (1627-28), had been fitted out and launched from Portsmouth; and the commander of these military misadventures, the Duke of Buckingham, was assassinated in the town for his pains. Plans were drawn up in 1628 to develop dock and storage facilities at Portchester Castle but were not put into action. The reputation of the town remained low. It still lacked the commercial infrastructure and the skills base to readily expand as a dockyard port; and a contemporary, Sir George Blundell judged the town to be "a poor beggarly place, where is neither money, lodging nor meat".

Strangely Portsmouth's fortunes were revived by actions that were favourable locally and catastrophic nationally. To assert sovereignty over the Narrow Seas (the English Channel and the southern North Sea between England and the Netherlands) and to combat piracy and the Dutch plundering of herring fisheries, Charles I built up fleets using money from the collection of a tax known as ship-money. In origin this was a tax levied on ports and maritime towns that dated back to the fifteenth century. Portsmouth benefited from the fitting out of the new ships. But as the construction costs of fleets escalated, the levy of the tax was extended to all towns and parishes in the country—a policy enacted when parliament was not sitting. There was local resistance to the collection of this new tax; and after parliament was recalled the House of Lords declared ship-money illegal in January 1642. Parliament then ordered the removal from that year's fleet of any captains with royalist sympathies. This has usually been acknowledged as the signal for the start of the Civil War.

During the post-war period of the Commonwealth shipbuilding returned to Portsmouth after a lapse of a hundred years with the launch of the 38-gun fourth-rate *Portsmouth* in 1650. The dockyard then expanded under the supervision of Commissioner Francis Willoughby, who was arguably, in Ray Riley's words, the "father of the dockyard". A double dry dock was built together with a mast wharf and tar-house. The expansion of Portsmouth's capacity and ship-building role continued after the Restoration. In part this was due to the support given by the Secretary of the Navy Board, Samuel Pepys (1633-1703), notable diarist, bibliophile, collector of female companions, composer and player of the flute, viol and flageolet ("music and women I cannot but give way to whatever my business is"). He was also an assiduous and forward-thinking naval administrator. Pepys worked hard to combat corruption and encourage professionalism in the seagoing officers; he sought to encourage a wider professionalism in naval affairs, something he himself displayed through the impressive mastery of his brief. He was a regular inspector of the dockyards; on one visit to Portsmouth with his wife Elizabeth, they walked the walls and viewed the house where the Duke of Buckingham was murdered. He was forced to tack with the wind in turbulent political times; and despite coming under suspicion of involvement in the fictitious Popish Plot and later of harbouring Jacobite sentiments, he survived to live on in retirement organising his library.

The Glorious Revolution of 1688 ushered in a new monarch, William of Orange, a Protestant Dutchman with an antipathy towards the French. Portsmouth was thus well situated to benefit from this shift in foreign policy; and the following year saw the start of a dock building programme supervised by the Surveyor to the Navy Board Edmund Dummer (1651-1713). A gentleman farmer's son Dummer had the sort of background experience that made him an exemplary civil engineer for the Navy. He had served a shipwright's apprenticeship at Portsmouth Naval Dockyard and later was first assistant Master Shipwright at Chatham Dockyard. Between times he was a midshipman for two years serving on HMS *Woolwich* in the Mediterranean, constantly making drawings of arsenals and ships observed. Dummer became Surveyor in 1692 and stayed in post until dismissed by the Lords of the Admiralty in a case of bribery and "indirect practices" counter claims. He had by then overseen the establishment of a naval dockyard at Plymouth and the enlargement of existing dockyards, arguably the largest engineering project of the seventeenth century.

Dummer oversaw the doubling in size of Portsmouth Dockyard with the first naval stone dock built with stepped sides, a centralised storage area with the more logical location of buildings, a second rope house and reclamation of land from the harbour. Dummer's post-Navy Board career was a less happy story, however. He was elected MP for Arundel but his enterprises, including an ironworks near Beaulieu and a mail service to the plantations of the West Indies, ended in failure and cost him dear. Dummer was declared bankrupt in February 1711 and died in Fleet Prison two year later.

Portsmouth had become a leading ship-building yard during the reign of William III, and in the second decade of the eighteenth century became, according to Riley, "possibly the largest manufacturing enterprise in the country". The growth of a company town is confirmed by the contemporary journalist, novelist (*Moll Flanders, Robinson Crusoe*), satirist, essayist and pamphleteer Daniel Defoe (1660-1731) in his book *A Tour through the Whole Island of Great Britain* (published 1724 -1726). He had set out in his 62nd year to complete a number of "circuits or journeys" through Britain "giving a Particular and Diverting Account of Whatever is Curious and Worth Observation"— this he deemed to include "A Description of the Principal Cities and Towns, their Situation, Magnitude, Government, and Commerce, The Customs, Manners, Speech... the Trades and Manufactures, The Sea Ports and Fortifications..." Defoe modestly added: "With Useful OBSERVATIONS upon the Whole." His account he intended to be "a celebration of the country's strong trading position, written by a patriot with no satire".

Arriving at Portsmouth he found "the largest fortification, beyond comparison; that we have in England", chosen "for the best security to the navy above all places in Britain; the entrance into the harbour is safe, but very narrow, guarded on both sides by terrible platforms of cannon..." Defoe was among the first to recognise and record Portsmouth's status as a prototype company town:

> These docks and yards are now like a town by themselves and are a kind
> of marine corporation, or a government of their own kind within themselves; there being large rows of dwellings, built at the public charge
> within the new works, for all the principal officers of the place; especially
> the commissioner, the agent of the victualling, and such as these; the

tradesmen likewise have houses here, and many of the labourers are allowed to live in the bounds as they can get lodging.

The dockyard's oldest building remaining intact is the Porter's Lodge from 1708. The first resident was Ellis Markant and his duties included opening and shutting the dockyard gate, and being on the lookout for pilfering dockers, thus keeping a weather eye open for suspect great coats and large trousers after he had crucially attended to the early morning ringing of the dockyard muster bell—the wake up call for the local community. As porter he was able to supplement his pay by selling small beer in the summertime, within reason, and by cultivating his garden to produce medicinal herbs and vegetables for sale.

More than ever the growth of the dockyard and the town beyond was driven by war or the fear of it. Portsmouth's fortunes might be measured by any barometer that could determine the pressure of international relations. Expansion and contraction of ship-building activity and the size of its workforce and that required by the Navy followed the inevitable cycle of war and peace.

In the eighteenth century there was a succession of conflicts between European nations. The War of Austrian Succession (1740-48) grew out of the rivalry between Prussia and Austria over the control of the German states and after four years a colonial dispute spawned a conflict between Britain and the Franco-Spanish alliance; then the Seven Years War (1756-63) was a re-run of the previous war between Austria and Prussia and the struggle for colonial supremacy in the New World and the Far East between France and Britain; this conflict was followed by the more self-explanatory War of American Independence (1775-83). By the latter part of the eighteenth century the sequence of warship construction changed. Increasingly the Navy Board put out the work of building hulls to private contractors in Bursledon, Cowes or Bucklers Hard on the Beaulieu river, with the fitting out to be done at Portsmouth.

Given this was a highly combustible working environment, the dockyard authorities were ever-alert to the threat of fire. On the afternoon of 7 December 1774 a blaze started in the rope house. The alarm was raised and this brought hundreds of men to the scene. The rope house was gutted but the fire contained, so saving workshops, ships in dry docks and vessels under construction on slipways. Evidence was recovered to support the suspicion of arson and the hunt was on for a dock worker called John the Painter.

Edinburgh-born John (or James), a man of many aliases, was an American Independence sympathiser and had been recruited as an agent for the revolutionary cause. Fortunately he turned out to be a comparatively incompetent arsonist. His original matches were damp so he had to go and buy more. Still, while on the run he did manage to cause damage at Bristol docks. Enquiries at his previous lodgings in Portsmouth revealed a French passport and instructions from his American minders. A reward and details about him were posted. It was a vigilant policeman at the lock up in Odiham, north Hampshire who recognised his description as fitting a recently arrested housebreaking suspect. Two dockyard workers travelled to Odiham to identify him. After a trial at Winchester he was found guilty of arson, convicted largely on the evidence of the lady who sold him the matches. Sentenced to death he was hanged on the 64-foot mast of HMS *Arethusa* erected as a gallows near the dockyard's main gate. Within an hour his body was rowed across the harbour to Fort Blockhouse and there on the beach was hung in chains by the harbour mouth—as a warning.

THE FIRST INDUSTRIAL SITE

The Royal Dockyards, primarily Portsmouth and Plymouth, were the industrial hubs of the country. At the time of the Napoleonic Wars 15,000 men were employed in the dockyards, including a third of all the shipwrights in the country. These were then the forges of industrial revolutionary change in the early nineteenth century. From royalty to citizenry, visitors came to the dockyards to see the future in possibly the first example of industrial tourism; Princess Victoria was brought to Portsmouth aged twelve as part of her education—a very prescient move.

What the dockyard of the late Georgian period has bequeathed to the present is an inspiring townscape more coherent than most civilian developments. Among those structures that have survived are the quarter-mile-long brick-built Great Rope House (1770) and Nos. 9, 10 and 11 stores (1778), each a red-brick rectangular three-storey block with a rhythm of rounded keystone arches. No. 10 was originally grander—it still retains its rusticated stone central arch but the clock tower and cupola were victims of a Luftwaffe raid during the Second World War (but replaced in the 1990s). Thomas Telford's Short Row (1787) is a terrace of five three-storey brick houses and the former Cashiers Office, which later contained the Royal Naval Film Corporation, was built in 1798 by Sir Samuel Bentham. The Samuel Wyatt- designed Commissioners House, later Admiralty House 1784-86, was built as the residence of the Commander-in-Chief Portsmouth, with a yellow brick three-storey central block fronted by a huge porch (from 1900) and crowned by an octagonal cupola. The building of the house was supervised by Telford (1757-1834), the son of a Scottish shepherd who went on to become a notable road builder and canal maker. Wyatt (1737-1807) came from an architect's family and also designed lighthouses including the Longships Lighthouse in Cornwall for Trinity House.

Amid the functional buildings designed for productive use—the Sail Loft, the Rigging Store and the Hemp Tarring House—were two buildings that became iconic. St. Ann's Church, designed by architect John Marquand in 1785 with its construction supervised by Thomas Telford, suffered from extensive bomb damage in a 1940 air raid, and was restored fifteen years later. The light interior is dominated by the sweep of a balcony that curves in a U-shape two-thirds along the body of the church. Ensigns,

The Semaphore Tower

memorials and a window bear testimony to the church's unusual parish. One encased ensign is that flown by Admiral Sir Charles Madden's flagship HMS *Revenge* as it escorted the German Baltic Fleet to Scapa Flow in 1918. Memorials include one to Admiral Sir Leopold McClintock who made voyages to the Arctic in the mid-nineteenth century to discover the fate of Franklin's expedition, and one to the naval officer brothers of Jane Austen. The East Window by Hugh Easton serves as a memorial to all who worked in Portsmouth or sailed from there and lost their lives in the Second World War; it displays Christ Triumphant over the dockyard possibly from the vantage point of the Semaphore Tower. That landmark tower, built between 1810 and 1824 and located on top of a five-storey block, was completely rebuilt after a mysterious fire in 1913. Designed for communication it also signals to the harbour entrance and the Solent beyond the leading edge of the dockyard.

Looking across Basin 1 from the stern of HMS *Victory* cradled in its Portsmouth Naval Base dry dock it is possible to see a set of Georgian industrial buildings adjacent to Dock No. 6. These are the former Block Mills. Here in 1803 the production of ships' blocks included use of a set of machine tools. This was the prototype of the production line and arguably was *the* pioneering production site of the Industrial Revolution. The neighbouring dry docks and basin had evolved in the eighteenth century and form what Jonathan Coad calls "the oldest such group in any European naval base".

Through the eighteenth century the Royal Navy grew in terms of ship construction and maintenance so that by the outbreak of war with revolutionary France in 1793 it was "the largest, best equipped and most experienced navy in Europe". The Royal Dockyards had a monopoly over the building of larger ships, with the result that these became hubs for all the specialist skills required to construct warships, to fit them out and supply and maintain them. By 1793 Portsmouth, as a key naval base and dockyard, had ancillary centres of specialist support: its naval hospital at Haslar, the victualling supply depot in the Royal Clarence Yard and an ordnance yard at Priddy's Hard.

The conflict between European nations spread to far flung theatres of war, and the Royal Navy accordingly had to develop bases overseas. By 1800 it had Mediterranean bases at Gibraltar, Menorca and Malta. Across the Atlantic it was developing harbours and bases in Antigua, Port Royal,

Jamaica and Halifax, Nova Scotia. The increasing size and reach of the Navy meant that home dockyards, especially Portsmouth, had to expand their facilities to include new dry and wet docks and new paint shops, roperies, rigging and mast houses, smithies, sail lofts, wood mills and block makers' workshops. The start in 1793 of the protracted Napoleonic Wars was the signal for a review of the dockyard's capacity and modernity.

Two individuals were key to the development of Portsmouth Dockyard in this period. The first was Samuel Bentham, who was appointed Inspector General of Naval Works in 1795. Brother of the more famous utilitarian philosopher Jeremy Bentham, Samuel had collaborated on his brother's scheme to develop the Panopticon—a model prison layout with factory wings radiating from a central hub where warders acted as overseers as the inmates worked on machinery in the wings. In part Samuel's collaboration was motivated by his desire to advance promotion of his own designs for woodworking machinery.

After serving as an apprentice to a master shipwright at Woolwich, Samuel spent two years on mathematical studies at the Naval Academy in Portsmouth and a year at sea with Admiral Keppel's fleet. He left for Russia in 1780 and spent eleven years surveying natural resources on a tour of the Russian Empire, working to manage Prince Potemkin's estate, helping in the construction of the new Russian Navy and specifically the development of Sebastopol as a Black Sea naval base. He saw some action in Turkey's war with Russia and commanded his own cavalry regiment in Siberia. He returned to England in 1791 and was set on going into naval administration. His combination of extensive, even exotic, trouble-shooting experience and some of his brother's utilitarian ideas applied to organisation eventually paid off. The Board of the Admiralty liked what they heard about dockyard modernisation, and by creating a post specifically for him made Samuel Bentham into one of those figures of modern suspicion—the Government Inspector.

At Portsmouth he oversaw developments that included the enlargement of the Great Basin, introducing a new "hollow floating dam" or caisson at its entrance and overseeing the construction of new dry docks, new wood mills and steam-driven woodworking machines and steam water pumping machines to send water round the whole yard in part to provide more effective on-site fire fighting capacity.

The second person to enter this hothouse of engineering innovation was Marc Brunel. He had come to Britain in 1799 after first fleeing revolutionary France as a political émigré to America where he had been appointed chief engineer of New York. He was looking for a chance to put a particular project to the test. His engineering inventiveness focused on designing block-making machinery; and there was a huge demand for ships' pulley blocks in the sailing Navy for rigging and the working of the guns. By the start of the nineteenth century it is estimated that the Royal Navy required 100,000 blocks each year. Brunel collaborated with Henry Maudsley, the leading contemporary mechanical engineer and manufacturer of machine tools, to make working models of the projected machines to interest potential backers. Through Bentham he approached the Admiralty Board and they agreed to his proposals. Work to start on the building to house some of the new block-making machinery was slated for August 1802. For the next five years Marc Brunel worked on the Block Mills project and during that time lived with his family in a terraced house in Britain Street, Portsea; it was there on 9 April 1806 that his son Isambard Kingdom Brunel was born, destined to be another titan of civil engineering.

It took that period of time to sort out all the problems associated with the innovatory production process—problems of supply of component parts and introducing engines of sufficient capacity; but by 1807 Brunel could predict that the mills would soon be capable of producing 130,000 blocks a year and so supplying "all the Blocks for the Navy". And by 1808 they were. One casualty was the future of many craft workers; one estimate suggested that ten unskilled men at the Block Mills displaced 110 skilled men.

The Block Mills were visited by Admiral Lord Nelson on 14 September 1805, the day before he joined his flagship HMS *Victory* in the Solent to sail south to the fateful encounter off Cape Trafalgar. Subsequently the building became a magnet for visitors, including in 1814 a royal party comprising the Emperor of Russia, the King of Prussia and Marshal von Blücher who were inspecting the fleet as part of the post-Treaty of Paris celebrations. In 1831 Sir Walter Scott took his daughters to Portsmouth Dockyard and "the girls contrived to secure sight of the Block Manufactory".

Samuel Bentham was sent by the government as an envoy to Russia to try and persuade the tsar to allow British warships access to Archangel—without success. He was dismissed from his inspector's post in 1812 and given a pension, while the post was abolished. He took his family to live in France, only returning in 1826. He kept working on new designs, and died in April 1831 from "exhaustion". He was conscious of being inadequately recognised, but as the naval historian Jonathan Coad concludes: "his small department was the seed from which ultimately grew the great civil engineering and architecture departments of the Admiralty".

Marc Brunel continued as an inventor and entrepreneur, designing wood-making machinery for the government mills at Woolwich and later completing a scheme at Chatham Dockyard which connected a sawmill and a timber pond via a canal tunnel and a wide-gauge rail track; but a failed scheme to stitch soldiers' boots by machine resulted in his committal to a debtor's prison in 1821. Friends came to his rescue and the government awarded him an honorarium recognising previous unrewarded work. This did not prevent the Navy Board from reneging on an agreement over designs for steam-driven tugs, leaving Brunel to bear the costs of design and experimentation.

He was always looking for pioneering solutions to engineering problems. In 1816 observation of how the mollusc *Teredo navalis* used a muscular action to bore through navy timber gave him ideas for a tunnelling shield. He was able to put his ideas into action when he was made chief engineer of a scheme to link the docks at Rotherhithe and Wapping by a tunnel under the Thames. It turned out to be a heroic endeavour. Tunnelling was started in December 1825 but the tunnel was not finally opened until March 1843. The first phase saw the tunnel half completed when in January 1828 the money ran out and work was suspended for seven years. At the end of his life Marc Brunel had received many decorations, including a knighthood and the Légion d'Honneur, in recognition of his contributions to engineering. He died in December 1849.

During the first phase of the Rotherhithe tunnel Marc had worked in collaboration with Isambard, who was the resident engineer. Brunel *père* was a hard act to follow but it was his driven son, Isambard Kingdom, who went on to be the more renowned engineer. The son only survived his father by ten years.

THE AGE OF STEAM

For almost thirty years after the end of the Napoleonic Wars in 1815, the dockyard experienced stasis rather than change. It was not a war that changed this situation but a technological breakthrough. Steam had already been harnessed to drive paddle steamers but these were never going to be converted into viable or convincing warships. The situation was altered by Francis Pettit Smith (1808-74) from Hythe. In 1836 he took out a patent for a screw propeller and by 1839 had built a screw-propelled steamer, the *Archimedes*. The Admiralty was persuaded that this might represent the future and encouraged him to build a warship, HMS *Rattler*, which proceeded to beat the paddler HMS *Alecto* in trials. The two ships had different systems of propulsion but otherwise shared identical specifications. Most famously the sloop *Rattler* pulled the *Alecto* backwards at 2.7 knots in a tug of war as both ships were at full steam ahead. The naval establishment was now on board and steam was the order of the day henceforth. The consequence for Portsmouth was the start of new programme of work in 1843; and the programmes would keep coming for the rest of the century as shore-based infrastructure had to be continually updated to keep pace with the acceleration of change in naval architecture.

The centrepiece of the new programme was the seven-acre Steam Basin completed in 1848 within five years, four days ahead of schedule. "Swan neck" steam-powered cranes were introduced; this tag alluded to their single curved metal jib. Two new docks were built that could serve as another entrance to the Steam Basin as well as a necessary combination dry dock that could take the new longer steam ironclads such as HMS *Warrior* (launched in 1860).

The expanding docks of the 1840s were also acquiring new buildings. An example of the iron-framed structures to come was the Boat Store (latterly No. 6 Boathouse and currently an interactive visitor attraction and cinema). Completed in 1844, its upper floors were supported by circular iron columns and girders. Boats could be hauled up on rails through arched doors from the Boat—former Mast—Pond. The building leviathan of the 1843 plan was the Steam Factory, stretching 600 feet along the western quay of the Steam Basin, built of fire-proof brick and metal girders. Inside a gantry crane eased the movement of heavy boilers and engines; sections of the factory announced the requirements of the new Navy: the heavy turning shop, the boiler shop, the punching and shearing shop. The nearby smithy contained swan neck cranes, hearths and a giant steam hammer. The Iron Foundry included railway access through Portland stone arches.

A limited granite tramway had existed prior to the new build of the 1840s built in 1828 by convicts brought over from the prison hulks with haulage of trucks powered by horses. The Steam Basin scheme included a standard gauge railway around its perimeter but a coherent steam locomotive railway was still some way off. Steam locomotives did bring supplies to the reception yard in the northern part of the dockyard on a line from the town station opened in 1849. It was another twenty years before a locomotive was working in the dockyard while trucks were still shifted by horses and probably hydraulic capstan.

Just as the increased pace of marine research and development made warships obsolete more quickly the same process was at work with dockyard and support facilities. In line with previous developments, the threat of war with the French was enough to trigger a further period of dockyard building—a scheme spanning a decade from the middle of the 1860s referred to as The Great Extension.

In 1864 the Admiralty was given the go-ahead by parliament to set in motion a programme of work that would treble the size of the dockyard, of which half (95 acres) would be reclaimed land. This last target and the size of the works intended would test the civil engineering skill of the contractors, Leather Smith & Co. John Towlerton Leather was already well-known to the Admiralty as contractor for the Portland breakwater. In 1861 Leather was also made the main contractor for the Spithead Forts.

The main phase of the work lasted from 1867 to 1876 and was accorded a budget of £2½ million in contemporary money. At the centre of the scheme was a 22-acre Repairing Basin accessed from a tidal basin through two locks and supplemented by two other fitting out basins—a true production and repair complex for ironclads. A temporary building site was crossed by between seven and eight miles of railway, peopled by 2,400 workmen and dominated by huge machines such as the steam gantry cranes used to carry heavy stone loads in the construction of the docks; each "Goliath" steam dredger dominated the mudflats like some giant iron mantis.

The workforce included up to 800 convicts from a prison just outside the dockyard wall, many employed in the on-site brickworks. Dredged clay was used to make bricks and surplus mud was deposited just to the north of the site of the emerging Whale Island which would later become the shore establishment HMS *Excellent*. As part of a second phase to the

Extension the quay where ships received their new supplies of coal, Coaling Point, was taken over in 1881 by ten thirty-cwt hydraulic black cranes standing on four curved legs and looking like creatures from a science fiction novel.

In the year of the completion of phase one (1876) the rail extension from the town station reached the harbour station and a single-track branch line ran out across the Common Hard into the dockyard; a swing bridge allowed boat access to the Hard. South Railway Jetty was created to allow twin tracks and the building of two railway waiting rooms and belatedly (1893) a Royal Shelter. Other buildings followed the excavation work of the Great Extension in the 1880s and reflected changes in armaments technology: thus the Gun Mounting Shop and the Torpedo Store. The largest workshop built in the dockyard was finished in 1905; known as the Factory and five times the width of the Steam Factory, its size was a testimony to the complexity and scale of engineering changes in the intervening decades.

In the following year an event signalled a more dramatic revolution in war at sea. On 10 February HMS *Dreadnought* was launched at Portsmouth Dockyard. Laid down on 2 October 1905, she had been built in record time. The speed was deliberate. As her design represented "a quantum leap in all-round performance" her arrival meant, writes Andrew Lambert, that "other battleships were rendered obsolescent". Her name became the generic term for the new big gun battleship; she was faster than her predecessors and had twice the firepower and twice the effective range (beyond the threat of torpedoes). With her rapid launch and the subsequent building of more battleships in her class, Britain hoped to dismay other naval powers and discourage them from continuing in the arms race. Only the US and Germany started to build Dreadnought class fleets; but as Germany had been preoccupied with the reconstruction of the Kiel Canal joining the Baltic and North Seas, Britain was still the major European naval power in 1914.

The first Dreadnought missed the Battle of Jutland, the big set-piece naval battle of the First World War, but she did manage the unusual feat of sinking a submarine in March 1915. Placed in reserve in 1919 and sold for scrap in 1922, she was broken up at Inverness the following year.

The Dreadnought project had been masterminded by Admiral Sir John Arbuthnot "Jacky" Fisher (1841-1920), a forceful even ruthless Navy reformer and radical. His career seemed to connect with much of contemporary naval experience. At fifteen he was a midshipman on the China Station; he studied navigation at HMS *Excellent* and became a gunnery lieutenant in HMS *Warrior*. By 1883 he was commander of *Excellent's* gunnery school and its first torpedo school. The following year he gave an interview to the *Pall Mall Gazette* for a series of articles entitled "The Truth about the Navy", an exposé of the Royal Navy's decline caused by underfunding. Promotions and increasing power ensued: in 1891 admiral superintendent of Portsmouth Dockyard; in 1896 vice-admiral; in 1899 commander-in-chief of the Mediterranean Fleet; in 1901 full admiral; in 1902 Second Sea Lord, where he brought in training reforms (as commander-in-chief Portsmouth he was a promoter of submarines); in 1904 First Sea Lord. He was instrumental in the Dreadnought programme and insistent on the importance of torpedo boats and submarines in home waters defence.

He retired as First Sea Lord in 1910 to be replaced by Winston Churchill. His opinion was still sought by Churchill and the two would meet clandestinely to discuss naval affairs—once walking around Portsmouth Dockyard at night; and it was Churchill who brought him out of retirement in 1914. He initiated a big ship-building programme and was decisive in the despatch of two battle cruisers to destroy a German raiding squadron at the battle of the Falkland Islands. He resigned from his post in 1915 after disagreements with Churchill over the Dardanelles campaign and the unsuccessful amphibious assaults on the Gallipoli peninsula. John Fisher died in 1920 after completing two volumes of dictated memoirs. He claimed his motto was: "Fear God and Dread Nought". Yet perhaps his decisive self is better reflected in advice he offered in a letter to *The Times* in 1919: "Never contradict, never explain, never apologise."

Two Navy ships berthed at Portsmouth Dockyard serve as symbols, emblems and reminders of Britain's naval glory and design ingenuity: HMS *Victory* and HMS *Warrior*. As they have become an integral part of the dockyard scene they warrant two brief post-active service biographies.

The epoch-making naval triumph at the Battle of Trafalgar ushered in a century of British naval supremacy and made national icons of Horatio Nelson and HMS *Victory*. Nelson's inclusion in the pantheon of heroes was immediate, the afterlife of his flagship rather more prosaic. *Victory* was removed from the active list in 1823, survived a threat of disposal in

HMS *Victory*

1831 and played a variety of flagship roles. In 1840 she was moved to a mooring off Gosport and by 1870 had started to receive public visitors who were taken round on unofficial tours by naval veterans. *Victory* was accidentally rammed by *Neptune* as that ship was under tow to the breaker's yard. This event in 1903 and the Trafalgar centenary two years later prompted questions about *Victory*'s future.

It was not until 1910 and the formation of the Society for Nautical Research that the Admiralty was lobbied over the preservation of the ship and a fundraising drive was launched; a key figure in this campaign was the Portsmouth-based marine artist William Lionel Wyllie. The First World War postponed any plans for the ship's recovery but finally in 1922 HMS *Victory* was taken to No. 2 Dry Dock and installed there. After restoration she was first opened to the public in July 1928. The ship is still in commission as the flagship of the commander-in-chief Naval Home Command and a potent naval heritage draw.

Charles Dickens, after visiting HMS *Warrior* at her launching in December 1860 commented: "she is a portent; the warship as gun machine". He was right about her significance but this battleship was never required to fire a shot in action. Her design ratcheted up the cycle of warship obsolescence, a cycle that would soon claim her as a victim. The *Warrior's* commissioning was a response to the 1858 launch of France's first ironclad *La Gloire* and to Prince Albert's question to the Admiralty: 'What have we got to meet this new engine of war?' The ship's design, formulated by Chief Constructor to the Navy Isaac Watts and iron shipbuilder John Scott-Russell, was centred on an armoured box or "citadel" which housed the main guns, boilers and engine and was made of iron plates bolted to solid teak, with the added bow and stern clad to a lower specification. She was fast and as her length was 100 feet longer than contemporary warships her design could include a more stable single gun deck. The French emperor Napoleon III described HMS *Warrior* as "a black snake amongst rabbits".

After only ten years of active service she was transferred to the Reserve Fleet in 1871 as a coastguard "gobby ship"—supposedly a soft option for older sailors—and then withdrawn from sea service twelve years later. For the first two decades of the twentieth century, *Warrior*, minus guns and masts, served as a floating workshop and power plant as part of the Vernon Torpedo School in Portsmouth. Subsequently the ship languished in Fareham Creek's Rotten Row, attracting no buyers until in 1929 she was towed to Milford Haven's Pembroke Dock to serve as an oil jetty: Oil Fuel Hulk C77.

The rescue and full restoration of HMS *Victory* and then the SS *Great Britain* and the *Cutty Sark* had demonstrated how these ships could be given new roles showcasing a more imaginative sort of nautical history. The Maritime Trust was founded in 1969 with the restoration of *Warrior* as one of its objectives and ten years later ownership of the ship was granted to the Trust. Hartlepool was identified as a site for the restoration work; it was in a development area and qualified for government funding and a skilled workforce could be recruited from workers made redundant by the closure of the town's Grays Shipyard. So in August 1979 the neglected and damaged hulk of the *Warrior* was towed 800 miles to her re-fit berth in the north-east port. Over the next eight years the ship was stripped of accretions such as the two hundred tons of concrete lining her upper deck and reconstructed as a replica of the HMS *Warrior* of the 1860s complete with new figurehead. The original ship's plans and plans from the log book of a midshipman—fourteen years old when serving aboard in 1862—pinpointed the locations of many fittings.

On 12 June 1987 *Warrior* was towed out to sea on her four-day journey to the designated home port of Portsmouth. She arrived there to a triumphant welcome. The local paper was not indulging in journalistic hyperbole when it ran the headline "Emotional Welcome for the Ship They Wouldn't Allow to Die". Now berthed across the Common Hard from the Harbour Station, she is a kind of sentinel for the dockyard and a symbol of the ascendancy of the Victorian Navy.

VISITING THE PAST

The dockyard did not start to change fundamentally until the 1960s. The age of the Cold War ushered in a new tactical emphasis with reliance on nuclear submarines and a scaled-down fleet of medium-sized warships. A review in 1981 spelt out that only two main naval bases were needed: Plymouth and Rosyth. Chatham would be closed and Portsmouth downsized to a yard carrying out maintenance and repair. Portsmouth's demotion was temporarily postponed by the urgent need to fit out the Falklands Task Force in 1982; but a workforce of 8,000 would soon be scaled down to 2,800. The yard was privatised and most of the oldest parts of the dockyard came under the ownership of the Portsmouth Naval Base Property Trust in 1985. Income was to be generated by converting buildings into tourist attractions to supplement visitors' experience on board HMS *Warrior* and HMS *Victory* and by making a feature of the wreck of the Tudor warship *Mary Rose*—hence the Mary Rose and HMS Victory Museums, an Action Stations activities centre and cinema in the former No. 6 Boathouse, a café, a shop and a Dockyard Apprentice Museum. These various attractions are managed by Portsmouth Historic Dockyard Ltd., a body that aims to preserve and protect the dockyard heritage. Navy Days and Festivals of the Sea have allowed visitors to explore the further reaches of this extensive maritime real estate.

Chapter Six

OSBORNE HOUSE

A HOME OVER THE WATER

Victoria had become queen at the age of eighteen. Now less than a decade into her reign she needed a country retreat, a grand dacha where the family could live away from the ceremonial of court and state and from the popular gaze of London, the Home Counties and Brighton. In 1831 and 1833 the queen had stayed at Norris Castle, a late eighteenth-century Romantic neo-medieval castle sited on a hill in East Cowes surrounded by a picturesque landscape attributed to Humphrey Repton. With its views over the Solent, Victoria had been entranced by this setting and when Prime Minister Sir Robert Peel learned through discreet enquiries that the nearby Osborne estate had became available, Victoria made a reconnoitre and wrote to Prince Albert: "It is impossible to imagine a prettier spot— we have a charming beach quite to ourselves—we can walk anywhere without being followed or mobbed." Victoria and Albert bought the house in 1845 and with it a thousand-acre estate. By then the completion of a branch line linking the mainland town of Gosport to the rail network had put the Isle of Wight within easier reach.

Albert was an architect manqué and unlike the contemporary heir to the throne who pursues a quest to slay the dragon of Modernism the nineteenth-century prince consort could be forward thinking in his design ideas. Whatever the constitution said or implied Prince Albert of Saxe-Coburg acted in effect as a dual monarch taking over much of the administration work when Victoria was frequently indisposed through pregnancy. He headed a royal commission to promote the fine arts, set up a model dairy farm at Windsor, made clear his anti-slavery position and so helped keep Britain out of the American Civil War; it was through the Royal Society of Arts that Albert became the prime mover behind the Great Exhibition project of 1851. The prince had recognised the architectural "genius" Joseph Paxton in the form of his great greenhouse at Chatsworth and recruited him to design the Great Exhibition building for the first world fair.

Thomas Cubitt (1788-1855), the builder and developer of Belgravia, Bloomsbury and Pimlico, was commissioned to design and build the new Osborne House. Starting with the Pavilion in 1845 and consulting with Prince Albert throughout, Cubitt added the Main Wing and the Household Wings and brought the job mostly to completion by 1851. The two additional wings were designed to house the royal household in one and to provide spaces in the Main Wing for the affairs of state including a Council Room and an Audience Room. The Privy Council of ministers would be convened in the Council Room several times a year and the Audience Room was for the queen to receive ministers prior to the Privy Council meetings.Osborne House could be a sort of functioning government over the water.

The Pavilion was essentially a large Georgian-style town house designed with enough rooms to meet the royal household's family and entertaining needs while staying domestic in scale. It included a nursery bedroom of dormitory proportions and the Queen's Sitting Room where two writing tables were pushed together so she could work on her dispatch boxes; Albert, her private and personal secretary, would hand her memoranda for her perusal. Victoria wrote in her journal about watching the moonlight on the Solent from the balcony and hearing the nightingales sing in the trees nearby. Downstairs there was a billiard room. Albert had designed the billiard table's side panels and legs. Victoria was known to play billiards with her ladies in waiting.

To the west across two lawns from the Household Wing is the walled garden. This was used primarily as a kitchen garden and then increasingly as a source of flowers for the house. The gothic lean-to glasshouses from 1854 were copies of those Prince Albert had erected at Frogmore in the previous decade. He oversaw the planting to improve the pleasure grounds designed to be strolled in. Albert also took a lead role in the tree planting. Directing operations from the Pavilion's flag tower, he would signal gardeners where to place flags to position the intended trees. By the year of his death in 1861 the estate's woodland had reached 400 acres. The result consisted of clumps of oaks and elms, together with Mediterranean pines, ilexes, cork trees and cedars.

South of the house in woods close to the shore of Osborne Bay a playground and study was constructed for the children. The Swiss Cottage, shipped over from Switzerland, was completed in 1854. Prince Albert had

been the instigator of this project, intending it to be a Tyrolean learning chalet where the children could learn the basics of domestic science and where a room would enable the children to create their own natural history museum. Their building of collections was so successful that eight years later a separate museum was built to house them. It stands today—the epitome of the Victorian museum with glass cases full of pinned butterflies, stuffed birds and animals and anthropological artefacts gifted or acquired from far-flung parts of the Empire.

On the ground next to the Swiss Cottage playing at being British and Russians soldiers was taken to a new level. A brick-built barracks was the centrepiece of a fort complete with earthworks and a small gravel parade ground with its own flagpole. The whole scheme, supervised by Lieutenant Cowell of the Royal Engineers, had included the two older princes Bertie and Alfred working as navvies and was completed two months after the end of the Crimean War in the spring of 1856. Nearby was a garden area where the children were encouraged by the prince in the practice of market gardening, growing vegetables and merchandising their produce. Back-to-the-land utopians of the later nineteenth century would have applauded this initiative.

For today's visitor there are two other objects nearby. The green mobile edifice the size of a small bungalow on wheels was Queen Victoria's bathing machine, rescued from ignominy as a chicken shed in 1927. The queen confided to her journal the experience of her first dip in the sea, attended by a bathing woman; it had proved "delightful until I put my head under the water when I thought I should be stifled." Next to it is the deckhouse of the Royal Yacht *Alberta*, built in 1864 and still used by Edward VII until it was consigned to the breaker's yard. This bridge had adorned a Portsmouth garden for decades until donated to Osborne in the 1970s.

Queen Victoria was persuaded to adopt the title Empress of India in 1876. In the following decade her son Prince Arthur became commander of the Bombay army. Victoria conceived a "great longing" to go to India, but this journey never happened. If the queen could not go to India, however, then India would have to come to Osborne. In 1887 the queen recruited two Indian servants and one, Abdul Karim, was appointed to the post of *munshi* (language tutor) to teach her Hindi in 1889. The following year work started on an extension to the Pavilion, the Durbar Wing, to comprise family accommodation upstairs and a hall/state reception room on the ground floor: the Durbar Room.

Prince Arthur had met Lockwood Kipling (father of Rudyard) who was director of Lahore's Mayo School of Art. When in 1884 local Indian princes made a present of decorating the billiard room of Prince Arthur's Surrey home, it was Kipling who supervised the work of carver Bhai Ram Singh. In the summer of 1890 Kipling was asked to make a submission of designs for the projected room at Osborne House; he and Ram Singh came to Osborne in January 1891. Two years later the work was finished, the completed space a nineteenth-century medieval-style great hall complete with minstrel's gallery and walls and ceiling covered with plaster carvings from north India—the decorative art of Hindu and Jain temples.

As the land falls away from the terraces behind the house, hidden in the first copse on view is the ice house. Built into the side of the hill by Cubitt in 1846, it has a cavity wall for insulation, a floor with bricks drilled with holes so melting ice would drain away and, after 1853, an imposing classical entrance through a rusticated arch. Although this could not be relied upon for a continuous supply for ice to meet domestic need, the operation of the ice house does illustrate the hard work involved in maintaining the domestic regime of an upper-class household. Over sixty cart-loads of ice were transported to this cave compartment in two days during the severe winter of 1859.

To keep a large house and estate going required a considerable contingent of mostly unnoticed indoor servants and estate workers. Those in service were a significant part of the labour force; the 1891 census recorded the country's workforce of indoor servants at almost two million. At Osborne the table-decker's rooms were in the basement of the Pavilion connected to the dining room above by a steep servant's staircase. These servants were responsible for laying the tables for lunch and dinner, arranging displays of freshly cut flowers and making final preparations for the food brought from the kitchen a hundred yards away. All this was overseen by the lord steward. Off the first floor landing was the pages' alcove where the pages waited to be summoned from 8 a.m. until the queen retired for the night. The servants' rooms were with the nurseries on the second floor.

The out of doors workers on large estates would have included gardeners, foresters, gamekeepers, estate carpenters, saddlers, wheelwrights, grooms, coachmen and then chauffeurs. The laundry was often staffed by young women from nearby villages. For those in the more menial jobs, the days could be long and the pay meagre. But the alternative of unemployment and poverty was shameful and degrading and could be fatal.

Four miles south of the Osborne estate across the River Medina just north of Newport was the House of Industry (1771-74) or workhouse, serving the whole of the Isle of Wight. It had been an early example of local poor relief which was systematised by the 1834 Poor Law Amendment Act. Local Poor Law unions of several parishes administered by an elected Board of Guardians oversaw this relief. Relieving officers met poor families and gave them a ticket to the "house". On entry new residents were given a bath, a uniform and a medical examination and then the men were segregated from the women and parents from children. The women were put to work on domestic chores and the men assigned to work such as stone breaking and oakum picking (the similarities to a prison regime are hard to miss).

The conditions within the workhouse were designed to be "less eligible" (more intolerable) than those of the poorest labourer. Charles Dickens wrote to expose the reality of the workhouses in his fiction and through his campaigning journalism. He wrote in February 1860 of a visit to the decrepit building housing the "Foul Wards" of the Wapping Workhouse: "They were in a building most monstrously behind the time—a mere series of garrets or lofts, with every inconvenient and objectionable circumstance in their construction, and only accessible by steep and narrow staircases, infamously ill adapted for the passage upstairs of the sick, or downstairs of the dead." For the able bodied the work was monotonous hard graft—closely supervised and sometimes work for its own sake—endlessly cleaning the building's interiors and repainting walls. This was the workhouse after all.

A CULTURAL DESTINATION

During the second half of the nineteenth century a gradual but significant cultural development unfolded, twenty miles to the south-west of Osborne at Freshwater. It became a destination and a locale for writers, poets, artists and certainly one photographer. In 1853 Alfred Tennyson (1809-92), the Poet Laureate, moved with his family to the secluded house of Farringford two miles south of the village church, a mile from the bay and sited below the high down that would later bear his name.

Tennyson was born at the Somersby rectory in Lincolnshire, his father a melancholic man of the cloth with no sense of a calling. As a teenager Alfred discovered his ability to compose poetry and in his *Memoir* he recalled: "I used to compose 60 or 70 lines in a breath. I used to shout them about the silent fields, leaping over the hedges in my excitement." He went to Trinity College, Cambridge, but left without taking a degree on the death of his father in 1831. Arthur Hallam with whom Alfred had a deep friendship when they were undergraduates died two years later. As his biographer Christopher Ricks suggests, Tennyson's "morbid influence... resigned to but contemplated with creative courage, informs much of (his) deepest work... unhappiness current and unforgettable..." His engagement to Emily Sellwood, broken off after two years in 1840, was resumed at the end of the decade and they married in 1850, the publication year of Tennyson's great elegy to Hallam "In Memoriam" and the year he succeeded William Wordsworth as Poet Laureate.

At Farringford the tall figure of the poet garbed in a cloak and with his sculptured face under a wide-brimmed hat became familiar to the villagers; he engaged with the old men in discussions about God and sometimes ventured out to sea at night with the fishermen, reciting verse to them as they rowed. He was often found on patrol up on the down heading westward toward the Needles, awe-struck by "dead claps of thunder from within the cliffs, Heard thro' the living roar".

That decade was one of great creativity which encompassed first "In Memoriam", where landscape was enhanced by memories of his friend:

I climb the hill: from end to end
Of all the landscape underneath,
I find no place that does not breathe
Some gracious memory of my friend;

This was followed by "The Charge of the Light Brigade" (1854), the Crimean War episode of heroic folly when the cavalry were directed to ride into the Valley of Death, and his monodrama "Maud" (1855): "all by myself in my own dark garden ground, listening now to the tide in its broad-flung shipwrecking roar", and "The Idylls of the King" (1859), a popular sequence of poems based on Arthurian legend.

Tennyson was a public celebrity and he became a catalyst for other artists and writers. The historian and novelist Charles Kingsley, the artist and writer of nonsense verse Edward Lear, the children's writer Charles Dodgson (aka Lewis Carroll) and the poet Swinburne were all visitors. In 1854 Tennyson wrote an invitation to stay in verse to his friend the Rev. F. D. Maurice the controversial founder of the Christian Socialist movement. One verse—the poet's description of his locus—reads:

For groves of pine on either hand
To break the blast of winter, stand;
And further on, the hoary Channel
Tumbles a billow on chalk and sand;

The Poet Laureate visited Queen Victoria at Osborne and his wider circle of intellectual and artistic contacts included occasional visitor, naturalist and world shaker Charles Darwin (1809-82), the London-based historian and essayist Thomas Carlyle (1795-1881) and novelist and prime mover behind the introduction of the pillar box into England, Anthony Trollope (1815-82). Part of his circle and a close friend of Tennyson was

Ellen Terry at sixteen by Julia Margaret Cameron (1864)

the popular innovative symbolist painter and sculptor George Frederic Watts (1817-1904) who painted a portrait of a very introspective Tennyson (c.1863-4). Watts acquired a property on the Island and a wife, for a year, in the stellar form of the teenage actress beauty Ellen Terry (see p.201). But the key figure uniting this disparate group was Tennyson's friend and Island near neighbour Julia Margaret Cameron (1815-79).

Born the daughter of a senior East India Company civil servant, Julia Margaret Pattle, after an education in France, married a jurist and Benthamite liberal Charles Hay Cameron in 1838; he was twenty years her senior. Her husband became a member of the Supreme Council in India and on his retirement in 1848 at the age of 53 returned to London. Julia became involved in a salon at Little Holland House at Putney, a meeting place for artists, writers even eminent politicians; here she met and became friends with Watts and Tennyson. These two would be influential in her photographic work as would her lifelong friend, astronomer and pioneer of the chemistry of photography John Herschel.

Julia's friendship with Tennyson was instrumental in the Camerons moving to Freshwater in 1860 and taking a house yards from his house at

Farringford, named Dimbola Lodge after one of her husband's estates in Ceylon. Her career in photography began when her daughter Julia gave her photographic equipment as a present in 1863. In the following ten years Julia taught herself photography and became a pioneering portrait photographer—persuading, cajoling, and even suborning local village people and the famous to sit for her. The results included definitive portraits of Watts, Darwin, Terry, Carlyle and Tennyson, whose personal favourite was the one of him as the "dirty monk". These images and the photographic illustrations for Tennyson's "Idylls of the King" are arguably her masterpieces. Her portraits were unusually atmospheric and could be astonishingly frank. After her election to the Photographic Society and exhibitions in London, her prints were in demand.

Given weakening family ties with England and Charles' declaration that Ceylon was his spiritual home where he should be husbanding the family plantation business, she returned to Ceylon to be re-united with her husband and in the hope that a warmer climate might restore her to better health. Their china plates had been packed for the journey south in two big wooden coffins; it seems that they did not contemplate returning. In effect Julia Margaret Cameron's photographic career of nearly a decade was over. She died on 26 January 1879 at the Glencairn estate in Ceylon's Dikoya valley.

William Robert Hogg (1844-1928) was the son of a London shoemaker who migrated to Southampton and then Ryde. William worked for his uncle's bakery business in Ryde, was a porter when he married in 1865 and subsequently a photographic assistant learning the trade with Mr. Jabez Hughes, a London photographer transplanted to Ryde. Hogg continued to practise his photographer's art, taking family portrait commissions and using his plate camera to capture postcard views even when he worked as a postmaster. An album he left show images that would have been so typical of contemporary photography: the Portsmouth/Ryde paddle steamer at the pier head, churches inside and out, the auditorium of the Theatre Royal, the yachting scene on the Solent, a wagonette full of sailors, an army recruiting campaign by the pier gates during the First World War, family members arranged around the garden of their villa. Three images were taken on an early assignment in his apprenticeship when he was sent to Osborne. One shows the chapel at Osborne used by the queen and her household. A second photograph is of Queen Victoria's second daughter Alice, dressed in black. The third photograph is of the queen herself also in black, gazing into the middle distance, distracted but very human. Another photograph of Queen Victoria taken at Osborne during her last years showing a black-clad figure sitting solemnly in a horse-drawn carriage specially made for her as a conveyance for getting around the grounds.

The queen herself was interested in photography but she probably did not realise the extent to which so much of the Island and the mainland realm was being recorded by the camera: churches, rectories, seaside resorts, bathing machines, Blackpool's Big Wheel, steamers, shepherds with crooks and lambs, the carting of corn, milkmaids in boaters, castles, ruins, hotels, piers, fishermen, harbours, manor houses, horse-drawn omnibuses, rural postmen with pony and traps, the Thames, boat races, markets, town panoramas, viaducts, mountains, lochs—especially any picturesque subject or feature. The key mover behind all this photographic fieldwork was Francis Frith (1822-98), who taught himself to become a photographer of renown and who then set out to photograph Britain and sell the results to tourists as souvenirs. This entrepreneurial drive made him the godfather of the modern picture postcard.

Queen Victoria died at half past six on the evening of 22 January 1901 at the age of 83 in the 64th year of her reign. Most citizens would have known only her as head of state. As Lytton Strachey observed, "she had become an indissoluble part of [her subjects'] scheme of things." There were few towns in the land that did not have a statue of her or assigned her name to at least one local place—a street, park, theatre, hall, hospital or railway station. On 1 February after the lying in state at Osborne House the queen's coffin was carried out to the waiting gun carriage by sailors from the royal yacht and the cortege set off at a slow pace down to East Cowes to the Royal Yacht *Alberta* at Trinity Pier. Accompanied by two other vessels the *Alberta* headed westward, their seaway marked by two lines of battleships and cruisers stretching from Old Castle Point to Portsmouth. A train brought the queen to Victoria Station on the next day and during the short journey to Paddington the cortege passed through crowds (as photographs show) at times sixty deep.

The coffin journeyed from Paddington to Windsor. From there the gun carriage was hauled to Windsor Castle's St. George's Chapel by an honour guard of sailors after the horses had become unruly. On 4 February the queen was interred in the mausoleum at Frogmore, the resting place of Prince Albert. As her *ODNB* biographers remark, the queen had met everyone who was anyone in the Victorian world. She was one of the most "painted, sculpted, drawn, caricatured and photographed" subjects of her day. As they conclude: "In her sincerity, her enthusiasms, her effort to do her duty, Victoria was truly Victorian."

AFTERMATH

Queen Victoria wanted Osborne House to stay in the family after her death. But the new king Edward VII had his own residences and other surviving members of the family showed scant interest; Princess Beatrice was happy to stay in Osborne Cottage. The central apartments were then kept as a memorial to the late queen and the rest of the house and the estate were bequeathed to the nation. The stables and the paddocks became the nucleus of a Royal Naval College in 1903. The Main and Household Wings saw new service as a convalescent home for military officers.

The college was designed as a training establishment for young officer cadets to give then a two-year grounding from thirteen before they graduated to the Royal Naval College at Dartmouth. The college intake grew as demand for officers intensified in the decade prior to the First World War. Cadets included the future kings Edward VIII and George VI who wrote home with accounts of meeting the explorers Scott and Shackleton. Yet the day-to-day regime was harsh starting with a 6.30 a.m. dip into a cold plunge pool with a subsequent non-stop timetable of lessons and games. The college was infamously the setting for a *cause célèbre* expulsion scandal which was made into a play by Terence Rattigan, *The Winslow Boy*, and a film.

After the war the Navy contracted and the college was closed in 1921. Many of the buildings were demolished. The surviving petty officers' quarters building is currently a visitor's reception centre.

During the First World War officers were not sent home to convalesce as this took too long. The speedier option—to get the convalescents into a fighting fit state sufficient for their return to the Front—was to use a rehabilitation billet such as Osborne; and it was here that the poet and author Robert Graves was dispatched to recuperate from his near death experience on the Somme in 1916, having recovered sufficiently to read his own obituary in *The Times*. He recalled his stay there in his 1929 memoir

Goodbye to All That. After the trenches, Osborne must have seemed like a dream:

> ... we patients could take all Queen Victoria's favourite walks through the woods and along the quiet seashore, play billiards in the royal billiard room, sing bawdy songs in the royal music-room, drink the Prince Consort's favourite Rhine wines among his Winterhalters, play golf-croquet and visit Cowes when in need of adventure. We were made honorary members of the Royal Yacht Squadron. Another of the caricature scenes of my life: as pseudo-yachtsman, sitting in a leather chair in the smoking-room of what had been, and is now again, the most exclusive club in the world, drinking gin and ginger, and sweeping the Solent with a powerful telescope.

Despite a reaction against Victorian artefacts and architecture in the 1920s and a dip in visitor numbers, the rest of the twentieth century witnessed an increase in public interest. English Heritage took on the management of Osborne House from the Department of the Environment in 1986 and began to restore its design integrity. The emphasis was placed on authenticity within the building and on protecting and managing wildlife habitats and ecosystems. Albert's planting and woodlands were reinstated and the Victoria and Albert's family home reassembled.

By the early decades of the twentieth century Julia Margaret Cameron's work was largely forgotten. It took a German researcher in photographic history to revaluate her significance. Helmut Gernsheim came across some of her photographs, by chance, hanging on the walls of the waiting room at Brockenhurst station in Hampshire. Julia had donated them to the station to mark her reunion there with one of her sons after a four-year separation. Gernsheim and his wife Alison researched a book on Cameron and its publication in 1948 was instrumental in restoring her status as a pioneering photographer. The Julia Margaret Cameron Trust opened Dimbola Lodge as a photography museum in 1994.

Chapter Seven

THE HOSPITAL AT NETLEY

BIOGRAPHY OF A VICTORIAN INFIRMARY

On the morning of 19 May 1856 the Royal Yacht *Victoria and Albert*, flanked by gunboats, carried Queen Victoria across the Solent from her seaside residence at Osborne to the Netley shore on Southampton Water. Her duty that day was to lay the foundation stone of a new military hospital that would become, on completion seven years later, the largest hospital ever built. The impetus for this project had come from press exposure of the deadly incompetence of military medical care during the Crimean War, where it was estimated that for every soldier of the 1,700 who died from their wounds another nine would die from disease. The queen had viewed first-hand the lethal medical environment of a barrack hospital at Chatham's Fort Pitt; she had contacted the Secretary of State for War to enquire why invalid soldiers were treated worse than convicts (Prince Albert's reaction). This combined with Florence Nightingale's reforming and campaigning work in the Crimea prompted an official response.

The search was then on for a suitable hospital site on the south coast. Various locations were reconnoitred—near the original naval hospital at Haslar, the Portchester Castle site at the top of Portsmouth Harbour and the Appuldurcombe estate on the Isle of Wight; but these were found wanting. The site chosen, on the mainland near Netley Abbey, was suggested by the Queen's Physician. Plans were drawn up only to be met with criticism. The site was considered insalubrious; despite Southampton being promoted as a spa in the eighteenth century there had been outbreaks of cholera in the locality. These doubts were dismissed as were the criticisms of Florence Nightingale that the planned interiors of the hospital were wrongly devised and unfit for purpose. For her the projected huge main block with its small rooms instead of separate pavilions with large airy wards contradicted all she had learnt firsthand in hospitals and asylums throughout Europe. She lobbied her friend and Hampshire neighbour, Lord Palmerston, the current prime minister, to no avail.

The building was completed in 1863, over schedule by five years and over budget by £200,000 (£14 million today). It was a quarter of a mile long and capable of housing a thousand men in 138 wards. This was the archetypal total institution, a recuperative warehouse for the sick run according to military regulations. It was also a medical microcosm with its own wells and reservoir, gas works, electricity generating station, brickworks, fire station, shops, post office and its own railway branch line. The building's chronicler Philip Hoare likened it to the immigrant-processing facility at Ellis Island in New York harbour.

The hospital's reception jetty had to be replaced after a year with a pier designed by the doyen of Victorian pier construction, Eugenius Birch; but at 560 feet in length it was still not long enough for hospital ships to dock. With the construction of the branch line in 1866 and then Netley hospital's own station, patients could be transported directly there via Southampton Docks.

As a grand Victorian institution the hospital complex included a chapel large enough to hold the entire resident population. More bizarrely it also housed its own museum of natural history—in the main entrance lobby. A visitor would be confronted by a giant glass-fronted cabinet displaying mummified heads from different ethnic groups of the British Empire. Nearby glass specimen jars displayed the pickled corpses of snakes for the visitor's edification. The building was architecturally imposing in its contemporary institutional form and long corridors provided impressive vistas but required postmen to negotiate them by bike; yet it was faulty in its design as a therapeutic community.

Queen Victoria kept up her involvement with the hospital even during almost a decade of self-imposed seclusion after Prince Albert's death. She made an official visit to the completed hospital in May 1863—her first public engagement since the end of the Crimean War and her husband's death in December 1861. Her last trip to Netley was in May 1900. Eight months later she was dead.

Two Wars

On her last visit the queen had used the branch line and hospital's new railway station; and it was the railways that were to play a key role in the coming world war taking troops to the theatres of engagement and bringing the maimed back from the killing fields. The scale of the fighting on the Western Front and resulting numbers of casualties were etched on the hospital's campus. A contemporary aerial photograph shows a huge hutted encampment lodged behind the main hospital block, soon to be supplemented by a bell-tented community in the fields beyond. Over the duration of the war 1,200 ambulance trains arrived at Netley, and through the first weeks of the 1916 Somme offensive, 151 trains transported 30,000 casualties from Southampton Docks. Few locals could have harboured any illusions about the human cost of the fighting in Flanders fields.

That panoramic photograph included a building at the top of the picture screened by trees from the new reception camp for the wounded. This was the military asylum. Included in the original 1860s plans and in isolation from the main hospital, this was the first purpose-built military lunatic asylum. Cloaked in official euphemism and clerical anonymity it was simply referred to as D Block. Many of the men who passed through this place in the First World War were suffering from psychosis induced by prolonged exposure to artillery bombardment, identified in 1915 as "shell shock". This was new psychiatric terrain and in 1917 it was decided to make a "kinematographic record" of these patients. What survives are celluloid images of men in hospital uniform negotiating their way through the grounds with obsessive spasmodic movements—reacting still to front line nightmares.

The hospital was essentially a closed environment, but it was breached on one occasion in 1917 by the shipyard workers from Thornycroft in nearby Woolston. The men at the works had heard that the German prisoner of war patients were receiving preferential treatment and they marched into the hospital grounds to protest. A potential riot was defused when the commandant assured them the German prisoners would be moved out of the hospital's main block.

One of the thousands who were processed through Netley's clearing station during the war was the soldier-poet Wilfred Owen. A survivor of the Somme he was suffering from neurasthenic damage caused by an exploding shell (one of his poems recalls "The shrill demented choirs of wailing shells"). Owen was shipped out from Étretat back to Southampton in "a luxurious West Indian liner". While at Netley he wrote to his mother: "the town is not far off, and we are allowed to go in... I just wander about absorbing Hampshire." He saw his vocation as a poet and had written in an earlier letter: "Do you know what would hold me together on a battlefield? The sense that I was perpetuating the language in which Keats and the rest of them wrote." In his first collection of poems published two year after the end of the war he had written in the preface: "All a poet can do today is warn." He wrote of physical ordeal endured by soldiers trying to survive in the demented world of the Front.

> Bent double, like old beggars under sacks,
> Knock-kneed, coughing like hags, we cursed through
>   Sludge,
> Till on the haunting flares we turned our backs
> And towards our distant rest began to trudge.
> Men marched asleep. Many had lost their boots
> But limped on, blood-shod. All went lame; all blind;
> Drunk with fatigue; deaf even to the hoots
> Of tired, outstripped Five-Nines that dropped behind.

Wilfred Owen came to epitomise the "doomed youth" of the Great War generation. After Netley he was sent to Craiglockhart Hospital in Edinburgh where he was mentored on poetry by his fellow inmate and writer Siegfried Sassoon. Owen recovered enough to be sent back to France in September 1918. He was killed crossing the Sambre-Oise Canal on 4 November—one week before the Armistice.

By the late 1920s the hutted settlement behind the main hospital had been dismantled. Just over a decade later this seaside institution had acquired a new more urgent therapeutic purpose. From 1940 the city of Southampton was a target for Luftwaffe bombing raids with the hospital's domed tower a possible landmark as the planes traced their flight path along Southampton Water. After the evacuation from Dunkirk the hospital was filled with the rescued sick and wounded. As the country braced itself for invasion pillboxes were built on the shore and barrage balloons swung over gun emplacements. By January 1944 the tide had turned and the whole of the Solent coast and hinterland was to become the launch pad for the Allied invasion of Normandy. The Americans arrived and Netley became the 28th US General Hospital. They took over the new prefabricated treatment complex built in 1940 at the northern edge of the hospital grounds and the American flag flew over the US Army 110th Station Hospital. The Americans were impressed by the landscape but depressed

by the main hospital's archaic form; it is reputed that jeeps were a favoured means of transport negotiating the long corridors.

In the aftermath of D-Day the whole Southampton area became a transit camp for Allied and German wounded and POWs. The American colonisation of Netley ended in July 1945, and the antiquated main hospital continued in use through the 1950s but the future was more clearly symbolised by the new oil refinery towers across Southampton Water on the New Forest shore. The main block increasingly fell out of use, despite the temporary housing of some groups such as refugees from the Hungarian uprising against Soviet rule in 1956. Trespassers and incendiaries helped propel the buildings toward its inevitable fate. Additional signs of the building's imminent end were the arrival of a BBC documentary crew and, in its final year, the use of the hospital in scenes for a film of *Alice in Wonderland*. Demolition of the main block began in 1966 and continued for that year. Only the Royal Chapel was kept. It is now a heritage centre.

A footnote to the hospital site's biography relates to the military asylum and concerns a key part of the life story of the controversial psychiatrist, psychoanalyst and counterculture shaman of the 1960s R. D.

Laing (1927-89). In books such as *The Divided Self* and *The Politics of the Family* he challenged some of the prescriptive orthodoxies and analytical judgements of psychiatry. Part of Laing's post- medical school training involved him spending a year (1952-53) at Netley's former D Block, then P Wing (P for "psychotic").

Laing was repelled by the practices he found there—inducing comas in patients through insulin injections, the use of electric shock treatment and administering the "truth serum" of sodium pentothal to get patients to talk about their malaise within a culture where only doctors could talk to patients while other staff were forbidden to initiate or encourage talk. Laing was alienated by this institutionalising regime which took in traumatised men and contrived to make them worse. His anti-psychiatry clarion call was an over-simplified but perhaps necessary challenge to old practices and was in keeping with his own practising skills; one biographer Charles Rycroft testified to his "remarkable gift for rapport with the mentally disturbed".

In 1980 the foundations of the main hospital were turfed over and the site was made into a country park—a closed world opened as a place of recreation.

The asylum had been shut down two years earlier and then given a new role as a training centre for Hampshire Constabulary, a development that Laing might have seen as an ironic continuation of the building's social control purpose. The prolonged survival of the smaller pavilion-like asylum perhaps vindicates Florence Nightingale's criticism of the design of the main hospital block and her alternative vision of what best contributed to a suitable therapeutic landscape.

Chapter Eight

THE RAILWAYS

FROM BRUNEL TO BETJEMAN

In 1830 there were fewer than a hundred miles of railway in Britain. By 1901 this had increased to 19,000 miles and by then railway stations, trains and lines had become part of the British identity and countryside. As the late Tony Judt judged, "Railway tracks reinvented the landscape." They also reordered time. By the 1840s the railway timetable and the railway clock were part of the modern perception of time. Photographs and lithographs and steel engravings in the popular press brought the new technology and the new feats of construction to life and so boosted civil engineering and made engineers into celebrities, even heroes.

And none was more heroic than Isambard Kingdom Brunel. He was born in Portsmouth in 1823, the son of Marc Brunel, initiator and inventor of revolutionary production processes in the Naval Dockyard. As engineer of the Great Western Railway he was responsible for the construction of the line from Paddington to Bristol, the two-mile Box Tunnel, the development of the locomotive works and railway village at Swindon, the stations at Paddington, Bath and Bristol Temple Meads and a sequence of rail bridges including the Royal Albert Bridge at Saltash where two huge bow-shaped tubes of wrought iron acted as trusses to carry the bridge high over the River Tamar. During the 25 years of planning, designing and supervising this whole GWR project Brunel was known to put in twenty-hour days. He designed a carriage that could contain his plans and instruments and afforded him room to catch some sleep. Brunel dubbed his moveable office the "Flying Hearse". He worked contemporaneously on designs for the Clifton Suspension Bridge and three ocean-going ships, the SS *Great Britain*, the *Great Western* and that steamship giant, the *Great Eastern*. How he found time for all these projects is not clear but certainly his demise in 1859, aged 53, could be seen in retrospect as an early death foretold.

Yet the rail network did not develop as a coherent whole. Brunel's Great Western line was built to broad gauge while other lines were mostly built to narrow gauge, and by 1866 there were thirty places where there were breaks in the gauge. When Queen Victoria travelled from her Deeside castle at Balmoral to her seaside residence at Osborne on the Isle of Wight she would have needed to change at Gloucester and Basingstoke. As the network was run by different companies, operating practices were not standardised or integrated. The consequence was that using the first and longest lasting rail timetable for England, *Bradshaw's Railway Companion* (later *Guide*) could be something of a challenge—a coded puzzle that had to be deciphered.

Writers could scarcely ignore the phenomenon of the age, and railways featured in Charles Dickens' writings and dramatically in his own life. In a short story *Mugby Junction* (1866) he writes of the confluence of railway lines as "the work of extraordinary spiders that spun iron; of iron-barred cages full of cattle... the drooping beasts with horns entangled, eyes frozen with terror"; of a new landscape where there were "half-miles of coal" and signalmen "popped out of boxes in perspective and popped in again". The speed of trains—sometimes over fifty miles an hour—provided a new, intoxicating experience of the countryside. Dickens, an inveterate train traveller, attempted to put this experience into words: "Everything is flying. The hop gardens turn gracefully towards me presenting regular avenues of hops in rapid flight, then whirl away. So do pools and rushes, haystacks, sheep... corn sheaves, cherry orchards, apple orchards, reapers, gleaners, hedges, gates, fields that taper off into little angular corners, cottages, gardens... Now a wood, now a bridge, now a landscape..." The railways started as a threatening innovation and became the subject of fascination.

The poet John Betjeman, the revisionist writer on English provincial life and the suburbs of Metroland and campaigner for the Victorian built legacy, is the person to sum up this re-evaluation of railway landscapes. He maintained that "Roads bury themselves in the landscape. The railways carve out a landscape of their own." Although driving along B roads does provide a stronger sense of being in the countryside, it is railways that "were built to look from and to look at."

Betjeman made a series of short films after the Second World War to illustrate the joys of rail travel through the English landscape, including hymns of praise to rural stations. In the later 1930s rail companies were keen to commission black and white promotional films to celebrate the railway through the inclusion of poetry, prose and music. *The Night Mail* is well known; less so is *The Way to the Sea*, a short film about tourists and trippers on their journey from London to Portsmouth and the Isle of Wight with some music by Benjamin Britten and words by W. H. Auden. It traces the dash from Waterloo to visit some of the Royal Navy ships in a precursor to Navy Days; one helpful sailor on film is a crew member of HMS *Hood*—a poignant image as that ship would meet a catastrophic fate in the coming world war. Then it is on to the Isle of Wight by paddle steamer and Punch and Judy shows and deckchairs on the beaches of the island's south-eastern coast.

RISE AND FALL: RAILWAYS IN THE ISLE OF WIGHT AND PORTSMOUTH

The history of railways on the Isle of Wight can be concisely described as a hundred years of network expansion, operation and then decline. The first line built in 1862 connected Newport and Cowes along four and a half miles of the west bank of the Medina. In 1864 the line from Ryde to Shanklin was built and extended to Ventnor two years later. By 1875 Ryde, Newport and Cowes were linked. There followed a Freshwater, Yarmouth and Newport railway, and in 1897 the Newport, Godshill and St. Lawrence Railway. The lines were initially run by different companies, and competition meant that companies made misleading claims about the efficacy of reaching certain island destinations using their railway.

The operating problems included the familiar ones of idle rolling stock in off peak hours. The problem for the island's network was compounded by a surge in demand during the summer months followed by winter when assets were idle, especially unused rolling stock which could not be transferred economically to the mainland. There were closures in the 1950s with the main cuts coming in 1966 in the wake of the Beeching Report.

That report and its aftermath marked a turning point in this country's post-war transport planning, downgrading rail and boosting roads. Dr. Richard Beeching was one of the first technocrats of the modern era, brought in from the private sector to sort out the railways. He might not have known much about transport policy but he did know about business. Beeching had worked his way up to the position of Technical Director in the multinational corporation ICI. In 1957 he was co-opted onto the British Transport Commission by Ernest Marples, the Conservative Transport Minister with personal interests in road haulage. Marples be-

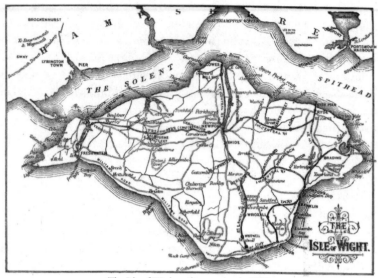

The Isle of Wight railway network, 1898

lieved that the railways should be run as a business and Beeching agreed. The head of the Commission, who believed the railways should be run as a public service, was retired early with Beeching his replacement tasked to modernise the railways and make them profitable. Research into the current performance of the network, which some critics complained had used some dubious methodology, revealed that half of the seven thousand stations generated only two per cent of total rail traffic, that a third of the track carried only one per cent of traffic, and that only a third of rail carriage stock was used all year round.

Beeching's report, *The Reshaping of British Railways*, published in 1963, listed 2,000 stations and 250 lines that needed to be closed on economic grounds with a resulting loss of 70,000 staff. Dr. Beeching resigned in 1965 after the election of a Labour government the previous year but the new administration pressed ahead with cuts. By 1969 track mileage had been cut by a third to just over 12,000 miles and the number of stations reduced from 7,000 to 3,000. The closures and the emphasis on road building transformed the English countryside and cities just as the "railway mania" of the Victorian period had done. Four decades later potential road gridlock and environmental concerns are prompting a fresh look at these ripped out country rail routes.

All that remains of a commercial service on the Isle of Wight is an ex-London Piccadilly line electric train that takes passengers the eight and a half miles from Ryde Pierhead to Shanklin and back. It is a good service but the train is too low to offer an inspiring ride even if it can be interesting to watch the conductor insert his large frame between the doors of two carriages and propel himself from one carriage to the other over swaying couplings. Rail enthusiasts have toiled to resurrect part of the old network and it now possible to join a Victorian steam rail experience travelling the ten miles of track from Wootton (north-east of Newport) to Smallbrook Junction (south of Ryde). Many of the small country stations at Godshill, Whippingham and St. Helens have been converted into houses and the one at Yarmouth into a youth centre. Some railway carriages have enjoyed a new lease of life as beach huts and one saloon coach has become a holiday chalet.

The reason the railway was relatively late arriving at Portsmouth was due in part to the entrepreneurial vagaries of competing rail companies and in part to the military. The latter did not want to see the northern defences—the Hilsea Lines—breached and thus effectively denied access to the island of Portsea. During the early years of the "railway mania" the city had to endure the indignity of being served by Gosport which was then the terminus of a branch line connected to Bishopstoke Junction (now Eastleigh) and the London & Southampton Railway. A siding ran from the town station in Gosport down through the Royal Clarence Victualling Yard to the Royal Station. This was used by Queen Victoria for her steamer voyages to and from the Isle of Wight and sometimes by her prime ministers. Gosport's rail pre-eminence was reflected in its magnificent station opened in 1842 and designed by Sir William Tite (architect of Exeter, Carlisle and Southampton stations among others). Passenger services finished in the 1950s and a fire soon after reduced most of the station to a ruin. Still the architect's fine fourteen-bay Tuscan colonnade in Portland stone can still be glimpsed through railings.

After 1838 rail passengers journeying from Portsmouth to London had to use the floating bridge or take a boat to cross the harbour to the Gosport side, and then walk the three-quarters of a mile to the terminal station. The floating bridge had to stop to allow passage of HM ships and it did not run at night. The eastern route to London via Chichester and Brighton connected directly with Portsmouth in 1847, the western route to London via Fareham and Eastleigh arrived the following year.

Some civic pride was restored when Portsmouth obtained its own dedicated line and town station in 1847. The station was jointly operated by the London Brighton and South Coast Railway (LBSCR) and the London and South Western Railway (LSWR). The distance to London was 95 miles by either route; travelling LBSCR via Brighton took three hour and ten minutes and the fastest LSWR train via Bishopstoke arrived there in two hours and fifty minutes. In the 1830s the most optimistic estimate for a mail coach journey time between the port and the metropolis was seven hours. Life had speeded up and the coast and capital made more accessible. When the direct line to London Waterloo via Guildford was finished in 1859 the distance was reduced to 74 miles and the time to two hours and fifteen minutes.

This direct route was overseen and fashioned by the most eminent railway contractor of the day, Thomas Brassey, bypassing the existing rail companies. As with Brunel, Brassey was the epitome of the enterprising Victorian civil engineer. This former land surveyor's apprentice oversaw rail schemes throughout continental Europe and in Argentina, Australia and Canada—notably the difficult brief for a line linking Toronto, Montreal and Ottawa. His work to build a seven-mile supply line linking the port of Balaklava to the allied forces besieging Sebastopol was crucial to the outcome of the Crimean War (1854-56). In Britain his entrepreneurial efforts added around 1,900 miles to the network. This project was a more cut rate affair with severe gradients and curves and for the first twenty years a single track. Deals also had to be struck with established companies to use sections of their lines.

The railways engineered social and economic change while also signifying existing social realities. The rail companies initially catered for the well-off who could afforded to travel and the entrepreneurial classes who needed to travel. In the 1840s LBSCR added flat wagons and horse boxes to their passenger trains so that their patrons could take their coaches with them; and to facilitate such travel special loading docks were built at some of the stations. Initially the differences between different classes of compartment were stark in terms of space, upholstery and protection from the elements or lack of it. An act of parliament was needed to require rail companies to provide one train a day in each direction that included third-class carriages. Demand then forced supply and by 1875, 75 per cent of all passengers travelled third-class and that figure was 96 per cent in 1911. The rail companies developed their fare policies to anticipate types of demand and build that demand, offering day returns for businessmen, special tickets for evening theatre trips, reduced fares for commercial travellers, concessionary fares for rail workers and their families and "market tickets" to encourage the residents of cities such as Portsmouth to travel out to towns on market days. Money saving periodical tickets were devised, with special first-class season tickets on offer to Portsmouth-based naval and military officers and reduced day and three-day fares for servicemen.

Transferring passengers from their station on to make their ferry connection became a particular problem for Portsmouth with increasing numbers of holidaymakers journeying to the Isle of Wight. A melee of horse-drawn cabs outside the town station vied for business to take these travellers down to the Hard at Portsea. In 1861 Clarence Pier opened on the southern shore of the island and provided a docking facility for two paddle steamers from the IOW Steam Ferry and the IOW Steam Packet companies; this became the preferred route for rail passengers in transit—an urban journey that was made easier when a (horse-drawn) tramway route was opened between station and pier in 1865. But Gosport had stolen a march on Portsmouth. By 1863 passengers were taken from the terminal there by branch line to Stokes Bay to be transferred to a paddle steamer bound for Ryde. Still this pier was exposed to strong south-westerly winds which could prevent steamers coming alongside.

In this competition for passengers the long-term solution for Portsmouth proved to be the extension of the railway line to a terminal at the harbour. Enquiries into its feasibility had to take into account the concerns of the Admiralty and the military. Eventually a harbour extension line was designed and built; fortifications were breached; a high level station was added to the existing town station to take the line up and over the busy thoroughfare of Commercial Road and the line constructed to curve along an embankment above the glacis of the defence works and snake towards the harbour foreshore beside the old Gun Wharf. The Extension Line and Station opened in 1876. The railway company bought the ferry companies and added new vessels. A branch taking traffic across the mud of the foreshore by the Hard to the South Railway Jetty was added later. By the late 1920s annual passenger traffic between Portsmouth and Ryde had reached two million.

One other line opened in 1885—a mile and a quarter branch line from Fratton Station to a station just north of South Parade Pier. This seemed designed for both holidaymakers and residents of the new estates such as Craneswater Park. It struggled to compete with the electric tram and services were stopped on the outbreak of the First World War in August 1914 and the line subsequently abandoned.

The rail infrastructures carved out distinctive features and affected local land use and building developments—what academics refer to as urban morphology. The railways brought services in their wake and made more ambitious retail distribution patterns possible. They revolutionised and expanded the postal service. By the 1870s there was a direct mail and a night mail service to and from London every day of the week. Electric telegraph companies decided to build their networks alongside railway tracks; so in 1845 a telegraph line linking the Admiralty in London with Portsmouth Dockyard was constructed along the LSWR route, then the longest telegraph link in the country.

Railways allowed goods to be distributed in a different way and created national markets. The increasing technological sophistication of Navy ships meant by the end of the nineteenth century equipment such as searchlights, radio transmitters and navigational aids would be delivered by rail to the dockyard. The first line into Portsmouth Dockyard dates from 1849 via a level crossing still standing at the corner of Victoria Park. Thirty years later another line joined the dockyard to the harbour station; and the yard itself developed its own internal network of 25 miles of track. Opportunities for Portsmouth's non-dockyard manufacturing sector meant that the brewers Longs could send their beer to Birmingham and South Wales and the corset makers Chilcot could export their goods to Paris and Chicago. Fruit could be brought in from anywhere in the country and fish packed in ice from Grimsby supplied to fishmongers and fish and chip shops. W. H. Smith showed the way in the development of high street chain stores and department stores such as Timothy Whites, Home and Colonial, Landport Drapery Bazaar set up shop in the streets near the town station.

The city was pulled towards Landport as walking distance from the station became an important factor in urban development. In the last decades of the nineteenth century six hotels and five banks opened for business in the immediate neighbourhood as did the head offices of the water and gas utilities, the Pearl and the Prudential insurance companies, the Free Library, the Theatre Royal and the new town hall. A new business district and civic centre coalesced round the first terminus. The main line and then the Portsmouth Waterside Extension Railway and the urban commuter line of the East Southsea Railway affected existing streets and the shape of further suburban development. Unlike many of the arterial road approaches to cities from the 1930s onwards, the main rail lines into cities took you behind the scenes to reveal the backstage life of the city. The main line from London down through the island of Portsea today takes you past allotments, overgrown defensive ramparts, the back gardens of terraced houses, Kingston Prison, the floodlight towers of Portsmouth Football Club's Fratton Park—across the former Goods Yard site, past St. Mary's Hospital and a cemetery.

St. Olave's Church, Gatcombe, Isle of Wight

Chapter Nine

RELIGIOUS LANDSCAPES
CHURCHES AND CHURCHGOING

Churches feel like a natural part of the English scene; they are, as Jonathan Meades describes them, "sculptures in the landscape". Many are now no longer in regular use and they in turn have now become one of the poor of their parish. The author recalls a trip in the spring of 2008 to visit three Hampshire churches in the care of the Churches Conservation Trust. Driving the B-roads east of Winchester I headed toward Itchen Stoke and the Church of St. Mary (1866). This church was commissioned by the then incumbent Rev. Charles Conybeare and designed by Henry Conybeare. Clearly both admired the thirteenth-century Sainte Chapelle in Paris, for here set on a rising churchyard site in rural Hampshire was a smaller but still grand Victorian version of that gothic extravaganza.

The key holder was a lady who lived in a bungalow nearby. This trustee trusted me with the key and wielding this hefty implement I let myself into the deserted church. The entrance was dramatic; from a small dark vestibule I climbed a few steps straight into the pulpit built into one of the side walls; it was like being thrust into a uniquely prominent box at the theatre. The nave really did soar and the windows of the chancel refracted light through multi-coloured geometric patterns. For a parish church tucked away in the Hampshire countryside this building truly did echo something of the gothic grandeur of the Parisian original. It was a privileged experience but any excitement was offset by the sense of a shuttered, largely neglected place with cobwebs visible between the pews. My reaction was one of sadness without being fully sure why this was so. I write this as a non-believer.

Philip Larkin's poem "Church Going" is partly about uncertain motive and trying to put into words the emotions religious places and buildings can evoke with their "tense, musty, unignorable silence".

Whippingham Church, c.1890

These places of worship more consciously now echo previous times when their users would have known all about the rituals they were designed for and been more familiar with the meaning of the church's interior, its architectural purpose and vocabulary. Many would not have needed to have recourse to a contemporary Pevsner's glossary to check the meaning of bellcote, hammer beam, high lancers, bar tracery, the chancel, reredos, squint, lectern...

Attendance at Church of England services has been declining since the 1890s. By 1999 only 1.9 per cent of the population in England went to church regularly on a Sunday. The Church of England has a membership whose average age is fifty; that figure is predicted to rise. Attendance figures may fall but the status of church buildings rises. Three-quarters of the 16,000 parish churches in England are listed as buildings of architectural and historic interest Grades I, II* and II. Nikolaus Pevsner gave churches the lead role in his architectural guides.

For believers and non-believers alike English churches are part of our architectural and spiritual present and part of our cultural past. For the traveller through England's countryside to encounter a village with no church is a surprise. Parish churches are an expression of the longevity of a village and its culture. Visiting a country church or churchyard usually supplies some evidence of the village's previous economy, history, even its wealth. These buildings are more than just "sculptures in the landscape" because stored up local experience is here.

Pevsner's contribution apart, it is John Betjeman (1906-84) who can be considered to be the patron saint of twentieth-century church visiting.

After various incarnations as a school teacher, secretary to the assistant editor of the *Architectural Review* and film reviewer for the London *Evening Standard*, he published *Ghastly Good Taste* (1933), an attack on the destructive threat of Modernism to English architecture but also on "unthinking antiquarianism". By the 1950s and early 1960s Betjeman was a recognised architectural campaigner (he was a key mover behind the saving of St. Pancras Station and in recognition there is a statue on its concourse today). He had also become a bestselling poet; in 1958 his *Collected Poems* sold 100,000 copies, and he was a radio broadcaster who had become a household name—in contemporary parlance a "media celebrity", but someone with something to say.

On Betjeman's church visiting, his biographer A. N. Wilson wrote:

> The great churches of Wren, with their gilded Commandment Boards and sword-rests; the varied styles, from medieval to Victorian neo-Norman of the Oxford churches, the sand-lashed mysteries of Cornish shrines, all held something for him, which could not, quite, be found anywhere else. At the same time, he felt it to be largely a longing for the past, certainly not a conscious search for God.

John Betjeman worked with the artist John Piper (1903-92) celebrating both built Englishness and churches in a co-editing partnership on the English county guides for Shell and the *Collins Guide to English Parish Churches*. In this latter book Betjeman included in his Isle of Wight selection the church of St. Olave's at Gatcombe—referring to its "well wooded setting" with the "only medieval glass on the Island"—and St. Mary's at Brading, the largest medieval church on the Island with its Oglander chapel off the chancel. In this family mausoleum is a collection of monuments and effigies none more striking than the wooden effigy of Sir John Oglander recumbent in armour atop his tomb with his helmeted head propped up by an arm. A recess in the wall behind contains a scaled-down version of this figure to commemorate his son George who died in his twenties. No one could deny the anonymous sculptor's subtle sense of humour; this was an example of romantic admiration for the Middle Ages as Sir John died in 1655.

Betjeman made radio broadcasts on the pleasures of "church crawling". Given all his championing of threatened Victorian buildings, he was

Sir John Oglander
and son, St. Mary's,
Brading

frank about the Victorians' penchant for "improving" churches: "nine out
of every ten churches in England have been terribly mutilated by the Victorians." Yet one area of church design they did make a significant contribution to was that of stained glass. In his essay for the 1944 Penguin
Modern Painters volume on his friend and colleague John Piper, Betjeman
writes about Piper's "passion for the English country, for living in it, for exploring it, for making lists and notes of every church visited. At the age of
twelve he was tracing stained glass in Surrey." There had been many developments in stained glass design in the previous eighty years.

In 1861 William Morris founded the firm of MMF&Co. with prestigious partners who included Edward Burne-Jones, Dante Gabriel Rossetti, Philip Webb and Ford Madox Brown. This enterprise was formed to
foster artistic co-operation and introduce the medieval ideals of crafts-
manship into the contemporary decorative arts, especially in church
design. One of the firm's first commissions in 1862 was for a stained glass
window at the Hampshire church of St. Michael and All Angels in Lynd-
hurst (under construction between 1858 and 1870). The firm designed a

composition for the east window which Burne-Jones called the Courts of Heaven. The result was a "tour de force" with Burne-Jones and Webb collaborating on design to a William Morris colour scheme—and all for £231. From this beginning more commissions followed in Hampshire and most other English counties. Here we will consider three on the Isle of Wight.

The commission at the Church of St. Olave, at Gatcombe south of Carisbrooke, was to feature work by all five of the firm's principal designers. The church serving the people of this hamlet set among chalk and sandstone hills is named after a Norse saint and probably dates from the thirteenth century with additions over the centuries and restorations in the early 1860s and around 1920. The firm's windows were not memorial windows but depicted biblical episodes as part of the 1864-65 restoration with one by Rossetti of the Crucifixion, small glass panels by Morris showing the Ascension, Burne-Jones' Baptism of Christ and Madox Brown's the Entombment of Christ with the overall scheme planned by Philip Webb.

South-east of Gatcombe and on the cliff just south-west of Ventnor the Royal National Hospital for Diseases of the Chest commissioned a window for its chapel in 1873 to show three saints and scenes of the healing of a woman by Christ (designed by Ford Madox Brown) and of raisings (e.g. of Lazarus). Prior to the hospital's demolition in 1969 these were removed and eventually found a home in the church at St. Lawrence (designed by George Gilbert Scott, 1878) further along the Undercliff towards St. Catherine's Point.

One commission for Morris & Co. just before the First World War (1913) was for a window at All Saints' Church at Freshwater, another Saxon church added to and changed over the centuries. The window was designed by John Henry Dearle (1859-1932) who became the firm's chief designer after the death of Burne-Jones in 1898. It is based on a painting by the artist George Frederic Watts, sometime resident of Freshwater, and depicts Sir Galahad. Some have suggested that the knight's profile in the left light was based on that of Watts' wife, the actress Ellen Terry, and that the face of the angel above the knight in the right hand window is a version of Tennyson's wife Emily.

One outstanding example of modern stained glass in an Island church is offered by the two small west windows featuring a peacock and a

The Sir Galahad window at All Saints' Church, Freshwater

phoenix in the Church of the Holy Cross at Binstead near Ryde. They were designed by Lawrence Lee, chief designer of windows for the new post-Second World War Coventry Cathedral. He died on 25 April 2011, aged 101.

QUARR ABBEY AND PORTSMOUTH CATHEDRAL

When Victoria and Albert acquired and transformed Osborne House they also bought land in the neighbouring parish of Whippingham, and one of Prince Albert's major projects there was the rebuilding of the parish church of St. Mildred. The architect of the new church was A. J. Humbert with Albert as a major player in the project. In his book *England's Thousand Best Churches* Simon Jenkins is critical of Whippingham's "overweight crossing tower" as part of its cruciform plan and of the "garish verticality" of the clusters of turrets and spirelets. He concludes that the church's outward appearance is "a cross between a college chapel and an asylum laundry". During a visit to Quarr Abbey the author was supplied by a helpful monk with the names of Island churches that should be visited, but he was singularly unchristian about the church at Whippingham.

Quarr Abbey stands close to Fishbourne and Wootton Creek on the Island's north-western shore, its coned-topped church tower visible as a landmark above the trees. Robert Graves visited there from his convalescence billet at Osborne House during the Great War. He befriended the French Benedictine Fathers who had built this new abbey in 1907-08, driven from France by anti-clerical laws. Graves wrote:

> The abbey had a special commission from the Vatican to collect and edit ancient church music. Hearing the fathers at their plain-song made me for the moment forget war completely. Many of them were ex-Army officers who, I was told, had turned to religion after the ardours of campaign or disappointment in love.

The modern abbey stands close to the site of a medieval Cistercian monastery and was formed round a large Victorian house. The abbey church was built in 1911-12 to the design of Dom Paul Bellot, a Benedictine monk and a graduate of the École des Beaux-Arts in Paris. An estimated one and three quarter million bricks were used in the construction of the abbey, chapter house and the adjacent entrance block

Quarr Abbey church

and refectory. When Nikolaus Pevsner was compiling his Isle of Wight volume in the mid-1960s he noted the use of Catalan motifs and the influence of Gaudi. He also wrote that "Paul Bellot was a virtuoso in brick," and that the abbey established him "as one of the pioneers of twentieth-century Expressionism".

Across the water, Portsmouth Cathedral was less pioneering architecturally but its biography as a building is certainly unique. It originated as a late twelfth-century chapel dedicated to St. Thomas of Canterbury. In the post-Civil War period it was restored after suffering damage from besieging parliamentarian cannon fire from the Gosport shore. Subsequently it was extended into a "classical"-style church through the next five and a half decades until 1750. When Portsmouth was set up as its own diocese, independent of the Diocese of Winchester in 1927, this church became a cathedral, and Sir Charles Nicholson was appointed architect to oversee the architectural transition from church to cathedral. Most of his scheme was completed (except for the nave) by the outbreak of the Second World War. And that is how it stayed for the next fifty years—the country's unfinished cathedral. Funds were raised in the 1980s to realise the plan's completion, with a fourth bay to the nave, two western towers, tower rooms, rose window, gallery and an ambulatory, stone altar and bronze doors—all completed in just under two years and consecrated on 30 November 1991.

The interior is light and airy with none of the gloom of many gothic churches. A new limed oak organ case in the organ loft dominates the newly-extended nave. On its two door panels are paintings depicting Night with a lighthouse beam on the waters and Day with the sun and a fishing boat hull. The cathedral has many fine sculptures, furnishings, paintings, icons, objects and memorials; I want to focus on three stained glass windows and two memorials.

In the chapel of Healing and Reconciliation are two memorial windows to Admiral Sir Bertram Ramsay (see p.160), director of the Dunkirk evacuation in 1940 and Allied naval commander-in-chief for the Normandy landings in 1944. The first window shows two Army personnel being rescued from the beach under shell fire by two sailors in an open boat. The second window is the antithesis of the Dunkirk reverse and shows British soldiers emerging from the landing beach at the start of the Allied liberation of France. The windows are dedicated in remembrance of Admiral Ramsay and "those under his command who were killed during these operations".

Another memorial window—a small roundel tucked away in the southern part of the Navy Aisle—is a memorial to the crew of the *Wilhelmina J*, a Portsmouth fishing vessel lost at sea in April 1991. A plaque lists the names of the crew and includes the observation: "Many waters cannot quench love, neither can the floods drown it." The small window shows a blue-hulled fishing boat—P742—eloquently empty at sea.

A large black and white marble monument to George Villiers, Duke of Buckingham (1592-1628), favourite of Charles I and failed military commander, now stands in the south chancel aisle. It was erected by his sister the Countess of Denbigh three years after her brother's assassination in a house further north along the High Street. Clearly he was mourned by his family and the distraught but doomed king, but apparently not by many others. Across the north transept from Buckingham's memorial is the recumbent bronze figure in relief of William Thomas Wyllie, second son of the painter William Lionel Wyllie, "killed in action at Montauban on the 19th July 1916 whilst acting as Brigade Major and buried at Mametz

Cemetery" on the Somme. He left a widow and three children. In the niche above William's memorial was where his father's painting, *The Miraculous Draught of Fishes*, had hung (now in the south transept tower). This had been painted in memory of his first son Robert T. M. Wyllie who was killed at the Battle of Messines on 1 November 1914, aged 26, and is commemorated at the Menin Gate at Ypres because he has no known grave.

Chapter Ten

ABOVE AND BENEATH THE SOLENT

FLYERS, SUBMARINERS AND WAR ARTISTS

Hampshire was the cradle for the birth and early development of British flying. Showman and ex-Texas cowboy "Colonel" Samuel Franklin Cody (1861-1913) made the first officially recorded aeroplane flight at Farnborough on 16 October 1908. In the same year Geoffrey de Havilland (1882-1965) built his first plane after an apprenticeship at Farnborough's Army Balloon Factory, converted into the Royal Aircraft Factory in 1912. In the following year a yacht dealer named Noel Pemberton-Billing set up a company to make marine aircraft on the River Itchen near Woolston, Southampton. Pemberton-Billing, who lived on a schooner moored on the Itchen, had once won a wager that he could gain his flying licence within twenty-four hours of his first experience of an aircraft cockpit. In the first year of the First World War Pemberton-Billing was part a naval team that put together and executed a dramatic plan for aircraft to bomb German Zeppelin sheds near Lake Constance. He was subsequently elected as an MP and so handed over the business to his partner Hubert Scott-Paine; and it was Scott-Paine who in 1917 hired as his assistant Reginald Joseph Mitchell, a 22-year-old engineer from Stoke-on-Trent.

This story would not have made the news in any era but the consequences of R. J. Mitchell joining the firm of Supermarine Aviation at Woolston would prove to be of national importance two decades later. As an aircraft designer and engineer Mitchell was a natural and within three years he was made Supermarine's chief engineer. Over the next sixteen years he was to design 24 different flying machines—everything from fighters, light aircraft and bombers to flying boats. Not every design took off from the drawing board but among those that did were the Stranraer flying boats and the Supermarine Walrus amphibian rescue planes. These were the standard RAF flying boats between 1925 and 1935 and both types saw service in the Second World War.

Supermarine Southampton, 1925

Supermarine was also involved in the Schneider Trophy. Launched in 1912 by a rich French flying enthusiast, it was a vehicle for the development of marine aviation. Britain won the race held at Monaco in 1914. The Italians won at Bournemouth in 1919 and again at Venice in 1920. A third win at Naples in 1922 would have resulted in the Italians retaining the trophy and would have been a propaganda coup for Mussolini and his new fascist regime. In the event Captain Baird won for Britain in Mitchell's and Supermarine's Sea Lion II biplane. The Americans won at Cowes in 1923. The race held at Venice in 1927 was another triumph for Britain and Supermarine. The next race was in 1929 and based at Calshot, the course describing a triangle across the Solent with the start and finish line just north of Ryde. Photographs of the event show packed crowds on Southsea beach and esplanade cheering on a British victory as the Supermarine S6 notched up the circuits at 328 miles per hour. One of the RAF's ground support team who was secretary to the wing commander in charge of the race was Aircraftman Thomas Edward Shaw—in retreat from his public celebrity as Lawrence of Arabia. He soon involved himself in the development of high speed air sea rescue craft at RAF Calshot.

Developments in flying kept the skies above the Solent busy in the two decades up to the Second World War. There were flying boat services from Southampton Water to Guernsey and to Australia and places in between. Lee-on-Solent had become an air sea training depot for the Sopwith seaplane in 1917 and continued in its Fleet Air Arm role. Charles Lindbergh landed his plane *The Spirit of St. Louis* on a visit to Gosport on 31 May 1927 after his pioneering solo trans-Atlantic flight. On 6 July 1936 the German airship *Hindenburg* flew over the Hampshire coast en route to America—its swastika decals prominent on the tail fin. A year later the airship was destroyed by fire as it came in to moor at Lakehurst, New Jersey.

Mitchell and Supermarine's involvement with the Schneider air races led the designer and the firm into the world of fighter aircraft design. Different types were trialled. In May 1933 Mitchell was diagnosed with bowel cancer and after surviving an operation he took up flying lessons in December of that year and gained his pilot's licence in May 1934—the better to understand how a pilot experienced a plane. Encouraged by the Air Ministry the firm worked on a new fighter, and on 5 May 1936 the prototype of a new fighter plane was ready to make its maiden test flight from Eastleigh airfield. By July 1938 the first production Spitfire was built at the firm's Woolston works. The aircraft's designer had not lived to see this landmark. His cancer had returned in 1936 and he continued to work on the project until he was no longer able to. R. J. Mitchell died on 11 June aged 42.

This brilliant designer's enduring legacy was a potent and iconic fighter plane designed in time and built in sufficient numbers to play a crucial part in the Battle of Britain, which halted and then forced the cancellation of Hitler's invasion plan for Britain. Currently plans are in progress to site a memorial to the Spitfire on Southampton's waterfront. Funds are being sought; and a design has been selected—a 131-foot (forty-metre) high structure comprising a polished steel Spitfire supported by a curved steel mast.

FERGUSSON AND RAVILIOUS

The modern submarine had some interesting prototypes: there was Dutchman Cornelius Van Drebble's oar-driven craft demonstrated for James I on the Thames in 1620; the Frenchman Louis De Son's 1653 submarine was built with battering rams; American David Bushnell tried in his barrel-shaped submersible *Turtle* to sink HMS *Eagle* in New York harbour in

1776 with a mine but without success; Merseyside cleric George William Garrett designed and built the first steam-driven underwater craft, *Resurgam*, in 1879 but the Admiralty was lukewarm. The Royal Navy's first submarine was built at Barrow-in-Furness to a design by Irish-American inventor John P. Holland (1841-1914) and launched on 2 October 1901. The *Holland 1* was an experiment for the Navy, and limited by her battery and fuel capacity and the cramped space for her crew of eight, she was restricted to harbour defence duties. The crew were joined by three white mice who acted as barometers of dangerous levels of carbon monoxide and dioxide.

The emerging new naval service needed a base for training and technical support and in 1905 it acquired Fort Blockhouse at the entrance to Portsmouth Harbour from the Royal Engineers. More commonly known as HMS *Dolphin*, it is still the "spiritual home of the Submarine Service".

By 1913 *Holland 1* had become obsolete. While being towed to the breaker's yard she sank. In 1980 the Royal Navy Submarine initiated a search and rescue operation and the boat was recovered and restored and can be visited at a special gallery adjacent to HMS *Dolphin*.

Many made deprecating remarks about submarines. The Controller of the Royal Navy had observed in 1900 that submarines were "underhand, unfair and damned un-English". Yet the marine artist William Lionel Wyllie deemed them to be a worthy subject, and excitingly captured these emerging craft in his dynamic work with a limited palette *Submarines A13 and C16 in Portsmouth Harbour*. By 1911 the D-class submarine—with a gun installed on its deck and a design that made it more seaworthy on the surface—now had the capability of ranging further afield as an offensive weapon. In the First World War the Germans used U-boats to devastating effect against merchant shipping and, most controversially, in the sinking of the liner *Lusitania*. After a cautious start British submarines were used in the Dardenelles campaign and in the Baltic to contain the German High Seas Fleet and maintain an economic blockade of Germany itself.

In the last year of the war Portsmouth was visited by Scottish Colourist John Duncan Fergusson (1874-1961). He had been called up at the age of forty-four. Realistically the Ministry of Information's Propaganda and Record Department decided to give him a six-week commission making sketches for paintings in Portsmouth Dockyard. In that year with a workforce of 23,000 Portsmouth Dockyard was one of the pulsating industrial powerhouses of the world. Fergusson was influenced by the colours of the pre-war Parisian Fauves and geometric shapes of the Cubists and Vorticists, and this can be seen in his paintings of 1918 *Portsmouth Docks*, with a giant overhead crane and a ship's prow dominating the composition, *Three Submarines*, with his use of white and black to emphasise their shark-like qualities and *Blue Submarine: Portsmouth Harbour* where swathes of bright colour give Portsmouth Harbour a Mediterranean feel.

In the Second World War Royal Navy submarines were operating from Murmansk to Tripoli and Alexandria and from Iceland to the Malacca Strait. Their roles in the war included attacking and protecting convoys, surveillance, laying mines, landing agents and commandoes, harbour penetration and laying channel markers for invasion forces. The introduction of sonar detection and thus the increased threat from depth charges and the unpredictably lethal hazard of mines made the submariners' working life an especially dangerous one. One in three of them lost their lives in the Second World War.

At the start of the war the director of the National Gallery Kenneth Clark had lobbied hard for artists' involvement in the war effort. He was appointed chairman of the War Artists' Advisory Committee which was given the task of selecting artists to record the war and to advise on how they might be employed. Rescued from his Observer Corps duties on Sudbury Hill, Eric Ravilious was one of the first artists recruited in December 1939.

The son of an Eastbourne antiques and second hand books dealer, Ravilious (1903-42) went to the town's School of Art and then to the Royal College of Art; one of his tutors there, Paul Nash (1889-1946), had been an official war artist in the First World War and as a captain in the Hampshire Regiment was posted to Gosport in 1916 en route for France. One of Ravilious' fellow students Edward Bawden (1903-89) became a friend and artistic collaborator. Both Bawden and Nash were also official war artists during the Second World War.

Eric Ravilious trained as a wood engraver and produced book illustrations (such as those for the Nonsuch Press 1938 edition of *The Natural History of Selborne*), bookplates and designs for magazines but in the late 1920s and 1930s he also worked in different forms: painting murals with his wife Tirzah Garwood for the new Midland Railway Hotel at Morecombe in 1933, designing lithographs of shop fronts for the sumptuous

1938 *Country Life* book *The High Street* and producing a series of designs for Wedgewood—for example, his garden series of bone china tableware and his boat race bowls. Ravilious was intrigued by unusual or discarded machinery, reflected in his watercolours of abandoned and working machines: *Farm Implements, Talbot-Darracq* and *Alpha Cement Works*.

In the 1930s Ravilious increasingly painted landscapes, in particular watercolour landscapes of Sussex and the South Downs in *The Waterwheel, The Downs in Winter, Chalk Paths, Train Landscape* (depicting the Westbury Horse hillside carving through a train carriage window) and a prairie-like *Wiltshire Landscape* (1937), culturally identified by a very English road sign and delivery van. He painted greenhouses, Dungeness Lighthouse, the harbours at Rye and Newhaven, bathing machines and the beautiful beachscape showing the launch point of *Lifeboat* (1938). His paintings and designs were accessible and idiosyncratic, re-assuring and subtly disconcerting at the same time and they were about England and Englishness. It is not hard to see why he might have been selected as an official war artist.

In his work as a war artist he painted seascapes such as *Leaving Scapa Flow, Norway 1940* and *HMS Glorious in the Arctic*, capturing the distinctive light in those latitudes. Sometimes he concentrated on the particular quality of objects such as *Ship's Screw on a Railway Truck*; and in *Submarines in Dry Dock* (c.1940) the boats are presented as strange sculptures. When Ravilious was sent to HMS *Dolphin* in the summer of 1940 he decided to concentrate on life on board a submarine. He acknowledged that there was no roll or movement but when submarines dive it was "awfully hot... and every compartment small and full of people at work". Still he admitted: "There is something jolly good about it, if only I can manage it, a blue gloom with coloured lights and everyone in shirts and braces. People go to sleep in odd positions across tables."

Eric Ravilious made a unique set of ten lithographs, most depicting life on board. One slightly surreal image shows the commander looking through the periscope and an inset of what he can see; and others such as *Ward Rooms 1 and 2* evoke the daily routine and that strange interior light. The artist visited other wartime landscapes and interiors that were environments replicated around the country. His painting of *Coastal Defences No. 2* show a gun battery near Newhaven that could easily be the Needles Battery on the Isle of Wight; and the artist's painting of *No. 1 Map Corri-*

dor shows part of the subterranean Security Control complex beneath Whitehall—a subterranean landscape similar to the control rooms of the D-Day operations in Portsdown Hill. He became increasingly interested in planes and flying; resulting paintings were *Walrus Aircraft on the Slipway* (1941) and in 1942 *Spitfires at Sawbridgeworth, Herts.* In July of that year Ravilious went up in a Tiger Moth to make drawings for a painting entitled *Hurricanes in Flight* (apparently they were Mustangs). Shortly after that his requested posting to Iceland came through and he flew to Reykjavik on 28 August. On 1 September Eric Ravilious was included in a three-plane mission to search for a missing aircraft. His plane never returned.

Ravilious, *Commander of A Submarine Looking Through A Periscope*, 1941

Portsmouth Naval Memorial, commemorating the dead of both world wars

Chapter Eleven

TWO WORLD WARS

PORTSMOUTH AND THE STRUGGLE FOR EUROPE

The American historian Barbara Tuchman called the pre-1914 Europe of interrelated royal families and parliaments dominated by the well-off middle classes the "Proud Tower". The German Kaiser Wilhelm II, after all, was a relative of the British Royal Family and had attended Fleet Reviews in the Solent and been present at Queen Victoria's death and her funeral. But the national rivalries within this "Tower" were real and centred on the struggle for commercial and colonial dominance and on a naval arms race. At the Fleet Review (or perhaps muster) held at Spithead in 1914 one month before the outbreak of war was a Royal Navy at its imperial peak; on display across the roadstead were 24 Dreadnoughts, 35 battleships, 49 cruisers, 76 submarines and 78 destroyers. One hundred thousand sailors or blue jackets were needed to man this fleet.

Spy mania was one element of the jingoism and popular alarm stirred up by the press. The year before William Clare, a Portsea dentist, had been charged with gaining a copy of the annual report on the development of torpedoes at HMS *Vernon* with the aim of selling it to the Germans. Found guilty he was sentenced to five years penal servitude. The Kaiser had become "the beast of Berlin" in the popular press. Foreigners became objects of suspicion and Russian shops were attacked although Russia was in fact an ally. The Alien Restriction Act resulted in some aliens being interned aboard the SS *Scotia* in Portsmouth Harbour, but Portsmouth MP Admiral Lord Charles Beresford, who did not believe there could be a friendly alien, enquired whether this incarceration did not afford these aliens a further chance to spy.

Dissent from the idea that the war was inevitable and necessary was drowned out. On the day after the 4 August official declaration of war between Britain and Germany, the Portsmouth shipyard worker and Labour councillor J. MacTavish was heckled and manhandled when he tried to make an anti-war speech in the Town Hall Square. The *Evening*

News headline simply declared "Ready". But we know now they were not. The anticipated conflict would be global. In fact, the first British officer to die in the war was Lieutenant Masterman Thompson of the Royal Scots, killed on 22 August while commanding a small force of Senegalese troops in German Togoland. Around 947,000 British and Dominion soldiers were killed in the Great War. The industrial scale of the war required ever more recruits. Posters attempted to provoke or shame men into doing their bit. Lord Kitchener's beady recruiting eye and "Women Say Go!" were supplemented by direct action and exhortation. Dockyard workers, manifestly involved in war work, were given white feathers by patriotic young women. The Rev. Bruce Cornford, a member of the board of Portsmouth Football Club, set up a recruitment wagon outside the Fratton Park ground to catch the crowd coming out after a match. Sergeant majors appeared onstage at the Kings Theatre; and Vesta Tilley, music hall entertainer, male impersonator and populariser of songs such as *Burlington Bertie*, included a direct patriotic pitch in her act at the Portsmouth Hippodrome:

> Boys, take my tip and join the Army right away,
> the money's good—not much but good!
> Who knows Perhaps you'll be a general some day.

It was hard for the civilian population in Portsmouth not to be fully aware of the war effort. It is estimated that between 25,000 and 50,000 troops were stationed in Portsmouth at any one time during the war. The St. Georges Barracks at Gosport served as a transit camp for troops scheduled to be taken by rail to troopships at Southampton.

The mortality of naval personnel through the destruction of their ships was concentrated in sudden and dramatic death tolls. The sinking of the Portsmouth-based HMS *Good Hope* at the battle of Coronel off the coast of Chile in November 1914 resulted in the loss of the entire 900-man crew. At the main set-piece naval battle of the war—at Jutland at the end of May 1916—the British losses were over 6,000. One week later HMS *Hampshire* struck a mine off the Orkneys and Lord Kitchener and all but twelve of a crew of 655 men were killed. There was a background dread in Portsmouth homes of the telegraph boy bringing the yellow envelope with the message: "Deeply regret to inform you that *** was killed in action."

Portsmouth had also contributed troops to the campaign on the Western Front and General Sir Douglas Haig used the 1st Portsmouth Battalion in a "diversionary operation" during the Somme offensive. On the first day of the Somme the total of British Army casualties amounted to 60,000—equivalent, as one historian has estimated, to the population then of the Portsmouth districts of Fratton, Buckland and North End. As the war casualties mounted the local hospitals—the Queen Alexandra Military Hospital on the slopes of Portsdown Hill and the infirmary at Milton—were used to full capacity. The Royal Navy Hospital at Haslar was extended in 1915 and some schools (such as the Fawcett Road Girls School) and private premises were pressed into service. The shell-shocked were confined and concealed within the extensive grounds of the Borough Lunatic Asylum in Milton (later St. James's Hospital).

There was economic hardship for the wives of Navy ratings and Army privates. One of the main industries in the city—the manufacture of corsets—contracted during the war, resulting in lay-offs and short time. Voluntary groups organised soup kitchens and charity drives such as the Boot Fund for poor children. But war work also provided new opportunities for women: the male preserve of the "dockyard matey" was invaded by females wearing badges "On War Service" recruited to work in the Block Mills. Women helped the war effort by working at the gasworks and female munitions workers were taken on at the naval armaments depot across the harbour at Priddy's Hard. These jobs were for the duration. In the last year of the war the Women's Royal Naval Service was launched and Wrens were employed typically on ordnance maintenance, making mine nets and signal duty. Women began to appear as delivery van drivers, tram conductresses and drivers, "lady bank clerks" and postal workers.

During the war it was felt necessary to hold in check some male behaviour traits, both natural and acquired. Whatever else it was, Portsmouth was not a temperance town; in 1914 there were 996 licensed premises. When it became clear that the war would be a prolonged test of endurance, increasingly severe licensing orders were introduced under the Defence of the Realm Act to counteract "drink-related slacking" in dockyards and munitions factories. At a time of marital separation and uncertain futures it might have been understood that there would be a rise in illicit sexual liaisons. Still the official message to the forces was "Don't!" The advice of the allegedly celibate Lord Kitchener to his men was to "avoid any intimacy' with women. However, after the 1917 Royal Commission on Venereal Diseases had submitted a report a VD clinic was set up at Royal Portsmouth Hospital.

In September 1916 Zeppelin L31 traced a flight path over Selsey Bill and East Wight, over the entrance to Portsmouth Harbour and north over the harbour, staying east of Southwick and heading towards Midhurst. It dropped its bomb load, which apparently fell into the harbour; nothing in the dockyard was hit. Six days later this airship was strafed by a fighter over Hertfordshire and caught fire; its crew were burned alive. Zeppelin raids were suspended, but in terms of the war in the air it was a portent of things to come. At the end of the war the German High Seas Fleet was escorted to and interned at Scapa Flow, the huge sheltered anchorage in the Orkney Islands used as a base by the Royal Navy. Most of these warships were scuttled by their crews in June 1919. By this time a flu pandemic was spreading throughout the world which would kill 25 million people. Its first appearance was in Britain among sailors at Scapa Flow.

The most common and visible built *memento mori* of the Great War was the war memorial, a version of which appeared in most British towns and villages in the years after the Armistice. On 19 October 1921 Portsmouth's War Memorial was unveiled before a crowd estimated at 30,000. Paid for by public subscription, the memorial included a central stone cenotaph within a U-shaped canyon of stone on which the names of the fallen were inscribed. The sculptor/designer Charles Sargeant Jagger MC (1885-1934), himself a twice-wounded Artists Rifles veteran of Gallipoli and the Western Front, was designing war memorials with no prior experience and to no accepted blueprint, but he understood from being in the trenches what he was putting into stone. The Great War by its singularity and scale obviated that. He went on to design other memorials and to sculpt public statues in the 1920s with arguably his greatest achievement the powerful Royal Artillery Memorial just south of Hyde Park. As with that memorial the Portsmouth design includes two stone figures of machine gunners, manning the Guildhall Square entrance to the site. These sculptures of men in action doing their duty and the friezes at the top of the stone column depicting war activity are strong statements of remembrance and the opposite of sentimentality.

Three years later the Naval War Memorial was unveiled; this commemorated the 9,700 Portsmouth officers and men who have no known

The Guildhall Square cenotaph

burial place. Sited close to the seafront on Southsea Common it became a prominent seamark. After the Second World War a walled garden was built on the landward side of the original obelisk, with the wall displaying the names of similar victims of that conflict and wartime mariners in stone keeping watch. This would be a significant site during commemorations of the fiftieth anniversary of D-Day in Portsmouth in 1994.

The Home Front

In 1938 Nevil Shute (1899-1960), an aeronautical engineer turned writer, sat in his house in Helena Road, Southsea completing a novel that he had written in part to "show what air raids really would be like". He hoped that *What Happened to the Corbetts* would alert the country's urban citizens and relevant officialdom to the reality of "the terrible things" that seemed imminent. When the book was published the following year it was not well received in Britain—perhaps understandably given the anxieties over a probable impending war. In the United States it was a Book of the Month choice and became a bestseller. The novelist's wife was lecturing in

Air Raid Precautions—part of a programme introduced in the late 1930s to recruit and train air raid wardens and run simulation exercises.

In the same year Brigadier Bernard Law Montgomery immersed himself in his work as garrison commander of Portsmouth, trying not to dwell on the tragic death of his wife Betty in October of 1937; despite his ambitions it is unlikely he could have foreseen his key military role in the coming world conflagration.

After Britain's declaration of war on 3 September 1939 Portsmouth's appearance changed to counteract the predicted aerial threat. Barrage balloons and their teams were made ready. Searchlight and gun crews on anti-aircraft batteries manned emplacements from Fort Southwick to Southsea Common. A sizeable tented camp on the Common for gun crews was recognition that the city's prime targets were clustered around the harbour, including the dockyard, HMS *Dolphin* submarine base at Gosport and the original Vosper shipyard in Old Portsmouth. The seafront area became an exclusion zone, with military policemen checking identity documents, especially rigorously in the summer of 1940 when invasion fears were highest and again in the lead up to D-Day.

If these forms of defence were visible and dramatic others were secreted away in the dense urban landscape. Heavy duty corrugated sheet panels half-buried in the grounds of 24,000 terraced house back gardens provided family air raid shelters. These gardens and allotments were pressed into service as posters urged people to "Dig for Victory" to offset the food rationing that the enemy U-Boat campaign enforced. Allotments became essential rather than recreational. The private plot Anderson shelters together with brick shelters, strengthened basements, public shelters and communal shelters, some capable of holding for 5,000 people, and the tunnel system dug under Portsdown Hill offered a range of emergency options to those going about their civilian lives. Sticky tape subdivided windows to minimise the effects of blast. Posters were pasted on city walls asking for volunteers, for instance, to fill sandbags: "volunteers should bring their own spade or shovel". The sandbags were then used to reinforce communal shelters, the posts of Air Raid Precaution Wardens and public buildings such as hospitals and the Guildhall.

Posters exhorted citizens to contribute to the war effort: 'Women wanted to help the children from evacuated area" or "It might be you— caring for evacuees is a national service". In the careless talk costs lives campaign one poster declared: "Bits of careless talk are pieced together by the enemy", showing a hand with a swastika ring on one finger fitting together incriminating pieces of a jigsaw.

The city began to display the marks of war and increasing signs of the global reach of the conflict: sandbagged shelters, white bands painted on the trees of suburban roads to guide drivers in the blackout, the presence of quasi-officials—ARP wardens, women police auxiliaries and special constables and increasingly the presence in the city and hinterland of American and Canadian troops, the Free French and Royal Indian Navy sailors. British Restaurants appeared, municipal restaurants where good cheap meals could be bought using ration books. Queues became a regular feature outside butchers and grocers as food rationing began to bite after January 1940 and people waited outside public buildings for applications and permits. Grimmer crowds would gather outside the Royal Naval Barracks to read the lists of the killed and missing whenever the loss of a ship had been announced. Such an event first occurred early in the war when during the night of 13-14 October 1939 HMS *Royal Oak* was sunk by a German U-boat in the naval anchorage of Scapa Flow in the Orkneys, with the loss of 833 lives.

The war mobilised the population. Men from 18 to 41 (later 51) were conscripted into the armed services unless they were in a reserve occupation doing vital war work, were medically unfit or were conscientious objectors. From 1941 the sight of women going to work in large numbers became commonplace as they could then be conscripted into war industries; this continuation of trends begun during the First World War meant that women became, for instance, postal workers, engineering apprentices, construction workers on motor torpedo boats and bus drivers; in 1941 Portsmouth supplied the first two women in the country qualified to drive double decker buses. Many women also volunteered to help the war effort. Organisations such as the Women's Voluntary Service organised drives to collect scrap—aluminium pots and kettles to be recycled into aircraft parts—and fundraising weeks for the war effort. The Auxiliary Territorial Service supplied drivers for essential services vehicles, while the Women's Land Army enlisted recruits to replace conscripted farm workers on the hinterland beyond Portsdown Hill. Pre-war women had been deemed unsuitable for certain occupations, but during the war years Wrens (from the Women's Royal Naval Service) could be seen operating the steam picket crossing the harbour to and from HMS *Vernon*, crewing tenders that delivered stores and as despatch riders and radio mechanics.

There was an attempt to carry on as normal. Portsmouth still went to the pictures to see David Niven and Bing Crosby in *First of the Few* or Clarke Gable and Vivien Leigh in *Gone with the Wind*; the Kings Theatre hosted vaudeville in 1944 with acts such as Murray and Mooney, the famous radio stars. Yet during the four years from July 1940 until July 1944 the citizens of Portsmouth, Southampton and the Solent region were all too aware that they were in the front line as the city around them changed.

Disruption started during the phoney war period. On the declaration of war an evacuation programme was activated and schoolchildren from Portsmouth and mothers with young children were evacuated to places away from the cities such as Winchester, Salisbury and the New Forest; three thousand were sent to the Isle of Wight. Yet over half of the city's 28,000 schoolchildren chose not to go and by Christmas many others were back. Evacuation of a different sort re-activated the transporting of children out of the cities. British and Allied troops had to be rescued from the beaches of Dunkirk and from northern French ports in the summer of 1940. Craft from Portsmouth played their part in this retrieval armada including the Hayling Island ferries and a Southern Railway Portsmouth-Ryde ferry paddle steamer. What the fall of France meant was that the Luftwaffe could operate out of airfields only sixty miles distant from the Solent coastline. When the plan to destroy the RAF through aerial engagement failed in the Battle of Britain, then the objectives were switched to the decimation of British industry and the demoralisation of the civilian population through the Blitz.

The radar station at Ventnor gave early warning of the approach of German bombers over the sea from the Luftflotte III bases in northern France; Ventnor itself became the target for Stuka dive bombing raids and later Cowes. The Isle of Wight, Portsmouth and Southampton were all in the front line. In the initial German invasion plans—Operation Sea Lion—Sandown Bay was highlighted as a possible landing area. In 1940 there were fighter aircraft dog fights off the Needles and above the Island.

As the enemy strategy was to target a wide range of industries and cities the bombers often flew over Portsmouth to other targets, and many of the 1,581 air raid warnings were false alarms locally. But in that period

Portsmouth bomb damage

there were 67 bomber raids on the city. The statistics of death and destruction are cold but stark: in all 930 people were killed, 1,216 were hospitalised and 1,621 people suffered less severe injuries. Ten per cent of the city's 63,000 houses were destroyed and a similar number severely damaged; almost 69,000 were less badly damaged. The military and industrial targets were clear. But were civilians deliberately targeted? As night bombing especially was an inexact science, the answer is not a straightforward one.

Arguably the worst raid occurred during the night of 10-11 January 1941. Possibly 153 aircraft bombed Portsmouth over a seven-hour period. Some 140 tons of high explosive were dropped on the city together with 40,000 incendiary bombs that started over 2,300 fires. Most of the Kings Road area of Southsea was flattened and as many as sixty water mains were cut. The most prominent built casualty was the Guildhall. The whole of the building was gutted by fire ignited by incendiaries, the most destructive of which fell down a ventilator shaft. One witness, Ernie Jolliffe of Ryde, recalled: "We watched Portsmouth burn. The sky turned red. One hundred and seventy one people died as a result and 430 were injured."

Prime Minister Winston Churchill visited the city at the end of January to witness the destruction and was met by cheering crowds. Whatever Churchill might have done wrong strategically it is difficult to gainsay the galvanising power of his speeches and broadcasts. The bleakness of experiencing aerial bombardment could be alleviated by communal resolve given voice by public oratory. One BBC employee who was present at the broadcast that included the line: "Neither the sudden shock of battle nor the long drawn out trials of vigilance and exertion will wear us down" recalled that Churchill's "genius is that while he puts into magnificent words what we ourselves are thinking, he manages at the same time to inspire. The closing passage was so intense that it kept a roomful of us silent for three minutes after he had gone."

That raid and subsequent attacks in the following months left a large swathe of central Portsmouth a ruined landscape of rubble and bomb craters. An ironic development came from the clearing and recycling of the rubble. Most of the salvaged hardcore was taken by lorries to Gosport via the Floating Bridge and used to make of ramps on the shore at Gosport and Stokes Bay—later used for the embarkation of troops and vehicles on D-Day. Whole chunks of people's city environment went missing, residents with their furniture out on the pavement or pushing salvaged possessions in prams were a common sight. After the worst raid on the city over 10-11 January 1941 the ideal of individual burials was abandoned and one contemporary photograph depicts the mass funeral and burial at Kingston Cemetery with the mourners, wreaths in hand, standing over a long trench lined with coffins.

D-DAY

War on the Home Front compressed contradictory moods and experience into the course of four years. At the time of the German invasion scare in the summer of 1940 the Southsea sea front was closed and the amusement machines from South Parade Pier were crated up and taken away. Four years later soldiers moved along that pier and a scaffolding walkway from the beach nearby to join their landing craft bound for the Normandy beaches. The city's population had spent anxious hours in those years crouched in shelters in their gardens and in tunnels under Portsdown Hill. In June 1944, in the subterranean Combined Operations Plotting Room below Fort Southwick further along that hill, the invasion of Europe would be tracked and controlled. A photograph of the naval plotting room shows figures moving objects over a sheet of glass covering a room-sized chart. This prefigures the typical nerve centre of James Bond film villains two decades later.

The retaking of France and the Nazi-occupied territories beyond required the largest amphibious military operation in history. By the autumn of 1943 the Allies had invaded the Italian mainland and Soviet forces had wrested Stalingrad from the Germans and were pushing them back—westward across the steppe and through the forests of the Russian Motherland. Preliminary planning for the invasion of Normandy was started in September 1943 and detailed operational orders were finalised by January 1944 through SHAEF (Supreme Headquarters Allied Expeditionary Force) under the overall charge of General Dwight D. Eisenhower. Included in his team of seven were Admiral Sir Bertram Ramsay in the role of naval commander and General Sir Bernard Montgomery appointed commander-in-chief of Allied Ground Forces. Time would be needed for training, assembling the men and equipment and building of landing craft. D-Day was projected for early June.

During the two months before D-Day 20,000 special trains brought troops and material south closer to the 24 marshalling areas and embarkation points dotted along the Solent coast between Southampton and Portsmouth. During the build up to the invasion upwards of three million men were billeted in forest encampments in southern England. Camps were set up at Emsworth, Cowplain, Rowlands Castle and most points west to the River Itchen such as the Forest of Bere. Men were confined to these camps, a security zone was established and a ban on non-essential civilian movement was imposed.

At the end of April Admiral Ramsay moved into Southwick House, a Georgian mansion set in parkland close to the village below the northern slopes of Portsdown Hill. This then became the forward headquarters of SHAEF. A plywood map of the target coastal area of Normandy, constructed by the toy firm Chad Valley, covered the east wall of the large drawing room. The Normandy beaches had been photographed by reconnaissance aircraft and surveyed by commando units under the cover of darkness. The picture of these target landscapes was further enhanced by civilian photographs and holiday postcards. The BBC had broadcast appeals for these and received a postbag of ten million in reply.

During May Ramsay was joined by General Eisenhower, Field Marshal Montgomery and their staffs. Ramsay's (1883-1945) role was to oversee Operation Neptune—the marshalling and despatch of the invasion fleet. He was a graduate of Dartmouth and the Royal Naval War College at Portsmouth who had seen service in the First World War on the Dover Patrol. He was brought out of retirement just before the outbreak of the Second World War and became vice-admiral, Dover. It fell to him to oversee the successful evacuation of the British Expeditionary Force from Dunkirk and other places on the French Channel coast in 1940—338,000 of them—and in July 1943 he had overseen the invasion of the island of Sicily by the Allies. He was a meticulous organiser and a systematic planner. He had the necessary form, skills and temperament to be naval commander of this expeditionary force, and he got on well with Montgomery—not a negligible quality. It was fitting, even ironic, that the man who organised the rescue of defeated Allied troops from mainland Europe should be a key player in the expedition to retake Europe four years later. He did not, however, live to see the final victory of the Allies as he was killed in a plane crash near Paris in January 1945.

Almost 7,000 vessels were involved in D-Day and Admiral Ramsay had assigned every vessel in the fleet specific orders "on what to do and when to do it". Midget X-craft submarines were to arrive at the beaches in advance of the invasion fleet and use their lights to guide the ships and landing craft in. Minesweepers cleared passages for the convoys. Battleships and cruisers would bombard the shore defences before the landing craft headed toward the beaches. Corvettes, destroyers and frigates acted as escorts to the troopships and to the landing and other support vessels. Requisitioned in their hundreds, these merchant ships helped to lay cables, ferry supplies and act as floating and command ships. All these ships, some coming from Belfast, Oban, the Clyde, Grimsby, Bristol, Falmouth, the Thames and most ports and estuaries in between, were given pre-arranged times of departure and their progress to the rendezvous area south-east of the Isle of Wight plotted in Fort Southwick's Operation's Control Centre. Over a hundred tugs would tow the concrete sections of an artificial harbour across the Channel.

As the occupied Normandy ports were so heavily defended, the Allies had decided to build their own harbours and take these over to France. Concrete and steel blocks were constructed locally in Portsmouth Dockyard, Stokes Bay and Hayling Island and stationed in creeks and inlets all around the coast. These blocks, when towed over to the invasion sites, were sunk offshore and protected by a wall of scuttled ships; they formed a sequence of piers where supply ships could be safely berthed. Pontoon bridges linked the piers to the shore. The capture of the damaged port of Cherbourg on 25 June was the signal for the start of a crucial logistical support project, PLUTO (pipeline under the ocean), designed to bring oil from southern England under the Channel to Normandy. Oil was taken by tankers from the Shell Mex BP oil storage facility at Hamble, piped ashore from these vessels anchored off Ryde, then pumped along the rail track bed to tanks in the woods near Brading. The oil was then sent from Sandown Bay via a flexible pipeline across to liberated Cherbourg.

In the days preceding D-Day Sherman tanks were backed up along the road from Horndean; it was said that Spithead was so packed with vessels that you could have walked over to the Isle of Wight from the mainland without getting your feet wet.

As there was a radio blackout on D-Day the news that the first troops were ashore was brought back to Thorney Island that morning by Gustav the pigeon. Another messenger reporting back was the Hungarian-born war correspondent and photographer Robert Capa (1913-54). Employed by the prestigious American news photography magazine *Life*, Capa decided to go in with E Company of the 1st Infantry Division as part of the first wave assault on Omaha Beach. Following his own maxim "if your pictures aren't good enough, you aren't close enough", Capa found himself photographing men of E Company under fire on the beach and in the surf. He soon escaped onto a ship offshore with his rolls of film. Back in London only eleven images survived as the darkroom technician dried the films too quickly. Even these were blurred but this accident in processing seemed to add to the authenticity of these photographs—something of the rush, even the fear, of battle.

These photographs, particularly one of a soldier in the surf near a steel "hedgehog" (a beach obstacle designed to rip open landing craft), were looked at by the artist Sandra Lawrence in her extensive research while designing the Overlord Embroidery (see p.61). This was the modern counterpart to the Bayeux Tapestry commissioned by Lord Dulverton in 1968 as an artistic tribute to the effort and sacrifice of those involved in D-Day. The 34 panels are a pictorial representation of all aspects of Overlord from the war work of industrial artisans to the military push east into Belgium; they depict the landscapes and seascapes of that campaign. It was perhaps right that Bayeux was the first town liberated after D-Day.

The Second World War has inspired a huge library of books and a vast archive of films. But I want to mention two books (and the film adaptation of one of them) that sought to describe the war at sea. Nicholas Monsarrat (1910-79), the Liverpool-born writer, served in the Royal Navy during the war, first as a sub-lieutenant on a corvette and later captaining a frigate in the western approaches. His most renowned book *The Cruel Sea* (1951), based on his own experiences of the Battle of the Atlantic, was made into a Ealing Studios film in 1953. Despite a stellar cast, all brylcreamed hair and duffle coats, there is a documentary feel to the film which depicts the harshness, tedium, danger, isolation and tension of wartime life at sea but also its potential camaraderie. Several of those collaborating on this production could look back at experience of wartime service, a common occurrence in the British films of the 1950s. The writer of the screenplay, Eric Ambler, served in a combat filming unit as assistant director of the Army Kinematograph Service. The commander of corvette K49 was played by Jack Hawkins, former 1930s matinee idol and respected stage actor. He had served in India with the Royal Welsh Fusiliers in charge of troop entertainment, and for the next decade went on to be typecast as a senior British officer in several war movies.

The pseudonymous Cecil Scott Forester (1899-1966) is best known for his Horatio Hornblower novels set in the Royal Navy between 1793 and 1823. A weak heart had ruled out Army enlistment in 1917, but he did subsequently write three novels about the First World War, two set in lonely outposts of imperial struggle—*Brown on Resolution* (1928) and *The African Queen* (1935)—and *The General* (1936). In the Second World War he was enlisted for a propaganda/public education purpose—to write an account of shipboard life on a Royal Navy ship during wartime. He sailed aboard HMS *Penelope* as observer and researcher—"embedded" in the modern parlance. The resulting book was *The Ship* (published in 1943), an accessible account of "trained individuals working as a team", the lives and back stories of some of the crew and descriptions of the reality of working life in the deep ocean: "as H.M.S. Artemis rolled and corkscrewed over the quartering sea the crow's nest swung round and round in prodigious circles against the sky."

Nevil Shute emigrated to Australia after the war and became an international bestselling novelist. One of his most famous books, *On the Beach*, published in 1957, tackled the subject of global nuclear war and annihilation by radioactive dust.

For Field Marshal Montgomery perhaps his finest hour was receiving the German surrender at Luneburg Heath in May 1945. Despite his failure to grasp the need for diplomacy in his dealings with allies during and after the war and the penning of his controversial memoirs in retirement, he could look back with the knowledge of mission accomplished. As Supreme Commander Eisenhower acknowledged: "No one else could have got us across the Channel and into Normandy... whatever they say about him, he got us there."

Any passenger on the Hayling Ferry departing from the landing stage at the tip of the land spit that shelters Eastney Lake can still see today a discarded concrete section from the 1944 Mulberry Harbour—part of an artificial dock complex that provided the Allies with a temporary haven and a stepping stone back onto mainland Europe.

Post-war Portsmouth Panorama

Chapter Twelve

AFTERMATH AND ARCHITECTURE

WHAT TO BUILD AND HOW TO BUILD IT

The architect and town planner Gordon Cullen (1914-94) was art editor of the *Architectural Review*, the prestigious house magazine of the profession, in the 1950s. Before the war he had worked with the modernists Raymond McGrath and the Tecton group, advocates of continental Modernism, and with Berthold Lubetkin, the émigré Russian architect whose designs included the north London apartment blocks Highpoint I and II and the Penguin Pool and other Regent's Park buildings. He was also a member of the Modern Architectural Research (MARS) Group, who had drawn up a plan for the complete reconstruction of London on a linear model. Through a series of visionary articles illustrated by original graphics and using towns such as Ludlow and Lyme Regis as models, Cullen had attempted to map out some planning composition guidelines and concepts that could be applied to the contemporary redevelopment of towns and cities. These articles were collected in a book *Townscape*, published in 1961, which became a popular primer for a new way of seeing in urban design. Here Cullen used photographs and drawings to illustrate concepts such as lines of advantage, enclaves and kinetic unity. He wanted to promote urban design where the resulting cities and towns could be experienced as a unique works of art—where a townscape presents a coherent narrative, even a sense of drama experienced by a pedestrian walking through sequences of unfolding spaces and streets.

In 1964 Cullen was funded by Alcan Industries to make four studies in town planning—essentially proposals for "linear circular" towns. One of these was for a Solent linear town, a development that would stretch from Portsmouth to Southampton and combine high-density, high-rise buildings with a linear urban parkland. Two features of this plan were a city park in the hinterland from the Solent shore and a continuous sequence of high-rise buildings on Portsdown Hill above Portsmouth's North Harbour.

The reality of planning in the post-war era was more a story of a fractured and incoherent ad hoc approach to urban renewal determined by the availability of funds, the need for fast and cheap public housing and the pressure of traffic in towns. The only comprehensive plan built in its entirety was that designed for the city of Plymouth. In the immediate aftermath of the war Portsmouth had to build quickly to try to alleviate two problems: homelessness caused by the bombing raids (almost ten per cent of the city's houses had been destroyed and eight per cent seriously damaged) and high population density which pre-war had reached seventy people per acre; in total, 10,000 Portsmouth citizens needed to be rehoused. Prefabricated bungalows had first appeared on the slopes of Portsdown Hill in the summer of 1945 and on bomb sites in the city. Seven hundred were in use by 1947. These prefab houses could be delivered to the site in three lorry loads and took a day to erect on a concrete base. Essentially they were corrugated-walled rectangular boxes for living in topped by asbestos-tiled low-pitched roofs. Functional containers they may have been but with their plumbed-in kitchens, inside lavatories, two bedrooms, basic central heating and Utility furniture they represented a huge improvement on previous living conditions in many of the cramped interiors of city terraced houses.

In the following year work was started on a new housing estate in Paulsgrove and in 1947 on a set of neighbouring estates—essentially combining to form a satellite town beyond the city boundaries at Leigh Park. Zoning decisions decreed the following: Commercial Road would be the city's main commercial and business area; the Guildhall (still a bombed out shell) would be the focus of a civic centre; the Camber near the harbour entrance would still be the city's commercial harbour. Old Portsmouth was to be an area of "high-class" housing, and there was an expectation that Langstone Harbour would be used as a flying boat base.

The planner's imagination has tended to prefer a site as a clean slate; and in many British city and town centres post-war planners, motivated by zeal for a new urban way of life, completed some of the destruction the Luftwaffe had started. Cities change and renewal is vital, but so too is some retention of the built past; the perennial question is always about what to replace and what to keep Many planners and architects in the post-war period had been influenced by European Modernism, most succinctly proposed by Le Corbusier in his 1923 manifesto *Vers une architecture*. He wanted architects to reject outmoded historic styles and building types and draw inspiration from the functionality of machines such as automobiles and aeroplanes and industrial buildings like factories and grain silos. "Engineers will be our builders," he asserted. Much needed to be swept away and replaced after the war but for British architects there were few existing buildings that could provide templates.

Architects in the 1950s might travel south to Marseille to draw inspiration from Le Corbusier's city-block-in-the-sky, the Unité d'Habitation. They could drive down to Bexhill-on-Sea in Sussex to study the 1935 De La Warr Pavilion designed by émigré architect Erich Mendelsohn (recently restored). In the Portsmouth area two Modernist houses (c.1935) still survive in Sinah Lane on Hayling Island as does Sunspan, a streamlined 1930s modern villa designed by former engineer, journalist and founder-member of the MARS Group Wells Coates, sited at the western end of Portsdown Hill. But these houses were private, bespoke commissions. Public architecture was represented by the Hilsea Lido (1936), a swimming pool and leisure park sited at the western end of Hilsea Lines, Portsmouth's northern fortification ramparts, where the Modernist vernacular was particularly well-suited to this kind of leisure landscape. Still British planners and architects in the 1950s had virtually no direct experience of designing and building large urban developments along Modernist lines.

The National Buildings Record was set up during the war to list the country's historic buildings—a necessary first step towards their protection. But in the immediate post-war period preservation was not on most local authorities' agenda. They did not have the money to fund ambitious redevelopment plans and this meant that land was leased out to property developers by competitive tender. The outcome of this "partnership" process resulted in the same predictable urban design scenarios. As architect Lionel Brett (later Lord Esher) described it: "The result would normally be a brand-new inner relief road feeding multi-storey car parks, a pedestrian shopping mall and lettable office slabs that paid for it all; and the trick was to gain all this without squeezing developers' profits out of existence. At its best the technique could finance a vital road improvement... At worst it could wreck a cathedral city like Worcester, or exchange decent low-rented houses for unlettable shops..." Lord Esher, who would be a consultant on the Guildhall Square redevelopment plan, could be describing some of the redevelopment of central Portsmouth.

The pre-Second World War Guildhall built by William Hill 1886-90 and its post-war reincarnation

An aerial photograph from c.1952 of the Guildhall Square quarter of the city shows the gutted remains of the Guildhall with the square virtually empty of traffic. The Municipal College behind stands unscathed. There are three cleared bomb sites but also in view plenty of trees, houses, a church and a theatre. Much of this was to be demolished as part of a later inner ring road development; one victim, off camera, was the landmark Water Company Building from 1883. The symbolic importance of the city's Guildhall, however, was clear. It had been a casualty of the Luftwaffe raid on Portsmouth during the night of 10-11 January 1941; burst water mains hampered the efforts of the fire services and an undetected incendiary bomb lodged in a duct ensured the complete destruction of the interior. The Guildhall remained a gutted and roofless shell until rebuilding work started in 1955. Four years later it was officially opened, not as a replica of the original but with a newly configured tower. There had been criticisms from some councillors over this change of design but these were rebutted by the scheme's architect E. Berry Webber (architect of the Guildhall at Southampton) who asserted his design autonomy: "Do you employ me as an architect or as a hack draughtsman?"

POST-WAR PLANNING

Mostly the schemes were piecemeal and not part of a larger vision. Government funding was limited so redevelopment became a process dragged out over decades. The author can recall bomb sites in central Portsmouth in the early years of the 1960s. Urban road building for the car took precedence over any other transport options and the road lobby grew more powerful. The dominance of Modernist ideas on housing among architects and planners resulted in developers finding cheaper system building methods for building tower blocks. The mindset of many contemporary urban design professionals seemed to include the idea that the historic built legacy of the Victorians was expendable. St. Pancras station, for example, recently refurbished as London's gateway terminal for Eurostar, had been a seriously considered as a target for demolition in the 1960s.

In the immediate post-war decades Portsmouth hence suffered from the planner's preference for clearance rather than restoration. The architectural historian Gavin Stamp in his account of the architectural vandalism in the second half of the twentieth century, *Britain's Lost Cities*, cites the verdict of David Lloyd, author of the Hampshire volume of the *Build-*

ings of England series, that the Portsmouth of 1965 was "as a whole, muddled and visually squalid". Stamp focused on the High Street in Old Portsmouth and neighbouring streets, an area that had been devastated by wartime bombing. The area was not rebuilt as a whole neither were the damaged buildings restored; instead these were demolished and new buildings filled the spaces. The result, according to Lloyd, was "a wretched hotchpotch of buildings that are neither modern nor even decently copyist but just unpleasantly nondescript". Any sense of a coherent city was lost.

By the mid-1970s critical reaction to the urban clearances gathered momentum nationally, articulated by books such as *The Sack of Bath* and *The Rape of Britain*, Colin Amery and Dan Cruickshank's accounts of the effects of demolition on the country's towns and cities. A pressure group Save Britain's Heritage was set up in 1975, European Architectural Heritage Year. Local authorities started to consider the alternatives of conservation and restoration of existing building and improvement of the housing stock. Change of use was also included in the planner's lexicon, and in the following decades surviving older buildings were assigned new roles. The classical brick building, for example, originally built as the Portsea Island Union Workhouse, became an old people, home and was then converted into flats for a local housing association.

The scaling down of the Navy and of Britain's global military commitments meant that the future use of Defence Estates properties in the Portsmouth area was on the planning agenda. In the dockyard the landmark industrial building, the Steam Factory, was converted into offices in the 1990s, and the No. 6 Boathouse from 1834, a dramatic cast-iron structure supporting a fine brick building used for the servicing of cutters and other boats, was converted into an a naval interactive visitor space and cinema; the top floor was occupied by a department of Portsmouth University.

The city's redundant barracks enjoyed contrasting fates. Most of Clarence Barracks, a military campus the size of a large city block, was demolished to be replaced by the private housing estate of Pembroke Park. Two barracks blocks were kept, one originally to house the City Records Office and the other, a powerful red brick chateau-like building incorporating strong circular towers topped by conical roofs, became the City Museum and Art Gallery. In contrast Eastney Barracks (built 1862-67), a military township for the Royal Marines commanding the seafront of the city's eastern shore, has survived the loss of its military role almost intact. The Officers' Quarters and mess was converted into a museum and the main barracks facing the sea across a long open terrain was converted into apartments for private sale, along with the brick water tower. One reason behind its survival is the site's architectural coherence and strong sense of identity. In his 1970 book on Portsmouth building Alan Balfour wrote: "As with many of the military and naval buildings in Portsmouth the forceful urban environment created here is much stronger than anything within the city itself."

Why some buildings are demolished and others saved has depended on factors that range from the existence of a neighbouring listed or famous building and changes in architects' and planners' thinking to shifts in the political agenda, the state of the economy or just serendipity. The precinct in which the Charles Dickens Birthplace Museum is located was improved in the late 1970s partly with money raised by the Dickens Fellowship and suggested how other city streets might have looked if restoration had been an earlier watchword. The Water Company Building, a minor "monument of commerce" from 1883 designed by the prolific Portsmouth architect A. E. Cogswell (of whom more later), was demolished to make way for a stretch of urban dual carriageway. However, a church which had lost its parish to a combination of bomb damage and urban clearance—the mission church of St. Agatha's—survived demolition after it was closed in 1950s, saw use as a naval store, was under threat again in the 1960s from the planned route of a dual carriageway which was diverted after a public enquiry and survives today in its restored state. The same fate was not in store for St. Agatha's unusual former neighbour.

The Brutalist megastructure known as the Tricorn was a multi-functional building the size of a city block. The product of the Owen Luder Partnership and completed in 1966, this structure was designed as a wholesale market, multi-storey car park and shopping development, together with two small blocks of flats and a nightclub. The principles of the New Brutalism had been articulated by the architects Alison and Peter Smithson, in part as an expression of criticism of the perceived smugness and conformity of architects and architecture in the 1950s, the slow pace of post-war rebuilding and its compromised nature. Their models were the architects Le Corbusier and Ludwig Mies van der Rohe, who were uncompromising and honest in their approach to design and in their stark

presentation of structure and materials such as shutter-patterned concrete or *béton brut*. Yet design manifestos do not always guarantee successful architecture. The Smithsons' Economist Buildings of 1964 created a high-quality, practical complex in a distinctive urban space. Owen Luder's Tricorn, on the other hand, was a building with a singular sculptural profile but one that, it can be argued, ultimately did not work.

The ground floor layout was difficult to read and negotiate and this made the building uninviting from the street level. The pub in its central space, the Casbah, signalled the architect's design intentions, but the key missing Middle Eastern ingredient there was sunshine, which rarely penetrated the central square. The raw concrete could be very grey in the winter light and the surfaces did not weather well over time. The scheme never took off commercially as no significant magnet store materialised and not all the shops were let. The flats suffered from damp and were eventually boarded up at the end of the 1970s. Despite these failings the scheme photographed well and some of the features such as the spiralling ramp of the car park created some visual excitement. Still the design and vision were too uncompromising to inspire much personal identification with the building or to allow it to be easily adapted to serve other purposes. Its daring design drew more attention than the many mediocre buildings in the neighbouring area, but negative stories in the local media always trumpeted its assumed unpopularity. The Tricorn was demolished in 2004.

Not all built mementoes need to be monumental. The author remembers Verrecchia's café and milk bar wedged up against the railway viaduct/bridge in the unreconstructed Guildhall Square. The café had been opened in 1933 by Augusto Verrechia, an Italian immigrant. Ice cream was made on the premises and the seating area was in a section raised above the kitchen. Here were rows of booths whose timber frames, inset with decorated glass panels, surrounded marble-topped tables and tip up seats. On the wall by each booth was an elliptical mirror. This meant that all the interior visuals were constantly changing. Verrecchia's might well have been just another café on a cramped site but inside it felt glamorous and continental. It was closed in 1970 and demolished to make way for a wing of the new Civic Offices. One booth is on display in the City Museum—a reminder for some but forlorn and out of context.

Why do the rescue, restoration and re-use of a city's old buildings matter? Cities and towns have grown organically and the survival of visual reminders of their former selves help prompt the imagining and even the re-reading of their histories. This is not just about nostalgia but about piecing together a past and an identity; many "new" trends in architecture and design have involved revisiting the past. A special edition of the *Architectural Review* published in January 1950 set out to champion the importance of the Functional tradition, best illustrated by the strong examples of seaboard architecture and design:

> The forms peculiar to the maritime way of life, the jetties, piers, lighthouses, bollards, buoys and a hundred other details demonstrate to a remarkable degree, not only the compelling requirements of this functional element, but also the freedom of form that is possible within this disciplinary code…

Photographic essays illustrating the magazine's theme included the unique functionality of the Cobb at Lyme Regis and the prototype for mass production of the pier and pavilion at Broadstairs, how objects such as bollards exhibit the qualities of both the ornamental and the functional and how the use of local materials and whitewash in walls and floors create a distinctive vernacular environment. Gordon Cullen contributed drawings to illustrate how Lyme Square and the town's Marine Parade could be modernised in a nautically functional way.

Such design thinking and advice was mostly ignored by property developers, local authorities and the architectural profession for the next two and half decades. A book by the architectural photographer Eric de Maré, *The Nautical Style* (1973), also set out to chart in more detail the importance of the built tradition of Britain's coasts and waterways and show how nautical buildings and artefacts could offer clear examples of how to combine the pleasurable and the functional in contemporary architecture.

Eric de Maré wanted to illustrate how the nautical style was still relevant to modern design with, for example, images of the supporting ironwork beneath piers, the sculptural possibilities of seawalls and the vocabulary and vernacular of dockside developments. He was also interested in the different forms possible in sea towers and lighthouses from the stone rocket tower of the country's oldest surviving lighthouse on the Isle of Wight's and St. Catherine's Down, its octagonal nineteenth-century near neighbour at St. Catherine's Point to the stone cylinder of the Needles Light and the thin column supporting the circular tower of the Southampton Water's coastguard tower.

De Maré also highlighted the incidental sculptures of the maritime scene. He celebrated derricks, cranes, hoists, buoys, signals, sluice and lock machinery and the different shapes and textures of bollards. They created focal points in dock environments and while fit for purpose they could also bring delight as "unintended pieces of sculpture". He championed the beauty in utility of docks, Victorian warehouses and boat stores, even the Georgian windows at the stern of HMS *Victory*; and the repeated message came at a time of increasing disillusion with contemporary architecture and urban design. These essays, by promoting greater recognition of the importance of the country's nautical architectural heritage, did help build an increasing interest in industrial archaeology and ultimately played a contributory role in the conservation of dock architecture in Liverpool, London, Portsmouth and other maritime cities.

The reaction against the drab uniformity of much modern architecture in the immediate post-war decades also brought back into the frame

A former Cogswell-designed pub in Broad Street, Old Portsmouth, now an estate agents

important local architects from the Victorian and Edwardian eras. One key Portsmouth architect was A. E. Cogswell (1858-1934) who was resurrected through the pages of a Portsmouth Polytechnic architecture course dissertation, which, printed and printed again in 1975, seemed to gather interest and generate almost samizdat-like demand.

Born in Peterborough, Arthur Edward Cogswell came to Portsmouth and started an apprenticeship at the age of fourteen in the firm of the city's foremost architect George Rake. The city was expanding and the firm's commissions were increasingly various, including the new prison at Kingston and the Lunatic Asylum (later St. James' Hospital) at Milton. From his early days as an apprentice Cogswell could witness the scope and range of architectural work that an expanding Victorian city generated. How to build and in what style had been matters of intense debate especially in the High Victorian period of the Gothic Revival, championed and articulated by Augustus Pugin both in his books and his interior designs for the new Houses of Parliament. In the latter part of the nineteenth century architects more typically used a mixture of historical styles—an approach best exemplified by Richard Norman Shaw. In his long career from the late 1870s until the 1930s Cogswell displayed a similar versatility and free use of styles; this adaptability was a practical necessity given the varied jobs that came his way.

Cogswell can truly be said to have put his mark on Portsmouth's cityscape. He built public houses, drill halls, churches, cemetery buildings, cinemas, newspaper and water company offices, shops, hotels and apartments, a Royal Navy school of physical training and a library. Of his surviving buildings just two serve to illustrate the variety of his design contributions to the city's built heritage. Byculla House (1895) was built for the brewing family of Brickwood in Southsea's Kent Road. Located on a small wooded site in a prime part of Owen's Southsea, it is a monied mansion that seems to make a nod to most stylistic devices including timber framing and a tower topped by a witch's hat; Alan Balfour dubbed the whole "Tyrolean Tudor". The former Palace Cinema (opened in 1921), its design possibly inspired by Cogswell's time in India during the First World War, features oriental motifs and forms—a skyline and frontage of ogee domes, two on stub minarets and flattened Islamic arches.

Architects like Cogswell working in the Victorian and Edwardian city paid attention to the importance of the texture of building materials and to details such as lettering—exactly those elements that Gordon Cullen returned to in his design primer *Townscape*. He argued that even with re-development the close grain nature of cities and the resulting enclosed places should be respected and contrast with the "prairie planning" of post-war out-of-town estates. The quality of urbanity depended on details such as the "calligraphy" of balcony ironwork, street furniture and significant objects such as post boxes together with enclaves and enclosures that could be accessed on foot but separated from the intrusion of traffic. Enclaves have been a feature of Portsmouth as the civilian city has grown used to co-existing with naval shore station townships—military ghettoes within a civic realm.

Cullen, from 1956 consultant to a number of British cities and local authorities, had some influence on town design in his lifetime but, ironically perhaps, more influence after his death. Portsmouth already had naval and military enclaves—places that were a built to a more coherent design than the city areas that surrounded them. So Gunwharf Quays on the site of HMS *Vernon* is a place with multiple uses, where the urban walker is set apart from traffic, a place that includs focal points and with an unfolding story that contained some drama and a sense of anticipation. Covered streets lead off an open urban square; a cluster of waterside cafés overlook a small marina and the harbour beyond; a lock, a canal and a crane are retained. Equally, the former Royal Marines barracks at Eastney is a waterside campus that contains an iconic water tower, with its barracks now converted into private apartments facing the sea and public access to a Royal Marines Museum in the former officers' mess.

This is especially apt in a city such as Portsmouth. In the 1950s and early 1960s the masses of workers converging on and emerging from the dockyard onto the streets of Portsea and beyond was a familiar weekday sight. Increased car ownership has since made the commuting cyclist increasingly rare, but the city's compactness and its largely flat terrain suggest that this is a mode of transport whose relevance really could come full cycle.

Two artists who were at work in the decades after 1945 were W. A. Jefferies and Garrick Palmer. Wilfred Avalon Jefferies (1907-70), a leading academic in the region, captured the Portsmouth maritime scene in the late 1950s and 1960s, especially with paintings such as *Car Ferry to the Isle of Wight* (c.1959), *The Construction of a Floating Dock, H. M. Dockyard* (1966) and *Floating Bridge* (1964). Garrick Palmer, a teacher at Winchester College of Art after being a Portsmouth Art College student in the 1950s, has photographed, drawn and painted that city over several decades; he is also a well-known wood engraver. The engravings have ranged from landscapes to maritime themes, illustrating, for example, Folio Editions of *Moby Dick* and *The Rime of the Ancient Mariner*.

CHANGING TIMES

From the later decades of the twentieth century to the present the city of Portsmouth has been forced to cope with the downsizing of its main service and industry—the Royal Navy and shipbuilding and maintenance. One significant new service provider has been Portsmouth University (formerly the Polytechnic), which has been a significant rescuer of existing real estate. Two central campuses have emerged. One is in Portsea, an area close to the dockyard and of such ill-repute that the Catholic Church deemed it necessary to introduce a mission of rescue in the later nineteenth century. Here the university hub includes new-build business and architecture schools, with other faculty and administrative services based nearby in the former Milldam Barracks. Less than half a mile away is Ravelin Park. This lies on land that once included the seventeenth-century defensive works of Bernard de Gomme: a moat, bastions and ravelins. In the nineteenth century these works were demolished and the resulting park became the Army's garrison HQ for the city. The Army moved out in the 1960s and in 1969 the site was transferred to Portsmouth Polytechnic. Today it is a park with green spaces and picnic areas. The Frewen Library and the Students' Union are landmark buildings joined recently by the university's Dental Academy.

In the south-east corner of the park is a house that was the former home of Field Marshal Bernard Law Montgomery when he was the Portsmouth Garrison commander (1937-38). It was a time of personal tragedy for him and a turning point in his military career. It is currently home to the university's Institute of Criminal Justice Studies.

Gordon Cullen's vision for a Solent linear town remained unbuilt— just a concept and a set of drawings. Yet a development of houses, maisonettes and flats, Portsdown Park, was built on the hill above Portsmouth between 1968 and 1973. The buildings suffered from serious water penetration from the start and the whole scheme had to be demolished in 1987. The nearby Portsdown Hill forts from the Lord Palmerston era (1857-80) have endured, their low slung building profiles matching the contours of their settings, almost natural features in their landscape now and given new leases of life as sports centres and a museum.

Part Three

PLEASURE AND LEISURE

Chapter Thirteen

BESIDE THE SEASIDE

THE BIRTH OF TOURISM

The seaside became a specific place and concept, and not just the edge of the land, in the early 1700s with the emergence of the spa resorts of Brighton and Scarborough. The fortunes of seaside resorts were improved by the publication in 1752 of Richard Russell's *Dissertation on the Use of Seawater in Diseases of the Glands*. He prescribed bathing in cold water and the copious drinking of seawater; as the doctor then moved to Brightelmstone (soon to become Brighton) this must be considered one of the earliest examples of boosterism. By the late 1780s King George III was visiting Weymouth and the Prince Regent was giving his patronage to Brighton. Londoners increasingly went downriver by steamer to Margate or Ramsgate. Queen Victoria considered Brighton too crowded and intrusive, finding the populace "indiscreet and troublesome", and in the late 1840s deserted the resort for the privacy of her own seaside estate at Osborne on the Isle of Wight. She got out just in time. The seaside holiday or trip was an experience being taken up increasingly by the middle classes. In the year of 1837 stage coaches brought an estimated 50,000 passengers to Brighton. By 1850 the railway could transport 73,000 travellers to the town in a single week.

Up until the mid-nineteenth century artistic representations of the seaside typically included either sedate scenes or outright satire. John Constable's *Brighton Beach* of 1824 shows Brighton's big sky, the fishing fleet in the distance and a few ladies with parasols walking the foreshore. Thomas Rowlandson's engraving made in 1813, *Summer Amusements at Margate, or A Peep at the Mermaids* depicts a group of lecherous, disreputable men on a cliff top focusing their telescopes down on the naked women launching themselves into the surf from bathing machines. But in 1854 a painting by William Powell Frith, *Ramsgate Sands: Life at the Seaside* changed attitudes toward the artistic portrayal of the seaside experience and possibly towards the experience itself.

The viewer is located a little way offshore. A sedate throng is arranged by the water's edge, almost a tableau of people waiting to have their picture taken. All the men, women and children are correctly dressed for mid-Victorian public display, with suits, hats, bonnets and parasols much in evidence. Newspapers are being read and telescopes focused. In the background towards the cliff and the town there is a puppet theatre and black or blacked up minstrels perform. A model townscape includes an obelisk, a clock tower, fine terraces and a modern castle with turrets. The painting portrays beach leisure pursuits as orderly and respectable. Queen Victoria bought the painting for the Royal Collection.

A year later, Abraham Solomon's painting *A Contrast* addressed a theme that others would return to. It shows a chance encounter between two young fisherwomen with their children and a middle-class family on a narrow shore below cliffs. The strong lustrous women carrying a basket and nets observe the family where a wan young woman in an invalid carriage is being comforted possibly by a brother while an older woman with a parasol looks concerned and a top-hatted footman looks alert. A gun dog stands guard beside another young woman who sits demurely on a rock immersed in a book. The painting did suggest that the seaside offered the possibility of encounters between people of different status and background—the democracy of the outdoors.

At its simplest the beach was an arena for playfulness. This is celebrated in Richard Doyle's 1864 engraving *At the Seaside*, one illustration for his series Bird's-Eye Views of Modern Society. The beach scene is full of people pursuing leisure: beach croquet, bathing machines being launched and retrieved, donkey races, boats approaching the shore and occupants being piggy-backed ashore, a quartet playing their musical instruments, beach combing, young women reading and sketching, and everywhere children—digging, building sandcastles and canals, dancing, testing the waters. The artist himself counselled the jaded adult to "find pleasure in contemplating their pleasure".

The seaside gave a licence to children and adults to be children and to get on. Charles Dickens on holiday in Boulogne in the early 1850s noted one aspect of the vacationing experience—how easy it was for different nationals to like each other and learn from each other. His stay at another "watering hole"—Broadstairs—brought out the contemplative observer watching children at play: "so busy burying their particular friends, and making castles with infinite labour which the next tide overthrows, that it is curious to consider how their play, to the music of the sea, foreshadows the realities of their lives."

Dickens certainly praised the "fine sea" as wholesome and profitable for mind and body. Not everyone agreed. While sea bathing was acknowledged as a pleasurable and healthy activity, some saw it as an incitement to voyeurism—women's voluminous shifts would cling to their bodies when wet. Others even considered the practice of women letting their hair down to get it dry to be an unseemly act. The seaside never quite lost its louche, low-rent, even seedy associations as evidenced by the naughty but popular comic postcards created by Donald McGill (1875-1962) and others which sold in their millions. Their garishly coloured saucy scenarios featuring cheeky chappies and children, hen-pecked husbands and prominently pneumatic women would stretch double entendres and sexual suggestiveness about as far as they could decently go. If part of the seaside prescription was for bracing sea air, showing you could have a risqué laugh was a necessary side effect. On the Isle of Wight Ryde's Union Street boasts a museum dedicated to the postcard king of the double entendre that contains a ceiling where over 2,500 of his postcards are on view, interactive displays and some of his original artwork (www.donaldmcgill.info).

PIERS AND PAINTERS

Soon the seaside was developing as a distinct environment with its own building types and furniture—an imaginatively constructed landscape of windbreaks, cafés, deck chairs, funfairs, holiday camps, rinks, bandstands, shelters, pavilions and piers. A postcard from around 1910 showing Southsea's South Parade Pier enhanced by distinctive Edwardian colouring, would possibly have been a more acceptable, even educational, alternative to McGill and Co.'s blatant bawdiness. In the picture a tram with an open top deck is passing by the new pier's huge glazed entrance canopy. Conservatively dressed Edwardians stride out along the promenade and across the ample decks of the new wooden palace. A skyline of towers and turrets signals the building's large interior spaces. The original pier of 1879 had burnt down in 1904—a common fate then as now—and local architect G. E. Smith (1868-1944) had been given the commission for designing its replacement. Smith was Portsmouth born and bred and though he was vir-

Skating at Southsea

tually anonymous on the national architectural scene he was able to apply his design talents to many and varied local commissions: hotels, banks, shops, schools, chapels, hospital buildings, cemetery buildings, a brewery, a gym and the Technical Institute and Free Library.

The new pier, opened in 1908, was indeed a people's palace and designed as much as a Winter Palace as a summer pier. Passing the shops and the kiosks selling steamer tickets, the visitor moved into the entrance hall with its tea room situated on the western side to catch the afternoon sunlight; beyond was the concert hall, a multi-purpose space, typically a concert venue at night and a roller skating rink in the day. From here doors opened onto the promenade deck. The pier's main internal space was next—the Pavilion Kursaal (a German word in popular use at the time referring to a rest room at a spa). The auditorium and the balcony could seat 1,700 people with further standing room taking the capacity to around two thousand. The main concerts and Pierrot shows were staged here. A large open deck beyond this pavilion was dominated by a bandstand. From the landing stage at the end of the pier steamers took passengers to various resorts and harbours along the south coast.

Southsea Beach, c.1890

Three photographic images tell something of the pier's own story. In the first (from around 1908) two young women and a girl with a straw hat roller skate confidently towards the camera along the pier's seaward deck. A photograph from 4 July 1940 shows amusement machines being crated up under the pier's entrance canopy after the imminent threat of German invasion had closed the seafront. A photograph taken from the esplanade in the summer of 1974 is a snapshot of the pier on fire, a blaze started during Ken Russell's filming of the rock opera *Tommy*. All that remained of the Kursaal was a burnt out shell. The pier survives today—a sub-Las Vegas one-armed bandit and games machine environment with dispiriting interiors and a tawdry replica of an Edwardian gem.

The pier and the nearby canoe lake marked the eastern end of the development of Southsea. In 1790 some houses had appeared to the east of the Portsmouth ramparts and in the next sixty years this suburb grew to house naval officers' families and other military personnel and, in the southern sector at least, the monied middle class. Its sea-facing boundary was always further inland than comparable resorts. The reason was the Common. This stretch of open land was strategically useful to the Army and so Victorian property speculators were kept in check.

The development of Southsea as the prototype for the garden suburb was due to one man, Thomas Ellis Owen (1805-62), architect, builder, surveyor, property speculator, local politician and the very model of a Victorian entrepreneur. Born in the year of the Battle of Trafalgar, he was the fourth of thirteen children who survived infancy. His father Jacob was a canal engineer and then clerk-of-works in Portsmouth Dockyard. An early part of Thomas' architectural apprenticeship was his involvement in the design of the Crescent at Alverstoke close to Stokes Bay. This elegant terrace of villas and a hotel, lauded by Pevsner and Lloyd as "a piece of urban planning of the early nineteenth century... unsurpassed in Hampshire", was designed as a centrepiece of the resort of Anglesey Ville. The Crescent survived but the resort project did not.

From 1829 until his death Thomas Ellis Owen was involved in many projects: campaigning for a direct London to Portsmouth rail link, designing chapels for the Highland Road cemetery, involvement in the failed Portsmouth Arundel Navigation, designing the Portsea Island Union Workhouse, surveying St. Paul's Church at Barton on the Isle of Wight, even assisting his brother-in-law with the design of Belfast's Crumlin Road Goal. Yet it was his architectural and urban design work for the suburb of Southsea that provided his legacy—crescents, villas, lodges, a church, curved roads and romantic, even picturesque, urban landscaping.

Thomas Ellis Owen built his own family home, Dovercourt, in Kent Road on a plot he had earlier reserved in a part of Southsea that was full of his architecture. He was happy to be a neighbour of the buildings he had designed—not something that could be said of all architects. The house has been described as "Picturesque Gothic" with arches over the entrance, gargoyles, a prospect tower, a family chapel with a stained glass window and an extensive garden behind the house complete with a grotto and a Greek Temple. In the last decade of his life Owen could have walked to the entrance gate of Dovercourt and if he had walked a couple of hundred yards to his left along Kent Road he would have passed fine lodges and a stuccoed terrace of town houses set behind white walls and behind these Sussex Terrace and other lodges—all his handiwork. Looking right from his gate he would see his Portland Hotel and the start of the sublimely classical Portland Terrace. By strolling a hundred yards to his right he would reach the church he designed, St. Jude's—the centrepiece of Owen's Southsea. Behind the church is a close of small neo-gothic houses with arched doorways, polychromatic brickwork, stone-dressed windows and decorative barge-boards. Good Victorian architects could do any style. On 11 December 1862 he died in the library at Dovercourt. Owenville was his legacy.

The green buffer of the Common keeps the seafront some way distant from the southernmost terrace of Southsea. Though this means a walk to the seaside, the intervening field does also provide an ample viewing platform and can be used as a showground, a circus venue and a parade ground. Brighton could boast an arcaded seafront prom, post-war Greeneland gangsters and, for a time, Magnus Volk's electric sea train (dubbed the "Daddy Long-Legs") but Southsea has never lacked for military and naval manoeuvres as spectacle or a lively seascape.

Portsmouth harbour entrance and the Point, Old Portsmouth, became perennial subjects for painters. J. M. W. Turner's *Gosport: The Entrance to Portsmouth Harbour* (c.1829) shows warships, sailing craft and rowing boats in a boiling sea under an explosive sky. In 1829 W. Clarkson Stanfield's painting similarly showed various craft coping with the tide race of the harbour entrance. In 1835 a George Chambers painting *Entrance to Portsmouth Harbour* was another take on this subject with a beautiful seascape depicting assorted vessels negotiating the harbour. William Smyth's *On the Point, Portsmouth* (1857) shows the current Old Portsmouth with the sails of a large ship off the seafront wall visible at the end of the High Street and Quebec House, the seawater bathing establishment. Turner returned to this location for his painting of *The Disembarkation of Louis-Philippe at Portsmouth* (c.1844-45). Turner would seem to have been going through a highly impressionist phase and the viewer benefits from an explanatory caption.

What Turner had highlighted was the increase in ceremonial attached to visits of royalty and heads of state and with it the institution of the Fleet Review. The first official Review was made by George III in June 1773. He spent five days in Portsmouth visiting fortifications, the dockyard, gun-wharf and the fleet at Spithead. In his yacht *Augusta* he sailed to Sandown Bay and back and anchored off Southsea Beach. A journalist wrote: "The sea and the shores were covered with an innumerable number of vessels and people each day."

Between 1842 and 1914—from the fifth year of Queen Victoria's reign until just one month before the outbreak of the First World War—

there were eighteen Fleet Reviews. Some were in honour of visiting royalty such as the Sultan of Turkey, the Shah of Persia and, in 1889, the Kaiser. The Review in the year of the queen's Diamond Jubilee in 1897 dwarfed all others. The British ships on review were stationed in four lines each five miles long. These were then flanked by one line of foreign naval vessels and one line of special merchant ships.

One engraving of the Fleet Review of 1856 depicts a fake gunboat attack on Southsea Castle. The artist's viewpoint is as if from an air balloon looking down on the Solent as far as Cowes and a distant Southampton Water. Two lines of warships extend into that distance and the Royal Yacht, here a paddle steamer, sails between them. On other occasions mock land battles, experimental naval attacks on port defences, the departure of an expedition such as that to the Arctic in June 1875 and even troop reviews would draw the crowds.

VICTORIAN TOURISM: THE ISLE OF WIGHT

There was also ferry traffic and regattas to observe. Every year the ferry boat men of Portsmouth harbour held a regatta, the Rowing Club held races and by the 1900s the Royal Albert and Royal Portsmouth Corinthian Yacht clubs held annual regattas. As the Isle of Wight became an increasingly popular destination there were ferries to watch. When Clarence Pier opened in 1861—essentially a landing stage with a pavilion built two decades later—the paddle steamers of the two steam packet ferry companies for the Isle of Wight crossing used that docking facility. By 1865 a new tramway service to the pier brought passengers clanking to and from the Town Station. Eleven years later passengers for the Isle of Wight could walk from the new Harbour Station to the attached landing stage. In 1880 the railways took over the ferry companies creating a business and a service that by the 1920s was handling two million passengers a year.

Passengers taking the steamer across to Ryde after 1864 would arrive at the pierhead, almost half a mile from the land. The original pier, the first in the country and extended between 1814 and 1842, now had a parallel structure to accommodate a horse-drawn tramway. By 1880 a third pier supported the steam trains that could disperse visitors throughout the Island. A Victorian guidebook did a good job of boosting the town's pier, commenting on "the elegance and beauty of the fair promenaders" and the rewards of this viewing platform: "The arrival and departure of steam

Ryde's pier, 1840s

packets; the numerous boats everywhere sailing about; the merchantmen constantly underway; together with the occasional naval salutes, announcing the arrival or departure of ships of war, compose a scene of unusual interest and excitement."

Ryde itself was a boom town of the Regency-Victorian era which witnessed a growth in its population from around 600 in 1801 to 9,300 in 1861. Architects Sir George Gilbert Scott with All Saints' Church steeple and Thomas Hellyer with his Holy Trinity spire gave the town distinctive landmarks on the hill. James Sanderson designed and had built the original town hall (1829-31) whose grandeur reflected the town that would be rather than what was. Thomas Westmacott's Royal Victoria Arcade (1835-6) in Union Street was named after the then Princess Victoria and is still in commercial use today largely unscathed: "one of the finest arcades surviving to this day", according to the 2006 Pevsner volume.

A brisk walk east from Ryde along the shore brought the rambler to a former maritime village which became in the Victorian era the small and fashionable resort of Seaview nestling on the north-east coast of the Island. The pier, opened in 1881, was a version of Brighton's original Palace Pier—

a sequence of suspension bridges. It fell victim to a storm in 1951. One of those strangely coloured Victorian postcards shows the beach lined with tents; the resort had adopted these rather than bathing machines. Seaview has some fine Victorian and Arts and Crafts villas including one, Horstone Point (1928), designed by the architect Oliver Hill

By the latter decades of the nineteenth century visitors were able to use the railway to access the Island's east coast resorts of Sandown, Shanklin and Ventnor. The sweep of Sandown's bay made it a natural location as a resort. Our guide hymned the delights of this locale: "lovely horseshoe bay, perfect bathing accommodation and the benefit of inland breezes". The railway connection with Ryde in 1864 provided the impetus for a small town to become a holiday destination. A pier was opened in 1879 and was a landing stage for paddle steamers; it remains the Island's only pleasure pier.

Neighbouring Shanklin did not have Sandown's sweep of beaches but what it did offer for early nineteenth-century visitors of a Romantic persuasion was the ideal picturesque landscape for a retreat, with its cliff top walks and ravine-like chines complete with a waterfall and situated nearby a bathing house in a fisherman's cottage. What is now the Old Village became a mixture of genuinely old cottages and nineteenth-century "cottages ornées", artfully designed small rustic houses collected into "a self-consciously picturesque group with scrolly bargeboards".

The resort town of Shanklin mostly developed to the north of this idealised landscape. Small hotels and villas were built in the early part of the nineteenth century. Just like small towns in America's Wild West everything changed with the coming of the railroad. In Shanklin's case this was in 1864. Four churches with built in the latter part of the century. St. Saviour on the Cliff, begun by Thomas Hellyer, is the dominant church of the town with its distinctive spire. Some of the stained glass is by Morris and Co. The town acquired a Literary and Scientific Institute in 1879, which became the town hall in 1913 and after a fire was converted into the existing theatre in the early 1930s. To the north of the town there were two "seafronts", one along the beach level esplanade and the other on the sandstone cliff above, the Eastcliff Promenade. The esplanade along the foreshore was completed by 1890 and had shelters sited at intervals along its length "with hollow broad-eaved roofs and ironwork cresting". The pier built at this time survived until its destruction in the south of England's

Great Storm of 16 October 1987. A lift originally built in 1892 and rebuilt in 1956 transports visitors between the beach and its upper cliff level. It might not have the brio of Bournemouth's West Cliff Railway but the shaft is a defining feature of Shanklin's beach life.

The Island's east coast resorts were all distinctively different in their location and their ambience; and Ventnor was something else again. The landscape provides the drama with this section of the Undercliff combining steep cliffs with shallow hollows. At the start of the nineteenth century this was a hamlet composed of a watermill, fishermen's and quarrymen's cottages, a farmhouse and a tavern. The development of a town in the 1830s and 1840s was built on the growing reputation of the place's benign climate—facing south-east and sheltered by the downs behind. Building started apace but in an ad hoc way with the architecture paying little reference to the potential offered by the irregular land forms. Amid all this under-planned development the town also acquired four churches, a zigzag road, a park, a short esplanade, a pier (1872-1993) where steamers could bring passengers directly from the mainland and take them for excursions along the south coast and, in 1935, a Winter Gardens Pavilion, described by David W. Lloyd as "a smaller-scale reverberation of the then new Bexhill Pavilion in Sussex".

Our Victorian guide said of this capital of the Undercliff that "its popularity is due to the remarkable salubrity of its climate, and the singular beauty of its situation," and added: "Ventnor is essentially a place that has been made by doctors." The author probably had in mind the eminent physician Sir James Clark who, in his book *The Sanative Influence of Climate on Diseases* compared the climate of the town to that of Madeira. Certainly this claim worked as the town increasingly became the destination of consumptives and tuberculosis sufferers. In 1868 work was started on the Royal National Hospital for Diseases of the Chest (designed by Thomas Hellyer) on a site west of Ventnor Park. When completed it consisted of eight substantial brick pavilions for patients and a chapel; at its height the hospital could accommodate 900 patients a year.

The medical regime encompassed the curative potential of plants and gardening so patients were encouraged to plant vegetables, build arches, create orchards and lay paths. Kew Gardens was asked to donate specimens and Queen Victoria planted a Chinese Fan Palm on the site. The hospital closed in 1964 and was demolished five years later. In 1972 the

Ventnor, c.1900

Botanic Gardens, now famed for its rare plants, was opened on the thirty-acre site.

The writer Henry James (1843-1916) cast a rather critical eye on Ventnor during a visit recorded in his *English Vignettes* published in 1879. Although the writer used it himself to get from Ryde to Ventnor, he disparages the "detestable little railway" with its tunnels and embankments which left a scar on a landscape that "is ornamental only", existing for "exclamation and the water-colour brush". As he arrived at the shimmering sea with the town hanging on the side of a steep hill behind, Ventnor did bring to James' mind "one of the bright-faced little [Mediterranean] towns"; but it lacked the right kind of villa and ultimately "it is a formed and finished watering place... reduced to a due degree of cockneyfication." For James it was not bosky or pastoral enough to be a summer retreat. However, he did find the nearby village of Bonchurch to his liking while acknowledging there was something absurd about it: "like a model village... kept in a big glass case". But it was on the walk from Ventnor to Shanklin that he discovered the best of the Island in the wide natural terrace of the Undercliff, "this long, blooming platform, protected from the north by huge green bluffs and plunging on the other side into the murmuring tides".

Given his literary skills, some of James' judgements can seem to the modern reader reactionary, self-absorbed, even contradictory. Karl Marx wrote to his friend and benefactor Friedrich Engels in July 1874: "This Island is a little paradise." Not a workers' paradise perhaps, but he urged Engels to visit. Marx wintered in Ventnor in 1881-82 for health reasons and again in the following year—his last.

SOUTHSEA, THE RESORT

In the course of the twentieth century the tourist potential of the seaside and seaside resorts grew and then stalled. In 1922 Portsmouth City Council bought Southsea Common from the War Department and over the next few years built ornamental and rock gardens, tennis courts, bowling greens, putting courses, football pitches and a giant paddling pool. The westernmost part of the Common was kept as open land and as a potential locale for training, parades and reviews. A striking addition to this landscape was the Royal Naval War Memorial on the Clarence Esplanade, a tapering column on a plinth with stone lions at each corner. It was erected to honour the 9,300 officers and men of the Portsmouth Division of the Royal Navy who gave their lives in the First World War, and was a potent reminder to those approaching or leaving the harbour or vacationing in Southsea of the tragic side of what the city was about. Navy Week and later Navy Days became an annual fixture.

The 1928 tourist season was Southsea's best on record and the resort's success at attracting visitors continued into the 1930s. Painters were still drawn to the subject of being beside the seaside. Edward Bawden's *By the Sea* (1929-30) depicted an archetypal beach scene in his own particular style—pier in the background, beach huts, ice cream kiosk and orderly rows of people in deckchairs facing orderly waves. Even the swimmers diving from a pontoon offshore look synchronised. In contrast Ernest Proctor's *Summer Holidays* (1934) shows some young people, some naked, wrestling each other into the waves with a sense of abandonment.

A Southern Railway poster from 1933, "The South Coast is the Sunny Coast", depicts two female sunbathers, one with arms raised in an almost worshipful gesture. A photograph of South Parade from 1932 shows crowds on the pier and the esplanade with waiting charabancs lining the road. The aerial photograph of South Parade Pier and its hinterland bathed in sunshine, used on the cover of the 1933 *Southsea Guidebook*, displays a packed beach east of the pier and a crowded Canoe Lake beyond. This last attraction had gained some international recognition earlier when the French novelist André Maurois, in a broadcast about his children's reactions to England on a family holiday, recounted how his youngest daughter had written to her grandmother to tell her that of the things they had seen—Salisbury Cathedral, the Tower of London, HMS *Victory*, the best were the "tin canoes of Southsea".

When Portsmouth and the Isle of Wight emerged from the trauma of aerial assaults during the Second World War and their front line role in the launching of the D-Day invasion fleet (South Parade Pier, for example, was an embarkation point for troops) and when some reconstruction could start, Southsea regained its role as a destination for holiday makers in the 1950s. The pier hosted West End comedy shows with Tommy Trinder, Radio Band Shows, daily Hammond Organ concerts and the hugely popular and slightly raunchy beach beauty and bikini contests on the pier's bandstand or the neighbouring beach. Southsea had moved decidedly down market.

Yet holiday makers' options and preferences were changing. Camping, caravanning and self-catering holidays all grew. The traditional seaside hotels and guest houses had to contend with the counter-attractions of the all-inclusive holiday camp, whose most famous exponent was Billy Butlin (1899-1980). Pre-war amusement park impresario and sole European agent for Dodgems, he became the holiday camp entrepreneur par excellence, building up his chain of' luxury holiday camps and offering full board, on-site entertainment and child care. A rail poster of 1940 advertising the Butlins camp at Clacton-on-Sea has the foreground dominated by a young female plunging towards the pool in a perfectly executed dive, with the poolside thronged by elegant young things and a landscape beyond of chalets, mini golf and tennis courts stretching to a Modernist main building and a beach beyond. It was all there. In 1939 there had been three holiday camps on Portsmouth's neighbouring Hayling Island and twelve on the Isle of Wight.

And the Island was no stranger to the holiday camp experience. The Brightstone Camp on Military Road was opened in 1932 and some of the

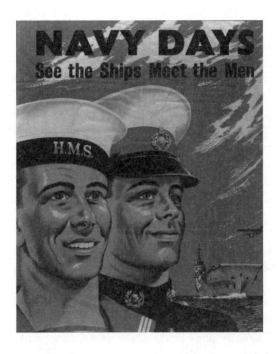

chalets still survive. In 1960 a Butlins had opened down the coast at Bognor Regis. Around that time, however, package holidays to Mediterranean resorts clearly signalled the coming trend in mass tourism.

Portsmouth City Councils from 1960 onwards found it difficult to decide what the seafront tourist landscape adjacent to Southsea Castle should look like—a winter garden, a hotel, an entertainment centre, a swimming pool, jazz cellar and motel… A grandiose scheme for an oceanarium was supported and then rejected on the grounds of costs needed to keep the mammals alive. A more localised emphasis on tourism was introduced by legislation in 1969 and gave the impetus to greater focus on the city's naval military heritage. In 1981 the government proposed "contracting activities" at Portsmouth Dockyard. The wreck of the Tudor warship the *Mary Rose* was rescued from the Solent seabed in the following year and moved to a dry dock next to HMS *Victory*. The brand was no longer Sunny Southsea but Portsmouth as the Flagship of Maritime England; the main visitor theme for the city would be as a place of unique naval historical interest.

To bolster this claim, the Royal Navy's first ironclad warship HMS *Warrior*, launched in 1860, was rescued from her ignominious service as an oil jetty at Milford Haven in 1979 and towed 800 miles around the coast to Hartlepool for a seven-year refit. In June 1987 she was towed—in a four-day voyage—to her new berth just inside Portsmouth Dockyard.

Three years earlier the D-Day Museum, located just inland from Southsea Castle, was opened with its centrepiece exhibit of the Overlord Embroidery—the unique and stunning sewn account of the Normandy landings of 1944. Three years later a modest Sea Life Centre was opened further west along the seafront. Certainly this added variety to the range of seaside attractions but it was no rival to Brighton's Aquarium from 1872.

The Isle of Wight likewise developed its heritage attractions including the English Heritage flagships of Osborne House and Carisbrooke Castle and the uniquely situated Needles Battery, run by the National Trust, while the Island's sea stories produced a shipwreck centre. Over the post-war decades two other forms of visitor attraction would be tried and tested: outdoor music festivals and hiking.

Musical festivals were a bold experiment which stuttered and died and were revived three decades later. The first Isle of Wight Festival in 1968 was followed by festivals in the next two years whose growth was exponential. The 1970 festival with the Doors, Joan Baez and Jimi Hendrix attracted a crowd possibly larger than the Island's population—and so proved unmanageable. This "tradition" was revived in 2002 and has been a regular fixture at Seaclose Park near Newport every year since then.

Thirteen years of the Isle of Wight walking festival has tapped into and revived a long rambling tradition. A Southern Railway poster from 1931 advertising cheap tickets to get you to the countryside quickest show a hiking couple striding out energised by their activity. James Walker Tucker's painting *Hiking* (1936) depicts a trio of young women hikers, with rucksacks, striking berets and sensible shoes, perusing a map on a hill above an archetypal English village set in lush countryside—independent and together. The twice yearly festival makes full, even exotic, use of the Island's 500 miles of maintained and signed footpaths with 300 walks to choose from.

Chapter Fourteen

THE LOCAL STAGE

THEATRES AND CINEMAS

Two major theatres have survived in Portsmouth into the early twenty-first century: the New Theatre Royal and the Kings. The first had been re-modelled and transformed several times since it was first opened in 1856, while the Kings has stayed essentially the same since it was built in 1907. Both are being restored and both featured in the projects portfolio of the doyen of late Victorian and Edwardian architecture, Frank Matcham (1854-1920).

The story of the New Theatre Royal could almost be treated as a drama with five acts: two substantial design makeovers, several decades of changes of use and loss of identity, a further period of darkness and vandalism followed by decades of rescue and restoration—a theatrical rebirth. Certainly any biography of the building would include architectural and entrepreneurial flair and imagination involved in creating magical theatrical environments, the entrances and exits of many of the leading actors of their day, the difficulty of keeping a provincial theatre afloat when faced with competing challenges from new media and the vagaries of official attitudes toward supporting the arts and conserving the built heritage of theatres.

Circus owner Henry Rutley bought the Swan Tavern in Commercial Road and its neighbour the Landport Hall, which he converted into the Theatre Royal in 1856. Small as the theatre was, it managed to stage a varied repertoire including opera. Twenty years later after Henry Rutley's death in 1874 a new company took over the Theatre Royal; John Waters Boughton became its manager and subsequently its new owner. He would go on to be the major player on the city's theatre scene when in the early 1900s he was the founder of the Kings Theatre and he worked in the interim to make the Theatre Royal the major playhouse in the south. To realise this ambition and remodel the theatre he hired the foremost architect of the day C. J. Phipps (1835-97).

Phipps was the "establishment" architect for London theatre land in the later 1800s. He did not use one consistent decorative style but could design using Greek or gothic—whatever was in vogue—and he designed particular theatres for the leading players of the West End stage: the Savoy for Richard D'Oyly Carte, the Lyceum for Henry Irving and Her Majesty's Theatre for Herbert Beerbohm Tree. He was adept at bringing the job to completion in good time and at making all the functional requirements of a theatre from front-of-house to backstage fit into limited spaces. In fact he liked to design a "domestic-scale" lobby and front-of-house space to provide a reassuring home-like atmosphere. His standard plan for the London theatres he designed or altered became the model for many other theatre projects throughout the country.

The New Theatre Royal included a gas-lit auditorium with three tiers seating a capacity audience of 2,000, a white and gold interior with painted murals and a domestic-style lobby and front-of-house. It was opened on 4 August 1884 with a production of Gilbert and Sullivan's *Princess Ida* whose cast included principals who were D'Oyly Carte Opera Company professionals, an amateur chorus of one hundred and a Royal Marine Artillery Band. The theatre's subsequent success over the next sixteen years encouraged Boughton to embark on another remodelling project—to enlarge the auditorium and stage and essentially to design a third theatre. For this work he chose Frank Matcham (1854-1920).

Born in Newton Abbot in Devon, Frank Matcham's career progression was a classic Victorian era example of success coming from learning and doing the job while immersed in a professional world rather than from time served at an academy. At fourteen he joined the office of a Torquay architect and served as an apprentice to a London quantity surveyor. Having joined the firm of an influential theatre architect Jethro Thomas Robinson and married his employer's younger daughter, he inherited his father-in-law's practice on Jethro's death in 1878. In the next 35 years Matcham built or remodelled more than 150 theatres. These ranged from the grand houses such as the Coliseum (currently the refurbished London home of the English National Opera), the Grand Opera House in Belfast and the Hackney Empire and other "Empires" to more modest suburban and variety theatres.

As an architect he was not an especially technical innovator although he did include cantilevered galleries in his theatre remodelling and he worked to ensure good sight-lines and install improved ventilation systems. It was rather in the design of his interiors that the "Matchless Matcham" made his dramatic statements. The whole range of styles and motifs was pressed into service, often co-existing in the same auditorium, according to Iain Mackintosh: "Tudor trap work, Louis XIV detail, Anglo-Indian motifs, naval and military insignia, delicate rococo panels, classical statuary, robust baroque columns…" There were also nymphs, shepherds, cherubs and burnished domes—he was the supreme scenographer.

With the Theatre Royal Matcham's brief was to expand its capacity both in terms of seating and its ability to take the most ambitious sets that London productions might demand. Consistent with his skill and experience of working to demanding timetables the architect was able to bring the job to completion in four months. During that period of closure the theatre staff and booked companies were transferred to the Princes Theatre in Portsmouth, also owned by Boughton and previously rebuilt by Matcham.

Framed by a new proscenium arch the resulting stage was one of the largest in the country—65 feet deep and 56 feet wide and with exits wide enough to provide a necessary run for horses to make a galloping entrance across the stage. In the first decade of the twentieth century advances in set building and the shifting of sets encouraged more ambitious stage spectacles; one Drury Lane melodrama of 1909 *The Whip* featured a train crash and a version of the Two Thousand Guineas horse race. The redecorated fronts of the upper and dress circles included motifs that were suitably suggestive of Portsmouth's naval and military significance: dolphins, mermaids, anchors, shells and lifebelts. The boxes adjacent to the dress circle were separated by the bows of ships and their figureheads. The light fittings shaped as brass anchors continued this nautical theme.

Mostly Italian craftsmen were hired to do the plaster work and the marble installation. The new auditorium was decorated in cream overlaid with gold leaf and terracotta; tiered boxes were added either side of the stage and above the proscenium a mural was retained on a panel supported by "an arcade of engaged Corinthian columns and flanked by a pair of superb winged tritons blowing long trumpets (John Offord)". The theatre's façade and old portico gave way to new polished granite entrances with the addition of a cast-iron balcony to the front of the theatre. This balcony provided a new gentleman's smoking room joining the dress circle saloon. Part of the balcony was reserved for the ladies.

The expanded and remodelled Theatre Royal (it had become New in 1900) was better able now to include London shows on tour and "Flying Matinees" in its programme—an arrangement that gave provincial audiences the opportunity to see the current stars of the London stage. These actors who would travel down from London could be a big draw but something had to be sacrificed in terms of production values; there was necessarily an impromptu quality to the lighting arrangements, the provision of props and stage settings and the coherence of the performances as the supporting actors would not have rehearsed with the principals.

STARS OF STAGE

Any listing of the leading actors who appeared at the Theatre Royal between the 1870s and 1920s would, however, provide a roll call of the key players of the English stage, and would certainly include Ellen Terry, Henry Irving and Mrs. Patrick Campbell. It was Mrs. Campbell—the stage name of Beatrice Stella Campbell (1865-1940), daughter of a wealthy army contractor for the East India Company—who was one of the leads in the first performances when the Theatre Royal reopened on 6 August 1900, initially in *Magda*, then in *The Second Mrs. Tanqueray*. It was this role that first brought her fame when the play opened in 1893, but she was aware that the portrayal of a woman with a notorious past risked a perception on the part of the public that the actress' own life had followed a similar course. Perhaps her stage name was recognition of this. She was certainly a performer who dared to play roles that were socially unconventional at the time. Appearing in George Bernard Shaw's premier production of *Pygmalion* in 1914, she later claimed to have "invented the cockney accent".

The real lives of the actors and actresses who provided the top of the bill draw for the theatre audiences of the day were not as open to scrutiny as contemporary stars but newspaper coverage and popular gossip were part of their fame then as now. One performer who would have been known to Portsmouth audiences was Lillie Langtry (1853-1929). Born Charlotte Le Breton, she was the daughter of the Dean of Jersey. In 1874 she married Edward Langtry, a Belfast ship owner, and during the following three years they became a celebrated couple in London society. Her beauty made her an iconic model for contemporary painters, most famously in John Everett Millais' portrait *A Jersey Lily*. She was also the mistress of the Prince of Wales and on the strength of the public notoriety that ensued she founded her own theatrical company which toured Britain and America.

A theatrical life of a different trajectory was that of Dame Ellen Terry (1848-1928). She was the daughter of travelling actors, her father Irish and her mother the Scottish daughter of a Wesleyan minister in Portsmouth. Trained by her parents, she made her stage debut at the age of nine in a production of *The Winter's Tale*. Ellen was an experienced actress by her teens, schooled by then in the art of projecting a juvenile's voice that could be heard in the gallery. She was married at seventeen to the artist George Frederic Watts, thirty years her senior; the relationship lasted less than a year. Ellen Terry's grace and beauty made her a "cult figure" for poets and painters; as her biographer Michael Booth remarks, she was "as much an art object as an actress".

She felt ambivalent about a life on the stage and left for six years in 1868 to start a family with the architect and interior designer Edward Godwin, but financial problems drove her back working as a actress in 1878, and four years later she became one of the leading ladies at actor-manager Henry Irving's Lyceum Theatre in London. Their personal and professional relationship lasted 24 years and encompassed productions of Shakespeare, romantic melodrama and comedy in London and on tour in the provinces and America. Ellen Terry built up a large personal following among the theatre public in a career that spanned 69 years on the stage. Booth suggests that theatre goers found it easy to feel empathy for her "liveliness and irrepressible spirits".

The career of Ellen Terry's acting colleague and theatre manager Henry Irving (1838-1905) also illustrates in one lifetime the changing status of the theatre as a recognised art form in British life. Irving's real name was John Henry Brodribb, born in Somerset but importantly shaped between the ages of four and eleven by his foster parents on his mother's side in the Methodist culture and "hard romantic landscape of Cornwall". Irving began a taxing theatrical apprenticeship in 1856 at the Lyceum in Sunderland and at other "stock companies" in the north of England and Scotland. The actor's bohemian life involved poor pay and often poorer status, and he broke with his mother and his wife Florence over their disapproval of his choice of career. Yet after public recognition that he was one of the great Shakespearian actors and after almost two decades as actor-manager of the Lyceum Theatre he was awarded a knighthood by Queen Victoria. It was perhaps acknowledgement of the crucial importance of artistic input into theatre production—something that Irving believed in strongly, the imaginative *mise en scène.* This was the "imaginative element", Robertson Davies suggests, "that creates the atmosphere of phantasmagoria and dream grotto that was the mark of every Lyceum production." Irving was also a friend and professional collaborator of theatre architect Frank Matcham.

Irving's personal story showed success and status gained after real occupational adversity, but it could make anyone marvel at the lure of the stage as a career then for young men and women who, as one writer puts it, were willing to endure "long hours, burdensome memorization, fierce competition, draughty and often unsanitary working conditions, inadequate pay, uncertain and unsavoury meals, lost sleep, tedious and uncomfortable travel, unscrupulous managers, self-aggrandizing stars, victimization by charlatans of various stripes and the nearly palpable bias of society at large against their chosen profession."

One of the performers who embodied the riskiness of Edwardian theatre and was likely to offend some patrons in those times was a woman who explored the boundaries of censorship, the music hall entertainer Marie Lloyd (1870-1922). A singing star at sixteen, she had been schooled by her father John to observe the artistes at the Grecian Music Hall attached to the Royal Eagle public house where he worked. She sung about the realities of working-class life, particularly for women, and was able to make her audiences feel they were in on the act with the suggestive spin she could put on the most innocuous lyrics; a line about her "having to go all the way to Crewe" was not foremost about a railway journey mishap. She could lark about as a cockney girl in the countryside noticing how a bull "wagged 'is apparatus", but she was also a public figure who campaigned for more honest assertion and expression of female desire and found herself in collision with the forces of censorship such as the Social Purity Alliance.

Marie Lloyd was one of the music hall artistes who told it like it was twice-nightly at the Hippodrome Theatre, Portsmouth's premier variety venue and "the handsomest and most luxurious house" (opened in 1907).

The Kings Theatre, Southsea

Other performers in those days were the music hall star Vesta Tilley (married to the theatre impresario behind the building of the theatre), the escapologist Harry Houdini and, on occasions, circus elephants. The theatre was a victim of the mass Luftwaffe raid of the night of 10 January 1941.

Marie Lloyd also appeared at Portsmouth's Theatre Royal (just across Commercial Road from the Hippodrome) and at the Kings Theatre. This second venue was a new theatre for Southsea also opened in 1907 that the entrepreneur J. W. Boughton had envisioned even as Frank Matcham carried out his remodelling scheme for the Theatre Royal. During the second half of the nineteenth century Southsea had grown as a satellite suburb of Portsmouth, and a contemporary photograph of the theatre shows a fairly tranquil scene on Albert Road with a tram trundling by, a horse-drawn cart ambling across the tram lines and a man on a bicycle pursuing the tram. Southsea was also a seaside resort, and in the first years of the twentieth century several speculators investigated the possibility of building a theatre there. It was Boughton who got in first, covertly paying for the initial transactions out of his own pocket without consulting his fellow company directors and commissioning Frank Matcham to draw up the plans.

The new theatre was located on an awkward site within the angle where Albert and Exmouth roads join. With no possibility of including in the design a significant front façade facing the street, Matcham made the most of the theatre's entrance through a triangular porch of glazed terracotta under a hexagonal tower with a steeply pitched roof topped by a cupola and a statue (recently restored). This strong vertical statement designed out of necessity makes an emphatic declaration of the theatre's presence in the streetscape. A less visible feature of the site was a spring that was kept from flooding by a pump under the main stage area.

After building the Bristol Hippodrome in 1912, Frank Matcham designed some cinemas but no more significant theatres. The foremost theatre architect of his day, affable, personable and extrovert, he was able to work sympathetically with his clients and bring his projects to completion in good time. Always conscious of the importance of sight lines he worked hard to make sure everyone in the audience had a good view of the stage. He was also the very model of the vigorous Edwardian entrepreneur, travelling the country by train on regular visits to his various theatres under construction: the Kings, Glasgow, the Olympia, Liverpool, the Manchester Hippodrome and the Buxton Opera House among others. He reserved use of his car for visits to his London theatre projects such as the Coliseum, sitting in the back seat of his Daimler-Benz, cigar in hand.

Both the Kings and the Theatre Royal have survived to the present day but during the previous century their survival could never be assumed as they searched for audiences. In the 1920s the Kings offered a mix of films and variety and by the 1930s it included in its repertoire plays destined for the West End and international ballet. After a post-war heyday during the 1950s and 1960s as a venue for musicals, classical concerts and pre-London stage runs of plays that featured actors as diverse as Rex Harrison, Margaret Leighton and Paul Scofield, the theatre struggled to find a clear role as its ownership changed hands between local authorities and theatre trusts. It is currently a popular theatre for the whole spectrum of entertainments and is being restored inside and out.

The twentieth-century history of the Theatre Royal was also a story of changes of use and a more dramatic story of decline and rescue. The immediate years after the First World War were a difficult time for theatres. The increase in production costs, the advent of radio and the spread of talkies led to theatres closing and fewer companies touring. The owners of the Theatre Royal decided to convert the theatre to a cinema in 1932 and so it remained until 1948; in the 1950s it was intermittently a variety theatre and then a repertory theatre. During these reincarnations the colour schemes were changed and Victorian light fittings and paintings were taken out. From 1960 to 1966 the theatre provided a hall for bingo and wrestling. After that the owners, the Portsmouth Theatre Company, applied to the council for permission to demolish the building and this was given. The theatre had been listed so it was instead left unprotected to suffer long-term demolition by neglect. These were truly dark days for the theatre; during this time of vandalism and rainwater penetration the council and the theatre's owners did nothing by way of protecting the building or maintaining it. Squatters installed themselves in 1968 and thieves made off with lead from the roof and brass fittings.

It was during this period of neglect that the Southampton-born film director Ken Russell, famous, sometimes infamous, maker of films about classical composers, injected some life into the building. Much of his film *The Boy Friend* (1971) was shot in the abandoned auditorium. In 1972 children had started a fire which consumed the great stage and the technical block; the Fire Brigade had been able to save the auditorium. The following year vandalism involved the destruction of statues, plaster decorations, ceilings and stained glass windows.

When a government inquiry recognised the case made by the newly - formed Theatre Royal Society and turned down the council's demolition application in 1975, it was the start of a long process of protection and restoration. Society volunteers were able to go into the theatre to try and stop vandalism and to limit further damage to the building's fabric—advised on this by local architect Deane Clark. The Society had set up a trust company and was able to buy the theatre when the Portsmouth Theatre Company went into liquidation in 1980. Work started on creating a viable performance space. Four years later, with a temporary stage built out over the orchestra pit, a small staff and the involvement of many volunteers, the theatre was able to put on small scale touring and local productions. Over the next two and a half decades capacity was increased, the auditorium and the front façade beautifully restored and a bigger stage included.

Most theatres had to adapt and go with the times. The Empire in Edinburgh Road provided music hall and variety entertainment over fifty years (from 1891) as the Coliseum and then as the Empire again. In the 1950s its glamour repertoire featured plenty of beauty queens including Jane (aka Christabel Jane Drewry) who had been the model for the *Daily Mirror's* wartime strip cartoon of that name.

Theatres on the Isle of Wight currently include two establishments with interesting pasts. The Shanklin Theatre stands on a site with a varied history, originally the location of a Literary and Scientific Institute (1879) which was converted into the town hall just before the First World War and then rebuilt in 1933-34 after a fire as a theatre with a striking French classical-style façade. The Apollo Theatre at Newport is a community-based venture in another building that has undergone an unusual reincarnation. When the former Methodist chapel closed its doors in 1969 a plan was laid to buy the building and make it into a theatre; that was the year of the Apollo moon shot—hence the name with a accompanying nod to the God of the Muses. The play list of recent productions includes the work of Arthur Miller, David Hare, Noel Coward and Alan Bennett; a matinee showing of films from the 1940s and 1950s is free for theatre members.

MOVING PICTURES

While the first developments in moving pictures were unfolding at the end of the nineteenth century further eastwards along the south coast around Hove, Portsmouth had its own cinematographic pioneer in the form of Alfred John West. His movie *Our Navy* played to countrywide audiences and Queen Victoria commanded a screening at Osborne House. The early film venues were basic, even primitive, sometimes consisting of tents such as Arnold's Electric Bioscope, which appeared annually at the Portsdown Hill Fair. The first building to feature regular Cinematoscope screenings from 1900 was the Victoria Hall in Commercial Road. A contemporary photograph of the auditorium shows a huge capacity audience waiting to see *Our Navy*, with many of the women still wearing their hats. This cinema survived Second World War bombing and was demolished in 1960. The last screening was *Expresso Bongo* featuring the up coming rock-'n'roll singer Cliff Richard.

In the decade before the First World War, biograph and kinematic theatres, Electric Palaces and Pavilions began to appear in towns and cities throughout the country. The first national cinema chain, Provincial Cinematograph Theatres, dates from those years as does the oldest cinema still operating, Brighton's The Duke of York—a building that would still be recognisable to its earliest patrons from 1910.

In the 1920s larger urban cinemas were built with auditoria seating over 2,000 sometimes with an orchestra pit or a restaurant and more typically with a café or tea room. To pre-empt dominance by American cinema chains two home-grown chains emerged at the end of the 1920s, Gaumont British and Associated British Cinemas (ABC). Their corporate logos became familiar visuals in British towns over the next decades. With the coming of the talkies many of the city cinemas copied the American contemporary design idea of the "atmospheric" auditorium. Cinema goers found themselves seated in Moorish palaces, Italianate follies, the courtyard of a Spanish grandee's house, even in an underwater mermaid's house.

In the 1930s the influence of the Modern Movement became apparent in cinema design exemplified by the fin tower of Dreamland in Margate and the cinemas of the expanding Odeon chain—soon to be ever present in the country's towns and cities. One of the most spectacular examples was the Worthing Odeon built in 1934 with its clock tower and rounded café wing. This development influenced the other two British chains to develop distinctive interiors. The Gaumont designers produced perfect fan-shaped auditoria and curved proscenium arches; the ABC chain designed spacious foyers with side staircases and decorative grille work.

Two short biographies of local cinemas might stand as examples of the careers of many smaller houses. The Apollo Cinema in Southsea's Albert Road opened as the Apollo Kinematic in April 1912. Its film projectors were then hand-cranked and the spool-changing required intervals. In the 1930s it boasted a luxurious entrance foyer and carpeted auditorium with a restaurant in the upper foyer. It was taken over by the Essoldo cinema chain, which in turn was acquired by the Classic chain in 1972; it closed in November 1975. In the heyday of film it had been one of the city's thirty cinemas. Today the commercial cinema is represented on the island of Portsea by the Vue multi-screen complex at Gunwharf Quays.

Further west along the coast is the seaside town of Lee-on-the-Solent. During the inter-war years the town's ambition to put itself on the map as a resort was signalled by a modern seaside development that included a cinema with a palm court café and a 120-foot tower offering extensive views over the Solent and the north coast of the Isle of Wight; the sum of 6d would buy you a ticket to the viewing platform. Opened in 1935 it struggled commercially from the beginning. During the Second World War it was used by American forces, and after the conflict the council saw the complex as a white elephant. The cinema was closed in 1958 and the complex itself demolished in the late 1960s. It had included an early equivalent of Portsmouth's Spinnaker Tower and the Modernist architecture was right for the sunbathing and cinema-going trends of the 1930s. Yet this resort complex was in the right seaside location and the wrong commercial location.

During the Second World War cinemas were closed during the initial "phoney war" period and then re-opened because of their contribution to public morale. Still the bombing risks were real. The Carlton Cinema at Cosham suffered a direct hit during the bombing raid of 5 December 1940; a bomb exploded in the projection room and fifty people were killed or injured. The Palace Cinema in Old Commercial Road, hit by a bomb in a 1941 raid, was back in business in five weeks. Originally designed by Portsmouth architect A. E. Cogswell in 1921, its façade displays Islamic motifs and forms such as ogee domes. In the 1960s the cinema was called the Palace Continental and specialised in films from mainland Europe. As foreign, especially French, films were thought to be more raffish and explicit in an adult way, it attracted a large rain-coated male clientele. Quite what they made of Jean-Luc Godard's experimental New Wave films has never been recorded. The cinema is now a nightclub.

In the immediate post-war years cinema admissions figures reached record levels, but the advent of television, especially ITV, saw admissions nearly halved between 1957 and 1960. Cinema did fight back with technical developments such as Cinemascope which could provide an involving experience. Also going to the pictures could still be an event. The author recalls the local premiere of David Lean's 1962 film *Lawrence of Arabia* at the North End Odeon in Portsmouth. Commissionaires in long coats and peaked caps greeted the cinema goers amid the potted plants of the foyer, and lavish commemorative programmes were on sale. This cinema had a career of over seventy years (opened in 1936 and closed for demolition in 2008, currently a store). George Formby made a personal appearance there in June 1941 to help raise money for air raid victims.

Peter Sellers' birthplace, Southsea

After the war there were regular personal appearances from the stars of British cinema among them Jack Hawkins, Margaret Lockwood, Peter Sellers (born in Southsea to theatrical folk)and Alec Guinness (himself a star of David Lean's wide screen desert epic). Just across the London Road, but fifteen years earlier in 1947, the staff of the Regent Picture House posed for the camera—about forty people in the frame, most in the cinema's uniforms, the organist seated next to the manager in the front row. In its heyday the Regent could seat almost 2,000 patrons and also staged events such as beauty contests. In 1951 the Regent became the Gaumont and that Gaumont was demolished in 1973.

Gosport's Olympia Roller Skating rink became the Olympia Cinema in 1914. The cinema survived despite a leaking tin roof which resulted in the orchestra having to keep their feet off the floor. Refurbished and modernised, the small cinema survived until 1935. In contrast the staff for the 1,000-seat Ritz in Gosport posed for a formal photograph at the end of the cinema's first year in 1936. There is a complement of twenty with the entire front of house and auditorium staff dressed in distinctive showbiz uniforms. All the usherettes look glamorous and there are two uniformed boys whose job it was to sell chocolates. It is not hard to see why these picture houses would have been viewed by local people as an important part of their urban experience. The credit card transactions and popcorn bucket trading in the archetypal airport terminal foyer of most contemporary multiplexes can feel, in contrast, just an exercise in customer processing.

In the second half of the twentieth century cinemas became akin to actors looking for work—buildings looking for a new role. The Gaumont at the top of Southsea's Victoria Road North became a bingo hall in the late 1960s and is currently the Portsmouth Central Mosque. Multiplexes of unadventurous design dominates the contemporary cinema scene, but smaller chains of distinctive houses do exist such as Picture House which includes in its portfolio the dockside architectural gem of the Harbour Lights cinema in Southampton and the Edwardian era survivor, the Duke of York's in Brighton.

Chapter Fifteen

FIELD OF DREAMS

FRATTON PARK

A photograph taken on 30 April 1949 shows a section of the crowd in the upper tier of the south stand of Portsmouth Football Club's ground at Fratton Park. The then Pompey captain Reg Flewin holds the League Division 1 Champions trophy flanked by the club's president and Second World War hero Field Marshall Bernard Law Montgomery. "Monty", wearing his trademark beret and a British warm coat, signals the applause for Flewin and the team's triumph.

Montgomery (1887-1976) maintained his links with Portsmouth after the war—a city that was both the launch slipway for his greatest triumph and was connected to his greatest personal despair. Born into a staunchly religious family of Northern Irish Protestants he spent most of his childhood growing up in Tasmania, unhappy under his mother's strict regime. His experiences of the First World War schooled him as an independent military thinker, a talented teacher of military tactics and an officer whose loyalty to his men came first.

In his late thirties this professional soldier previously wedded only to the Army sought a wife and found her in the person of Betty Hobart, the widow of a Gallipoli casualty and a graduate of the Slade School of Art. Their marriage was a happy one with Montgomery finding himself a natural as an attentive and devoted husband and father. It was while serving as the garrison commander at Portsmouth that he tragically lost his wife when a delay in treating an insect bite resulted in the need to amputate her infected leg and Betty died of post-operative septicaemia. A close army colleague said that the only time he had ever seen Montgomery "less than in control of himself" was at his wife's very private funeral service.

From that point on Montgomery devoted himself to the arts of military command. His famous military achievements in the Second World War are a familiar part of British modern consciousness: the first Allied success in the field against the Axis armies at El Alamein—the "turning of the tide" heralded by Winston Churchill's order that all the church bells be rung across England; and in his pivotal role as the commander-in-chief of the land forces for Operation Overlord, the D-Day invasion launched from the Solent and other south coast staging points and masterminded from command centres in and behind Portsmouth's sheltering Portsdown Hill. Less well known and less heralded was Montgomery's key role in ensuring the successful evacuation of so much of the British expeditionary force through Dunkirk and that it was he who received the surrender of the German armed forces for the north in May 1945. He was a brilliant planner, strategist and leader but he was also egotistical, arrogant and especially critical of and tactless towards American commanders.

Montgomery's post-war home for the last decade of his life was near Alton in north Hampshire but through his presidency of Portsmouth Football Club in the years after 1944 he maintained a connection with the city that was crucially associated with his D-Day achievements. The players at the club in the immediate post-war years had been part of the war effort. The Portsmouth-born centre-half in those years whose name seems to identify an earlier historical period, Reg Flewin, had served during the war in the Royal Marines. Team mates included Jack Froggatt, who signed for the club on his return from the RAF in 1945, and Peter Harris, who was "discovered" while working in a local aircraft factory. Jimmy Scoular had been a sailor in the Royal Navy as had Jimmy Dickinson, the ever present left half for twenty years, never booked in over 760 league appearances for the club nor as an England international.

The inception of the professional club Portsmouth FC was recorded in a minute of a meeting held on the evening of 5 April 1898 at the house of solicitor alderman J. F. Pink at 12 High Street, next door to the house where King Charles I's minister and favourite the Duke of Buckingham met his demise. A syndicate of five local businessmen and sportsmen proposed the purchase of five acres of land used as cow pasture just north of Goldsmith Avenue to provide the site for a football club; and that they would be the club's directors. The syndicate contained archetypal local entrepreneurial and professional figures as founding fathers—men such as John Brickwood, head of Brickwood's brewery, and architect and surveyor Alfred Bone. Awareness of the recent successful re-incarnation of St. Mary's as Southampton's professional football club would have provided additional motivation for the Portsmouth syndicate. Pompey's first club strip featured eye-catching salmon pink shirts.

This meant that the current popular Royal Artillery team would become a footnote in history, as would the football "career" of struggling local GP and aspirant writer Arthur Conan Doyle. He had turned out for Portsmouth AFC sometimes as left back and sometimes as goalkeeper using the alias A. C. Smith. He recalled in his *Memories and Adventures* (1924) that: "I took up Association and played first in goal then as a back at Portsmouth when the famous club was an amateur organisation... I was always too slow, however, to be a really good back, though I was a long and safe kick." A colleague recalled how Conan Doyle had "captivated" his team mates on a long return journey from an away match outlining the plot of the historical novel he was working on, published four years later as *Micah Clarke*.

ARCHIBALD LEITCH, EMINENT ARCHITECT

As the country's professional football grew apace so did the architectural specialism of stadium design. The field of dreams would increasingly be defined by expansive terraces in iconic stadia—the built expression of ambition. The Fratton Park south stand that was the setting for the 1949 trophy presentation after the last home game of the season was designed by the firm of Archibald Leitch, the doyen of British football ground design in the early twentieth century.

Born in 1865, Archie grew up in a Glasgow tenement off Gallowgate.

He gained a scholarship to a grammar school but in fact was as much so-cialised by the industrial and engineering ferment that was contemporary Glasgow—an international mercantile hub. After three years at sea learning to be a marine engineer he got married and spent six years in the drawing offices of Glasgow companies before setting up on his own in 1896. His company's letterhead designated him as 'Consulting Engineer and Factory Architect' but it was as an architect of football grounds that he would be remembered.

The ambitious consulting engineer's stadium design career started with a prestigious job and could have ended there. He was engaged in 1899 by Rangers FC to design their new Ibrox Park stadium. Initially its full capacity was not fully tested until the international match played there between Scotland and England on 5 April 1902 when disaster struck. High up on one open terrace the timber joists split. Twenty-six people were killed and 516 spectators injured. The timber merchant supplier was tried and cleared. Rangers decided to retain Archibald Leitch's services.

In the years between 1902 and 1915 Leitch's client list expanded to include eight of the most prestigious clubs in the country. His preoccupation was with safety and with that in mind he increased the number of circulation routes and distribution passages in the new ground designs and he pioneered crush rails or barriers. He was engaged by deadly local rivals and worked on designs for Anfield and Goodison Park, Highbury and White Hart Lane, Stamford Bridge and Craven Cottage. At Old Trafford Leitch created what Simon Inglis calls "truly the first modern stadium of the twentieth century". In the early 1920s Portsmouth FC were on an upward trajectory through the League that resulted in their greatest successes in the immediate pre- and post-Second World War years. The ground was capable of containing crowds of up to 30,000 but Fratton Park boasted one corner pavilion with a capacity of only 1,000. In 1924 the club's financial advisor J. E. Pink wrote to a bank seeking financial backing for the building of a new stand as the overcrowding in the existing stand meant that a "very large number of the better class supporter" stayed away. He informed the bank that "the directors have therefore called in Mr Archibald Leitch… the eminent Architect for Football Grounds." This architect had enough entrepreneurial experience to be able to advise the club on how to play the loan procurement game and so the bank agreed to the loan. Building work started the following June; and the stand

Fratton Park's South Stand

was declared open on 29 August 1925. The architect's site visits allowed him to go down to the harbour to observe ships—an interest carried on from his first occupation as a marine engineer.

The South Stand was a classic Leitch double-decker, a smaller version of the design for the North Stand he was currently working on for the English Rugby Football Union's ground at Twickenham. The Fratton Park stand was restricted in height as there was a terrace of houses immediately behind it; for that reason too the glazing all along the back of the stand's roof is designed to bring enough natural light to the seating deck and the stairs and passages beneath. The trademark Leitch balcony detailing—currently obscured by advertising boards—now only survives here and at Ibrox and Goodison Park. There are also two survivals from Leitch's time and two decades previously. A narrow door set into a stadium wall is an example of a transfer gate allowing fans to change ends at half time from the Fratton End terrace via the South Stand. At the end of the ground's main approach road—the modest terraced street of Frogmore Road—is a half-timbered gatehouse that is the remnant of the club's original 1905 pavilion. On the right approaching the ground is the similarly half-timbered Pompey Shop, a building designed by renowned local architect A. E. Cogswell as a public house for the Brickwoods brewery whose owner also happened to be the first chairman of the professional club.

British engineers and architects are rarely given the kudos or recognition granted to them in other European countries and America. Yet so much of our built environment, our familiar townscapes and our machines for living in come from their imagination, vision and skill, however well or badly the original ideas are interpreted by financiers and politicians.

In the autumn of 1933 J. B. Priestley set off on his personal state-of-the-nation field trip, following in the tradition of William Cobbett and Daniel Defoe; his resulting book, *English Journey*, inspired the writer George Orwell and photographer Bill Brandt to mount their own expeditions of social investigation.

A contemporary photograph from the *Nottingham Guardian* used to illustrate the 1997 Folio edition of Priestley's book shows an open terrace at the Notts County FC ground—a sea of the trilbies and cloth caps of an almost exclusively male crowd. Priestley commented on a Saturday afternoon derby match at Nottingham Forest that the cold mist and drizzle "did not prevent the supporters of Notts Forest and Notts County, two distinct groups of partisans (though on what principle they elect themselves I cannot imagine), from filling the ground to the palings..." As a disinterested observer, Priestley makes some observations that would still resonate some eighty years later. "Nearly everything possible has been done to spoil this game: the heavy financial interests; the absurd transfer and player-selling system; the lack of any birth or residential qualification for the players; the betting and coupon competitions; the absurd publicity given to every feature of it by the Press; the monstrous partisanship of the crowds (with their idiotic cries of 'Play the game, Ref.' when any decision against their side has been given); but the fact remains that it is not yet spoilt, and it has gone out and conquered the world."

Priestley did not like the fans' "stupid partisanship" and "their dogmatism". Yet he appreciated that the fans were not 'indifferent lookers-on"—they suffered with their team and he recognised the happiness the spectacle could bring, allied to a "quick comradeship". The fans on the terraces might not have much control or influence in other areas of their lives but this "uproarious Saturday plaything" was their own.

Today's football crowds are drawn from more affluent working and middle classes and are more media-savvy; indeed, the game is now filtered and interpreted by a controlling media and the perspectives are more international than merely parochial; but the dreams of the fans are the same as they would have been in the 1930s as is spectator involvement and need for a collective focus. As then, the mass of spectators is still the other key ingredient of a landscape designed to make the crowd an integral part of the drama.

One aspect of the game Priestley did not mention was the status of female footballers. The First World War years and the immediate post-war period had proved to be a short-lived heyday for women's football. Locally a charity match between Gosport and Portsmouth ladies' teams was staged during the war to raise money for the planned War Memorial Hospital; the hospital was opened after the war by Earl Haig, a commander who contributed much to the need for more hospitals. The female munitions workers from the ammunition factory at Priddy's Hard made up the first Gosport representative team. Teams were typically drawn from workforces such as those at the Hants and Dorset and Southdown bus companies. Even the small suburb of Alverstoke had a ladies' team in 1919.

A Boxing Day match at Everton's Goodison Park in 1920 drew a crowd of 53,000 to see St. Helens Ladies play a Preston works team, Dick, Kerr Ladies FC. But by the end of the following year the Football Association had banned women from playing on pitches that were FA-affiliated—essentially all grounds with spectator facilities. This ban was lifted in 1971, two years after the formation of the Women's Football Association; and the women's game has had more official support in recent decades. Still the game had survived at a local level and more teams were formed in the euphoric aftermath of England's World Cup victory in 1966. Typically then a South Hants Ladies FA (Southampton and District) league match would see Southampton and Paulsgrove Ladies compete on a Southampton Common pitch.

SPORTING HISTORY

Public schools had played a major part in the development of the game. Winchester College certainly staged matches in the 1820s. Prior to that the game seems not to have evolved much beyond the medieval practice of whole male populations from adjacent villages trying to kick or carry a "football" into each other's territory for several hours. Hampshire's oldest club appears to have been the Fordingbridge Turks. By the 1880s local clubs included Lymington, Ryde, Cowes, Sandown, Total Abstinence of Basingstoke, the Mechanical Engineers and Woolston Works. In that decade football clubs often had to borrow or rent fields that were used for other purposes; the teams brought their own goal posts with them; the playing areas were marked out with sawdust; changing areas were distant or non-existent save for a nearby hedge. The team coach would often be a horse-drawn wagon and matches started earlier in the afternoon to get the game played before dark.

In October 1863 a group of representatives from London clubs met at the Freemasons' Tavern at Lincoln's Inn Fields to agree on a set of rules for the game and to inaugurate the Football Association. The Football League was formed in 1888 and the sport professionalised; all of the original twelve clubs were from northern and Midland towns. Although international matches were staged at Portsmouth and at Southampton's Archers Road ground (later the Dell) in the early years of the twentieth century, the south was a relative backwater in terms of the professional game. With the introduction of the professional game many amateur teams such as Corinthians were placed in a quandary. Competitions were not part of their mindset and they refused to take penalties as no gentleman would have deliberately fouled another player. In the first decades of the twentieth century public schools increasingly made their field of dreams an arena for rugby union and not association football.

Stick and ball games recognisable today were played as early as the sixteenth century. The county of Hampshire was certainly one of the cradles of cricket, with the inception of the modern game (between 1750-63) usually credited to the Hambledon club, making the ground at Broad-halfpenny Down a site of pilgrimage for modern aficionados. Initially the game attracted much gambling interest; by the end of the eighteenth century it had become the pastime of both gentleman and artisan alike. Two Portsmouth women's cricket teams competed at Milton in 1813. In 1854 Portsmouth property entrepreneur and architect Thomas Ellis Owen gave his workers the day off so that the firm's bricklayers' and carpenters' cricket teams could play each other.

In the later decades of the nineteenth century cricket had become an international game with the first ever Australian touring side playing three matches in Hampshire in 1868; this was soon followed by an all-Aboriginal touring side. One writer, John Simons in "A History of Cricket in Hampshire 1760-1914", described the period from 1880 until the start of the First World War as the Golden Age of cricket when the game "had become one of the defining elements of English culture". In the 1880s Portsmouth GP Arthur Conan Doyle was a leading local cricketer. Hampshire County Cricket Club was established in 1894 and five years later the visiting Australian team played matches at Southampton and Newport on the Isle of Wight. Cricket fans love their dreamy summer cricket pitches and grounds and they also seem to like facts.

Southampton FC or Saints were promoted to the Football League's Division 1 in 1966 and survived in that division and the Premiership until 2004, except for their Division 2 status between 1974 and 1977—a period that included winning the FA Cup in 1976. For a small club they have managed to attract international players such as Kevin Keegan, Matthew Le Tissier, Peter Shilton and Alan Ball, who would later become manager at Portsmouth. The Saints moved to a new 32,000-seat stadium at St. Marys for the start of the 2001-2 season. The club suffered a period of administration at the end of the decade which resulted in relegation, but the Saints moved back to the second tier in 2011 and, to the first a year later..

Winning the League Championship in two successive seasons (1948-49 and 1949-50) was the post-war highpoint for Portsmouth FC, or "Pompey". For the next four decades they slalomed up and down the four divisions. They were promoted into the Premiership under the management of Harry Redknapp in 2004 and stayed there for three seasons. Pompey won the FA Cup for a second time in 2008. Since then they have experienced the uncertainties of financial administration. Recent behind-the-scenes stories have included a Hong Kong-based businessman, bidders from the United Arab Emirates, a French businessman of Russian descent allegedly involved in arms sales, possible financial irregularities within the club, accusations of asset stripping and the reality of bankruptcy. The net effects of uncertainty and lack of continuity have been limited resources and inconsistent form as well as successive relegations.

The antidote to the business side of professional football takes the form of those keepers of the flame—the fans. One such, Mr. Portsmouth, otherwise known as John Anthony Westwood, has been an unmissable cheerleader for many years with his stove pipe hat, bright blue wig and ex-chef's chequered trousers, rallying the faithful with a bugle and a bell and frequently stripped to the waist to reveal some of his sixty Pompey tattoos. What does this talismanic Mr. Hyde do on non-match days? He runs his antiquarian and second hand bookshop in Petersfield.

Chapter Sixteen

LANDSCAPES OF LEARNING AND
SOCIABILITY

LIBRARIES AND PARKS

Andrew Carnegie was born in 1835, the son of a Dunfermline damask linen weaver who was of a nonconformist faith with Chartist sympathies. The Depression of 1848 put Carnegie senior out of work and the new weaving technology announced a future that did not need his skills; so the family emigrated to Pittsburgh. Andrew started work as a bobbin boy in a cotton factory; by fifteen he was a telegraph boy and three years later his job was as a clerk and telegraph operator to the assistant superintendent of the Pennsylvania Railroad Company, Thomas Scott. He rose through the company to become superintendent of its western division and invested (with the help of Scott) first in the burgeoning Woodruff Sleeping Car Company to make enough money to further invest in the business that became the biggest iron and steel works in the United States and would make his fortune. After the end of the Civil War in 1865 the demand for iron and steel, especially in the form of rails for the expanding railroads, grew and grew. In 1901 the banker and financier J. P. Morgan bought out Carnegie's share in the US Steel Corporation for $447 million. Carnegie's career had been an epic version of the American success story; and for a time he was the richest man in the country.

Carnegie moved to his estate at Castle Skibo in Sutherland and embarked on a second career as a pacifist and philanthropist. He took on the role of a campaigner for world peace and tried to follow the dictum articulated in his book *The Gospel of Wealth*: "a man who dies thus rich, dies disgraced." The personal story behind Andrew Carnegie's programme of cultural endowment of "free libraries" came from his memories of the messenger boy years in Pittsburgh when borrowed books had provided his education. The trust he set up oversaw the building of 1,946 libraries in the United States and 660 in Britain. Included in this programme were some

The Carnegie Library at Fratton

monumental branch libraries in the city of Pittsburgh, libraries with assembly rooms and children's rooms big enough for the largest primary school classes and gardens for outdoor story hours. Carnegie's largesse included a branch library built at Fratton—an inner suburb of Portsmouth—in 1905.

Designed for no fee by the Portsmouth architect A. E. Cogswell, the branch library introduced into Fratton an imposing local institution. The grandiose Edwardian "Renaissance"-style façade is red brick framed by stone, its entrance signalled by a deep-bracketed canopy with its semi-circle theme continued in the tall first-floor windows. A pediment at the top of the entrance tower announces the building's purpose and its provider. Two cartouches either side of the entrance doorway record the century and the year. The vestibule and hall lead to the main borrowing part of the library accessed through a wooden door with decorated glass screens above; open stacks radiate from a V-shaped issuing desk top-lit from a lantern in the roof. Large general reading rooms for newspapers and magazines are entered from the entrance hall; there was a separate ladies' reading room upstairs.

One reader was James Callaghan (1912-2005), a Pompey boy whose early family life was clouded by economic hardship after the death of his father when "Jim" was nine. He went on to become Chancellor of the Exchequer, Home Secretary and then Foreign Secretary between 1967 and 1976 and was Prime Minister from 1976 until 1979. He recalled that during his teenage years he disliked the regime at his school—the Northern Secondary School in Fratton Road—and pursued his self-education through books at the nearby Carnegie Library; it was here, he said, he discovered the "joy of reading".

On the morning of 10 September 1908 HMS *St. Vincent*, the latest, state-of-the-art and the fastest Dreadnought class of battleship, was launched at Portsmouth Dockyard. On the same afternoon, less than two miles away, a throng of local government and academic worthies was photographed standing on the steps of the new Municipal College, opened that day. Among the soberly attired, almost exclusively male contingent a little girl, dressed in white, stands out. She is Doris, the mayor's five-year-old daughter. This Technical Institute designed by local architect G. E. Smith (1870-1944), was located behind the former Town Hall. Clad in Portland stone, its central entrance tower acts as a hinge for two blocks housing classrooms, laboratories, workshops and art rooms. Also included in the complex was the Free Library (later the Central Library) with its own grandiose entrance staircase and magnificently large reading room.

Across the railway line and clearly visible from the upper storeys of the Technical Institute's east wing (containing the library) is Victoria Park. Conceived in 1878 this was the classic late Victorian urban park—a place of civic sociability and an arena for socialisation. Municipal parks evolved in the mid-1800s as pioneering, freely accessible open spaces for urban recreation and as gathering places for important events. They "represented ideal landscapes separated from the realities of their urban surroundings", claims Hazel Conway. The larger parks came with their own specific structures: bandstands, boathouses, lodges, pagodas, palm houses, refreshment rooms, drinking fountains, toilets and shelters.

Portsmouth's twelve-acre site was bisected by the railway with a recreation ground to the south of the tracks. More dramatic features such as a canoe lake were sited further east close to South Parade Pier, and Southsea Common provided a site for circuses and a platform to watch events and shipping movements in the Solent. Still Victoria Park could boast a horticultural oasis in the city with massed bedding plants, a bandstand and a tree-lined walkway. Certainly the park did offer the prospect of a walk for sailors on shore leave but they were more likely to prefer a run ashore—a pub crawl in civilian parlance.

TEMPERANCE HOTELS AND PUBLIC HOUSES

Someone who tried to offer an alternative to the ubiquitous pub was Dame Agnes Weston (1840-1918), philanthropist and temperance activist. Her family's wealth and her evangelical Anglican commitment had given her the opportunity to evangelise and organise independent of both "marriage and remunerative work". The target of her charitable work was the comfort and well-being of sailors; and she organised groups of naval wives and set up Sailors' Rests—large hotels or clubs—first in Plymouth then in Portsmouth. These projects were the Navy's first welfare arm.

The Portsmouth Royal Sailors Rest, which opened in 1882 just across from the park in Commercial Road, offered sailors the option of signing the temperance pledge and receiving 3d for a bun and a cup of tea. A 1909 photograph of this restaurant shows clean living sailors sitting in an elegantly spacious room with an attendant waiter in a long apron looking very French. When Dame Agnes Weston died in 1918 she was accorded a naval funeral.

Agnes Weston's commendable efforts did help promote abstinence but the counter attraction of pubs and of alcohol was formidable and part of the civilian and naval culture. At the time of the Public House Act of 1864, Portsmouth had 277 public houses and 545 beer houses—a drinking establishment for every one hundred residents. The Act set the mandatory closing hours for these places at between 1 and 4 a.m. The Still (now Still and West) in Old Portsmouth was a near neighbour of a daily fish market and this would justify its pre-dawn opening. The Navy and the dockyard workers supplied sizeable clienteles, and clustered on or near the Hard were the Ship Anson, the Ship and Castle, the Ship Leopard, the Keppels Head, the Navy Tavern, the Horse and Jockey, the Royal Navy Arms and the Cock and Bottle. Across the harbour in Gosport, research into the prevalence of pubs between 1800 and 1925 located over 75 such establishments in the Old Town alone. A 1920s aerial photograph of the harbour-facing Beach Street, just across from the dock for the floating bridge, reveals a continuous line of ten pubs. A drink was not hard to find.

The Ship Anson public house

Pubs in contrast to beer houses have never simply been drinking dens. They have always had the potential to act as social centres, meeting places for local groups and tradesmen, early labour exchanges (dramatically so in the days of the press gang) and venues for pub games and pre-music hall entertainment. By the late Victorian and Edwardian eras breweries wanted their urban pubs to be prestigious advertisements for the brand, and so hired architects to create this. A. E. Cogswell, who turned his hand to most building forms in his long Portsmouth-based career, was involved in the building or remodelling of ome sixty pubs and hotels. The most distinctive surviving hostelries are the Talbot, Pelham and Rutland hotels (1890s), the Pompey (1898) and the Eastfield Hotel (c.1905). The first four have street façades of intricate half-timbering and glazed brickwork; the Eastfield's (and the Pompey's) public fronts are enlivened by ceramics—pale-green glazed brick upper walls and dark green faience for the ground floor. The Talbot Hotel, located prominently on Goldsmith Avenue, includes in its distinctive skyline a gambrel-roofed (witch's hat) turret—an early example of branding by use of an architectural feature.

By the 1960s many pubs were too often depressing locals. Many were dives and boozers where the familiar archetype of a surly landlord would attract an equally surly clientele. The ubiquitous keg beer was as bland as the singer Val Doonican; the Portsmouth keg version then was made by Brickwoods, and its forgettable and regrettable taste earned the contempt of some and inspired the contemporary wall graffiti formula: Brickwoods = K9P.

In Memoriam

Community and civic remembrance of the fallen in battles, places and circumstances that could only be imagined is of a different order. The section of Victoria Park near to the entrance at the top of Queen Street—the location of the former superintendent's lodge—became in part the depository for campaign memorials rounded up from other city sites where new traffic schemes had threatened their survival. A column celebrates Admiral Sir Charles Napier (1786-1860)—"Ready Aye Ready"—and long forgotten exploits at Acre and Martinique. A small obelisk is dedicated to the memory of those who were killed in a gun accident on board HMS *Royal Sovereign* off Greece in 1901. Across the path an obelisk remembers the officers and men who lost their lives on board HMS *Victoria* on 22 June

1893. Even some of the names seem to go back in time or are apt in a Dickensian way: Fraser S. Stooks, George Dubber, painter, Edward Irons, J. Vittles, George Nelson… Nearby a scaled-down pagoda is a memorial to comrades from HMS *Orlando* who lost their lives in 1900 during actions in defence of Peking Legations, Taku forts and Tientsin. The centrepiece is a bell which was taken at the capture of one of the Taku forts. It bears the inscription: "Come pleasant weather and gentle rain, The Empire Happy at Peace Again."

One of the park's access and exit points is via a foot tunnel under the railway embankment and through a gate in the high stone wall which is the shielding corral of the city's First World War memorial site (unveiled in October 1921). Later additions were the figures of two machine gunners at their post flanking the Guildhall entrance to the site. They were made by the sculptor Charles Sargeant Jagger (see p.152), who created at this site a stunning place of remembrance. Yet there are just too many names to engage with—evidence of the Great War's industrialisation of military slaughter. Inscribed here are the names of 2,625 Army men from Portsmouth and 2,240 Navy men and three women.

Addendum

Victoria Park is still a welcome space among the surrounding urban density but its Victorian grandeur has faded and it now tells a story of relative municipal neglect. The bandstand has gone and its large green house is hidden and secured behind a hedge and fences. The lack of park keepers might have something to do with this.

At the time of writing there is a plan in train to close nine of the eleven public libraries in the Isle of Wight as an economy measure. One of those slated to close is the Carnegie Library at Sandown. The library at Fratton is still in business. The ground-floor interiors with their beautiful stained glass screens and the wooden check out corral remain. The upstairs rooms, formerly the ladies' reading room and later adult education teaching rooms, are neglected store rooms. The interior of the building is listed but not the building itself.

The Oxford-based children's author Philip Pullman in a January 2011 speech criticising the planned closure of many local authority libraries, recalled his thrill as the child owner of his first library ticket and made a plea for the community significance of libraries whose presence reminds him of "things that stand for civic decency and public respect for imagination and knowledge and the value of simple delight".

Chapter Seventeen

THE VIEW FROM THE DESK

THE WRITER'S TRADE

A painting made by Philip Burne-Jones in 1899 shows the writer Rudyard Kipling (1865-1936) seated at his work table pen in hand in the study of his house at Rottingdean. In the background are book shelves, a framed picture of a warship and a small globe. Kipling was already something of a celebrity as a children's writer, a popular versifier and "balladeer" of Empire, and groups of tourists would come out from Brighton to try and catch a glimpse of him over the hedge. Forced to search for a new residence the Kiplings found the perfect house.

This was the grey stone house of a seventeenth-century ironmaster half a mile south of the East Sussex village of Burwash. Kipling's new desk, in the book-lined first-floor study, was ten feet long, flanked by two globes and covered with writing implements and gadgets—a canoe-shaped pen tray, a pot of black ink, paperweights to hold down the loose pages of books he would dismember with a penknife. The desk faced a mullioned east window with a view across the small Wealden valley to Pook Hill. Kipling was a restless, serious smoker and visitors remembered the room's blue haze.

In the last few months of his life, at seventy, Kipling started to write his autobiography, *Something of Myself*. As he composed this account he will have recalled his time as a journalist in India, his attempt to emigrate to America to settle in Vermont, his return to discover the most marvellous country that was England "for the first time", his award of the Nobel Prize for Literature, the happy outcome of finding the current house with its good Feng shui, his war work for the Navy and the fate of his son John as one of the missing of the Great War. Yet when he thought and wrote about one house from his childhood it was with no sense of good Feng shui for this was Kipling's "House of Desolation" in Southsea.

Rudyard, then nine, and his sister were lodged with an old Navy sea captain and his wife in "the extreme suburbs of Southsea" in a "house smelling of aridity and emptiness". There had been no prior warning and his parents had then left for India; it was an arrangement that was to last almost six years. Kipling says he was beaten by the landlady and bullied by her son. Cross-examinations, he said, taught him to lie: "the foundation of literary effort". The captain was kind to him and they went on long walks. Otherwise he sought escape in reading, from *Aunt Judy's Magazine* to Tennyson's poems and the book sent by his father—a copy of *Robinson Crusoe* with steel engravings. He wrote that when he was in solitary confinement in the basement he used packing cases and a tin trunk to set up as a sole trader dealing with savages. In *The Light that Failed* the author says of the landlady: "Where he looked for love, she gave him first aversion and then hate."

Writing of his earlier childhood in India, one author has described him as having been "a very wilful child… used to bossing the servants around". For one month every year during that foster period, Kipling stayed with his aunt Georgie and her husband Sir Edward Burne-Jones in their house in the North End of Portsmouth. He never spoke to them of his fostering anguish. He was eventually "rescued" by his mother on her return from India.

WELLS AND CONAN DOYLE

A mile to the west of the House of Desolation's location at Lorne Lodge in Campbell Road, and a decade later, another incipient writer was about to experience his trial by indenture. Herbert George Wells (1866-1946) had moved from Bromley aged thirteen with his mother when she took up the post of housekeeper at Uppark, a seventeenth-century mansion set on the downs just over a mile from South Harting and seventeen miles northeast of Portsmouth. For a time Wells educated himself using the house's fine library, including Thomas Paine's *Rights of Man*, unearthed in a book collection secreted away in the attic, for understandable reasons. This was between two failed job placements at a local drapers and a Midhurst chemist. In 1881 he was sent to Hyde's Drapery Establishment in Southsea's Kings Road to serve as an apprentice.

Wells hated the daily boredom and drudgery and the dull future the work predicted. In his *Experiment in Autobiography* (1934) he wrote: "I still recall those two years of incarceration as the most unhappy hopeless periods of my life." In fact, he acknowledged that Mr. Hyde was a good

Uppark House

employer who provided cubicles in the apprentices' dormitory with their own furniture and a reading room and library. Wells tried to teach himself by reading but the long hours, the tedium of the work and the tyranny of the managerial staff ground down his ambition. Later, he would put some of this experience of early struggles into his novels, *Kipps* and *The History of Mr. Polly*. Then he needed to act.

So one Sunday morning in August 1883 Wells walked the seventeen miles from Southsea to Uppark to tell his mother he could not go on. What came from this was the offer of a post as a student assistant at Midhurst Grammar School, then a scholarship to the Normal School of Science (now Imperial College, London) and in 1890 a first class honours degree in Zoology. By the end of the first decade of the twentieth century H. G. Wells had become one of the first modern celebrity writers—a bestselling author of science fiction, a populist educator and later a high-profile political and social commentator with views on subjects as diverse as futuristic warfare, international cooperation and modern love.

When Wells was experiencing his anti-apprenticeship, just down the road from Hyde's Drapery in Southsea's Elm Grove yet another would-be author was trying to earn his living as a doctor. Arthur Conan Doyle (1859-1930) had stepped off the steamer at Clarence Pier one day in September of the previous year. He had left behind a failed medical practice partnership in Plymouth. After completing his medical studies at Edinburgh University Conan Doyle had been an apprentice ship's doctor on an Arctic whaler out of Peterhead and a medical officer and surgeon for a steamship line to West Africa out of Liverpool. Portsmouth in 1882 was where he hoped to start a successful practice and he put up his brass nameplate at the entrance to 1 Bush Villas. While he waited for the occasional patient he scribbled stories for publications such as *Boy's Own Paper*. At the start he could only afford to buy furniture for the consulting room.

Still Conan Doyle's gregarious nature and his sporting prowess brought him more consultations. He became captain of Portsmouth Cricket Club, bowling out the legendary W. C. Grace for a duck and was goalkeeper for a football team that would prefigure Portsmouth FC. Conan Doyle also joined the local Literary and Scientific Society and would become its secretary under the presidency of Dr. Watson. In 1885, the year of his marriage, Conan Doyle began work on a detective novel based on the practice of observation and deduction in diagnosis taught by his professor at Edinburgh Joseph Bell. This novel, *A Study in Scarlet*, was published in 1887 in *Beeton's Christmas Annual* and introduced Sherlock Holmes to the reading public. He went on to write and have published two historical novels—his preferred genre—*Micah Clark* (1889) and *The White Company* (1891), the latter a story from the Hundred Years' War set largely in the New Forest. But it was detective fiction the public wanted and with the publication of *The Sign of Four* (1890) and collections of Sherlock Holmes short stories from *The Strand Magazine* in 1892 and 1894, Conan Doyle's detective became, in modern parlance, a brand. *The Hound of the Baskervilles* was published in 1902 and has never been out of print.

This novel was written at Undershaw (a possible tribute to George Bernard Shaw), a house that Conan Doyle built surrounded by the pines and heather of the Surrey uplands at Hindhead. He involved himself as a doctor and reporter in the Boer War, lent his support to liberal social and political causes, publicly campaigned against miscarriages of justice and

Arthur Conan Doyle, doctor, sportsman and creator of Sherlock Holmes was a tireless proselytiser for spiritualism. He was also an advocate for the work of the writer George Meredith (1828-1909).

Meredith was born at 73 High Street, Old Portsmouth, the grandson of a flamboyant naval tailor Melchizedec who became the character Great Mel in the author's picaresque satire on class, *Evan Harrington, or He Would be a Gentleman*. (Portsmouth would seem to be the novel's location of Lymport.) Although his fiction was very much of its time, perhaps Meredith should be remembered for other reasons. As a reader for Chapman and Hall publishers he encouraged Thomas Hardy and George Gissing and was, as successor to Tennyson, an effective president of the Society of Authors. He was also a public intellectual, a "Republican Gentleman", according to George Bernard Shaw, supporting Home Rule and women's rights, advocating a probationary term for marriages and opposing the second South African war.

A contemporary of Meredith's was Portsea-born (Sir) Walter Besant (1836-1901). After an education at London and Cambridge Universities he was for six years a professor at the Royal College, Mauritius, until he returned to England to pursue a literary career. He published works on French language and literature and on the archaeology and history of Palestine. Most significantly he was a founding member of the Society of Authors in 1884 and was subsequently knighted in part for his contributions to its work. He also wrote novels with co-author James Rice, and one—*By Celia's Arbour* (1878)—is set in Portsea. He writes about the old sailors who sit every day on a wooden bench on the Common Hard overlooking the harbour and about Commercial Road, with its street market and "hundreds of men... loafing about, pipes in mouths" and those church-goers who acted as pew-openers and were allowed once a month to "finish the sacramental wine". Besant also details the social composition of the St. George's Square quarter.

It was to St. George's Hall in the same square that Charles Dickens (1812-70) returned to the city of his birth as it was a venue on his countrywide public reading tours in November 1858 and May 1866. Rumour had it that after one of these performances Dickens set off with friends to visit his birthplace but could not find 387 Mile End Terrace. The author had always loved acting and theatricals, and these readings gave him a third professional career after writing fiction and journalism and offered him the opportunity to meet and commune with his readers.

The appetite for and response to these performances was astonishing. On his tour of America in 1867 people queued round the block for tickets from dawn in the city of Boston, and New York's venue—the Steinway Hall (capacity 2,500)—was sold out. A review of one of his readings in Belfast in 1867 stated: "Mr Dickens... does not, except on very rare occasions, act thoroughly out; he suggests and suggests forcibly... he calls the imagination of his readers into play; they are to fill up what he leaves incomplete. This is just what the very best reading... ought to be." In 1868 the writer for *The Scotsman* went further: "Hear Dickens and die, you will never live to hear anything of its kind so good."

Dickens was successful as a reader because of his ability at mimicry and impersonation. He relished the chance to be someone else not like himself whether it was Sikes or Nancy, Mrs. Bardell or Mr. Pickwick. He once said enigmatically: "Most people are other People." The set for these two-and-a-half or three hours of virtuosity was designed by the author: his desk with side shelves, a side prop for the book and a cover of "lustrous maroon". The back screen and rug were of the same hue.

The city of Portsmouth is prominent in only one of Dickens' novels, *Nicholas Nickleby*. He visited the city in 1838 to do some research for the part of the novel where the hero and the rescued Smike fall in with the travelling theatrical company of Vincent Crummels en route for Portsmouth. Most probably he visited the Theatre Royal, then in the High Street, but there is no record. Much better recorded is the author's visit to the Isle of Wight in the summer of 1849.

Dickens had decided to try a different summer residence from his favoured resort of Broadstairs in Kent. In July he and his family travelled down to Portsmouth—four hours by train from Waterloo followed by a steamboat passage over to Ryde, a chance encounter with Thackeray on the pier and then a journey by stage coach to their rented villa at Bonchurch. He was delighted with the location, a house on the plateau of the Undercliff 150 feet above sea level with the down behind and a nearby waterfall where Dickens rigged up a shower-bath.

The author would work on his current novel, *David Copperfield*, between breakfast and 2 p.m. for at least the first couple of weeks of each month. Away from his desk, Dickens joined in the holiday fun of rounders, picnics, sea bathing, theatricals and conjuring displays and walks, especially up and along the downs from where the views were only equalled, in Dickens' estimation, "on the Genoese shore of the Mediter-ranean". The boys would go to East Dene to play with "the golden haired lad of the Swinburnes", the poet to be Algernon Swinburne (1837-1909). Yet Dickens came to find the climate in high summer enervating and in late September the family decamped to Broadstairs. Perhaps the author's disenchantment with the place found future expression in his novel *Our Mutual Friend*, particularly in the scene where after two weeks of honey-mooning at Shanklin, the Lammles' disillusionment is expressed by their moody walk along the sands:

> With that, they walk again; she, making those angry spirits in the sand; he, dragging that dejected tail. The tide is low, and seems to have thrown them together high on the bare shore. A gull comes sweeping by their heads and flouts them. There was a golden surface on the brown cliffs but now, and behold they are only damp earth.

A twentieth-century novelist who was born and brought up in unhappy family circumstances in Portsmouth but whose best-known work was based on experiences elsewhere was Olivia Manning (1908-80). She and her husband visited Romania shortly after their marriage in August 1939 and were then forced by world events to keep travelling down through the Balkans and live out most of the rest of the Second World War in Cairo. Manning used her wartime experiences to write two trilo-gies, the *Balkan Trilogy* and the *Levant Trilogy* (also titled in combination *Fortunes of War*), works which Anthony Burgess called "the finest fictional record of the war produced by a British writer".

In her novel *A Different Face*, published in 1953, Coldmouth doubles as the scarcely-disguised post-war Portsmouth, a city where "respect was not for the naval families cheeseparing on low pay, and less for widows with their mouse-meal pensions, but for the business-men who ran the city in their own interests and each year bought a bigger car, or a bigger house, and took it in turns to become mayor." Olivia Manning died sud-denly of a stroke at Ryde Hospital on 23 July 1980 and she was cremated at Whippingham. She had recalled that the Isle of Wight was the place she was happiest as a child on holiday with her brother. Otherwise she ad-mitted that she was only happy when she was writing.

The latter decades of the twentieth century and the first decade of the twenty-first saw authors of detective novels base their stories in particular British cities, for example Ian Rankin in Edinburgh and John Harvey in Nottingham. They brought more attention to those cities and Graham Hurley's crime stories did that for Portsmouth. Hurley worked as a researcher for Southern Television and then as a director making documentaries for ITV on subjects such as the search for the wreck of the *Titanic*. After writing a six-part drama *Rules of Engagement* he garnered a book contract and decided to work as a novelist full time. The resulting police procedural stories recount the investigatory casework of DI Joe Faraday, based in Portsmouth and working a south Hampshire beat. In his first Faraday novel, *Turnstone*, Hurley takes the reader to identifiable locations: the RSPB nature reserve at Farlington marshes, Langstone Harbour, the American Bar in Old Portsmouth, the Newtown Creek nature reserve on the Isle of Wight, and has the DI on one occasion watch the Fastnet yacht race from the Pennington bird reserve on the coastal fringe of the New Forest. Our hero considers the view from Portsdown Hill: "Faraday could see the hazy sprawl of the city stretching away towards the gleam of the Solent." The city's tourist officers must have begun to purr at all this. They might have been less encouraged by the novel's cover blurb describing "Faraday's squad of detectives battling with an ever-growing caseload of a city torn by violence, poverty, drug-dealing and petty crime."

In the end Portsmouth is a city that revolves around arrivals and departures; the poet Simon Armitage, sometime student of geography at Portsmouth Polytechnic, wrote about the departure of the Task Force for the Falkland Islands in his poem "The Stern", where the fleet felt "The shape and the taste of the heart in its mouth".

Further Reading

Bainbridge, Beryl, *Every Man for Himself*. London: Duckworth, 1997

Balfour, Alan, *Portsmouth*. London: Studio Vista, 1970

Barnes, Julian, *England, England*. London: Jonathan Cape, 1998

Basford, Vicky, *Historic Parks and Gardens of the Isle of Wight*. Isle of Wight County Council Cultural Services Department, 1989

Burton, Leslie and Musselwhite, Brian, *Crossing the Harbour: The Portsmouth Harbour Story*. Portsmouth: Milestone Publications, 1987

Chaney, Edward and Clearkin, Christine, *Richard Eurich (1903-1992) Visionary Artist*. London: Paul Holberton, 2003

Conway, Hazel, *Public Parks*. Oxford: Shire Publications, 1996

Cullen, Gordon, *The Concise Townscape*. London: The Architectural Press, 1971

Dicks, Brian, *The Isle of Wight*. London: David & Charles, 1979

Freeman, Michael, *Railways and the Victorian Imagination*. London: Yale University Press, 1999

Gray, Fred, *Designing the Seaside: Architecture, Society and Nature*. London: Reaktion Books, 2006

Hayward, Edward, *Upstairs and Downstairs: Life in an English Country House*. Stroud: Pitkin Guides, 1998

Hoare, Philip, *Spike Island: The Memory of a Military Hospital*. London: Fourth Estate, 2001

Hurley, Graham, *Turnstone*. London: Orion, 2001

Hyland, Paul, *Wight: Biography of an Island*. London: Victor Gollancz, 1984

Inglis, Simon, *Engineering Archie: Archibald Leitch – Football Ground Designer*. London: English Heritage, 2005

Lloyd, David W. and Nikolaus Pevsner, *Isle of Wight: The Buildings of England*. London: Yale University Press, 2006

Maré, Eric de, *The Nautical Style*. London: Architectural Press, 1973

Payne, Christiana, *Where the Sea Meets the Land: Artists on the Coast in Nineteenth-Century Britain*. Bristol: Sansom and Co., 2007

Phillips-Birt, Douglas, *Waters of Wight*. London: Cassell, 1967

Pike, Sue et al, *Thomas Ellis Owen: Shaper of Portsmouth, "Father of Southsea"*. Portsmouth: Tricorn Books, 2011

Platt, Richard, *Smuggling in the British Isles: A History*. Gloucester: Tempus, 2007

Priestley, J. B., *English Journey*. London: Heinemann, 1984

Riley, Ray (ed.), *Maritime City: Portsmouth 1945-2005*. Stroud: Sutton Publishing, 2005

Riley, Ray, Portsmouth: Ships, Dockyard and Town. Sutton, Tempus, 2002

Steadman, John (ed.), Portsmouth in the Twentieth Century: A Photographic History. Wellington: Halsgrove, 1999

Steele, James, *Queen Mary*. London: Phaidon Press, 1995

Surry, Nigel, *A Portsmouth Canvas: The Art of the City and the Sea 1770-1970*. London: The Fortune Press, 2008

Taylor, Miles (ed.), *Southampton: Gateway to the British Empire*. London, I. B. Tauris, 2007

Webb, J., Quail, S., Haskell, P., Riley, R., *The Spirit of Portsmouth: A History*. Stroud: Phillimore, 1989

Three especially useful sources have been the Portsmouth Papers, *The Oxford Encyclopedia of Maritime History* and *The Oxford Dictionary of National Biography*. The Portsmouth Papers were inaugurated by the Libraries, Museums and Arts Historical Publications sub-committee of Portsmouth City Council. Issue number 1 was published in June 1967. Portchester Castle was the subject of the essay, written by Professor Barry Cunliffe, who had been leading an excavation team at that site. There are now over seventy papers with topics ranging from theatres, breweries and public houses to smugglers, railways and votes for women. Four papers of particular relevance to this book are:

Riley R. C., "The Evolution of the Docks and Industrial Buildings in Portsmouth Royal Dockyard 1698-1914", Portsmouth Paper No. 44, 1985

Grundy, Nigel J.H., "W. L. Wyllie, the Portsmouth Years", Portsmouth Paper No. 68, 1996

Yates, Nigel, "Selling Southsea, Promoting Portsmouth 1920-2000", Portsmouth Paper No. 72, 2002

Francis, David, "Portsmouth Novelists", Portsmouth Paper No. 74, 2006

The Oxford Encyclopedia of Maritime History, published in 2007 in New York by Oxford University Press, has entries and essays on everything nautical from Sinbad to submarines. An index of 220 pages helps the reader navigate its four volumes.

I would also like to praise `. It offers a wonderful online research source—free to many local library card holders. With its collection of almost 58,000 biographies it is a compulsory port of call when trawling British history. One exemplar of its quality will have to suffice: Roger T. Stearn's exact, revealing and moving essay on the Unknown Warrior.

The following websites are useful sources of information:
www.visitportsmouth.co.uk
www.historicdockyard.co.uk
www.islandbreaks.co.uk

Index of Historical & Literary Names

Index of Places & Landmarks